Northern Ireland: Half a Century of Partition

Northern Ireland:
Half a Century of Partition

Edited by Richard W. Mansbach

Department of Political Science
Rutgers University (New Brunswick, N.J.)

FACTS ON FILE, INC.   NEW YORK, N.Y.

Northern Ireland: Half a Century of Partition

Library of Congress Catalog Card No. 72-81732
ISBN 0-87196-182-2

9 8 7 6 5 4 3 2
PRINTED IN
THE UNITED STATES OF AMERICA

CONTENTS

INTRODUCTION

C OMMUNAL AND GUERRILLA VIOLENCE in Northern Ireland has 3 principal causes: religion, history and geography. People of 2 Christian communities, a Protestant majority and a Roman Catholic minority, live in this 5,242-square-mile land but, tragically, seem unable to do so in peace.

Northern Ireland has been a recognizable entity separated for some 50 years from the rest of Ireland. Formed from 6 of the 9 counties of the Irish province of Ulster, Northern Ireland is a fragmented society of slightly more than 1½ million people, at least 900,000 of them Protestant and nearly 600,000 of them Catholic. Protestants are descended from Scottish and English settlers who took root in Ulster more than 3 centuries ago. The Catholic descendants of the native Irish of Ulster have been set apart from their co-religionists in the South by the experience of Protestant settlement and, more recently, the establishment of Northern Ireland as a part of Great Britain. The Catholic and Protestant communities have lived in uneasy juxtaposition, fragments detached from their origins, and as yet have been unable to establish a common identity or community in Northern Ireland.

The division of the "6 counties"—60% Protestant and almost 40% Catholic—has been, and remains, the most important political and social distinction in Ulster. The crisis in Northern Ireland reflects tensions and hatreds that date from the Protestant Reformation in the 16th century.

The English kings had claimed dominion over Ireland in 1169, but they made no serious attempt to control the island until the Reformation. In 1541, Henry VIII was proclaimed king of Ireland, and he set out to convert the populace to an Irish version of the new English Church. The attempt failed, but from then on the Irish hatred of English domination became identified with religious differences. Maintaining allegiance to Ireland's outlawed Roman Catholic Church became an act of patriotism as well as a religious decision, and the clergy of the Irish Church, outlaws themselves, became closely associated with the Irish people in their struggle against an alien crown and religion.

In the north and west of Ireland, Gaelic chieftains had retained their authority and control, but Henry and his successors were determined to subdue them. At the end of the 16th century, the Ulster earls, led by Hugh O'Neill and Red Hugh O'Donnell, attempted

1

unsuccessfully to throw the English out of Ireland. Defeated in the Battle of Kinsale in 1602, the Ulster chieftains, with their families and retainers, fled to the European continent. The crown confiscated their lands and brought in a flood of Scottish and English settlers. This "Plantation of Ulster" was established along the same lines as some settlements in the New World, and with more reason; the security of English naval power depended on a secure Ireland. The Ulster settlement, the English hoped, would thoroughly establish English control over this particularly restive part of Ireland.

But it was not to be so. The Ulster Irish rebelled again in the 1630s, and not until 1649 were the English, led by Oliver Cromwell, England's Lord Protector, able to subdue them. Cromwell devastated the countryside, leaving a legacy of intense hatred still bitterly remembered. Ireland has never been without rebellions against the English. The period's final serious Irish challenge to England's authority came in 1689. In that year James II, the Catholic English king, came to Ireland to raise an army to regain his throne, which had been taken from him in the Glorious Revolution of 1688. James Stuart and his Ulster Catholic allies were defeated in 2 important battles that are enshrined in Ulster Protestant history. In Londonderry (Derry to Irish Catholics), the Ulster Protestants successfully withstood a 3½-month siege, and in 1690, at the Battle of the Boyne, the Dutch stadtholder William of Orange defeated the Catholic forces when James panicked and fled the field on the verge of Catholic victory. English rule was assured for more than 2 centuries.

Irish lands were given to English peers, and laws were established to coerce Irish Catholics into submission. By 1700, only 14% of Ireland was owned by native Irish, and most of these had converted to Protestantism. Irish Catholics were forbidden to own property, to educate their children or to practice their religion. Ireland was treated as a rebellious colony, not as an integral part, of Great Britain. Not until after 1800, when Ireland became part of the United Kingdom, did conditions begin to change. In 1829, freedom of worship was restored to Irish Catholics, and gradually other reforms were undertaken. The "Irish Question" became one of the most burning issues in 19th century British politics. The great potato famines of mid-century turned Ireland into a liability to the British treasury and an embarrassment to English liberals. Millions of Irish fled Ireland for the Americas, and millions died of starvation. The population of Ireland, estimated at over 8 million in 1835, was reduced to little more than 4 million by 1900.

Ulster Protestants became increasingly alarmed as Irish reforms gave rise to a discussion of Irish Home Rule at the end of the 19th century. There had been recurring, but small-scale, sectarian violence throughout the century, and Protestants feared for their safety in a free Catholic Ireland. The Orange Order, founded in 1795 to protect Ulster Protestants, was dedicated to Protestant control in Ulster. Its members swore an oath to support the British Crown *only* as long as it maintained a Protestant Ireland. The Order was outlawed by the British for its violent activities, yet despite this it flourished and grew as the prospect of home rule became real. When full-scale rebellion against the English broke out in 1919, the Orange Order played an essential part in organizing and arming Ulster Protestants in their successful defense of Northern Ireland against the Irish Republican Army (IRA).

While many Irish Catholics had begun to work through the established régime as it liberalized, some Irishmen rejected accommodation with the British; they held that "good government is no substitute for self-government." Revolutionary movements were organized to free Ireland by force. Most important of these were the Fenians, organized in 1858, the precursors of the IRA. By 1900 violence was commonplace throughout Ireland.

British Prime Min. Herbert H. Asquith introduced an Irish home rule bill in Parliament in 1912. The bill included Ulster's Protestant counties in the notion of an autonomous Ireland. The House of Commons passed the measure by 367-267 vote in Jan. 1913, but the House of Lords rejected it. Still, the measure was not dead since passage twice more by Commons would make it law no matter what action the Lords took. (This new British constitutional feature stemmed from the provisions of the Parliament Act of 1911.)

The vested interests of Protestant Ulster readied resistance. Led by Sir Edward (Lord) Carson, the Ulster Volunteers—assisted by many prominent men on both sides of the Irish Sea—armed themselves and took steps to establish a separate government in Belfast when Asquith's bill became law. After the House of Commons in May 1914 again passed the bill, the House of Lords excluded Ulster from its clauses. King George V attempted in July to win an accommodation from the peers and Commons of Parliament but failed. The bill was again passed by Commons in Sept. 1914 and became law, but Commons also voted that the measure was not to become effective until after the war that had broken out that summer (World War I). The Asquith home rule bill never took effect.

In 1916 the IRA attempted to take advantage of Britain's preoccupation with World War I by launching the famous "Easter Rebellion" in Dublin.   The uprising proved abortive, but the resulting British reprisals created martyrs and gained widespread support for the IRA.

In 1919, the IRA led a full-scale rebellion that gained Irish independence after several bloody years. In Ulster, the Protestants, led by the Orange Order, defeated the IRA and maintained British control. Elsewhere, the IRA, led by Michael Collins, was quite successful in its guerrilla war against the British.

In 1920, the British, weary and unable to defeat the IRA, offered a compromise. Under the proposed agreement, Ireland would be divided in 2—Northern Ireland (made up of the 6 most Protestant counties of Ulster) and the Irish Free State (or Saorstát Eireann, composed of the remaining 26 counties of Ireland).   Northern Ireland, as proposed by the British (and as ultimately constituted), was to be made up of the counties of Antrim, Armagh, Down, Fermanagh, Londonderry (which Irish Catholics call Derry) and Tyrone and the boroughs of Belfast and Londonderry (Derry to the Irish Catholics).

Northern Ireland and the Irish Free State were to form a loose federation under a weak central government.   Collins accepted the British order, but many IRA members wanted a united Irish Republic or none at all. Civil war ensued between rival IRA factions. Collins' faction won, although Collins himself was killed in the fighting.

The Irish Free State came into existence as a commonwealth of the British Empire. The compromise agreement, however, was never ratified by the Free State, and no institutional connections were established with Northern Ireland. By rejecting the agreement, the Irish refused to give formal recognition to the partition of Ireland. The constitution of the Irish Free State specifically claimed applicability throughout the 32 counties of Ireland—although suspended in its enforcement in the 6 counties of Northern Ireland until some unspecified future date.

Although it was defeated in the civil war of 1921–3, the anti-Free State faction of the IRA refused to accede to the division of Ireland and continued a sporadic underground resistance against both the Protestant régime in the North and the Free State in the South. Even when Éamon de Valéra, a leader of the Easter Rebellion, became the prime minister (*taoiseach*) of the Free State in 1932, the IRA continued its activities directed at the Dublin régime. De Valéra banned the IRA as a result and set out to destroy it in the South. By the early 1940s, only diehard members remained active, but World War II provided an opportunity to attack British rule in Ulster.

The Nazis were glad to provide material assistance to the IRA, and a widespread terrorist bombing campaign was launched. The neutrality of the Free State was seriously threatened, and de Valéra feared British intervention. He redoubled his efforts to crush the IRA. 5 of its leaders were executed by the Dublin government, and many more were imprisoned. In 1947, the Irish minister of justice declared that the IRA was dead. It was close to the truth; most of its leaders were either dead or in prison, and there was little public support among Irish Catholics for its activities. The resentment of the IRA against the Free State, and especially de Valéra, remained intense. De Valéra and those who supported the Free State were pictured in an IRA song of the 1950s as "quislings who sold out."

The Protestants in Northern Ireland remained united with Great Britain as the only sure means of guaranteeing Protestant control. The prominence of the Orange Order in Northern Ireland reflects its strong defense of the principle of Protestant control at almost any price, a position shared by most Ulster Protestants. Most of the Protestant politicians have been members of the Orange Order, and the Unionists, the Protestant political party, has been dominated by Orangemen. For Protestants, the partition of Ireland in 1921 was a final settlement. The Ulster Parliament, in Stormont, a suburb of Belfast, exercised control over the internal affairs of Northern Ireland. Although London considered the 6 Northern Irish counties as legally a part of Great Britain, the Westminster Parliament was unwilling to interfere with the Stormont régime—partly because the British were fearful of raising a hornet's nest, partly because the Unionist members of the Westminster government (Northern Ireland sends 12 members to the British House of Commons) have often provided the margin of victory for Conservative governments.

The Northern Irish régime was controlled by the Unionist Party from its inception and thus is thoroughly identified with the Protestant community and not at all with the Catholics. As the first prime minister of Northern Ireland, Lord Craigavon, observed, it was a "Protestant government. . . a Protestant parliament for a Protestant people." The Unionist view of Catholics was simple. Only Protestants had remained loyal to Britain during the 1919 rebellion, and thus only Protestants were worthy of participation in the government. The support of Ulster Catholics was neither sought nor desired. Ulster Protestants saw Catholics as troublemakers at best, treasonous at worst, and the religious division was exacerbated by Northern Ireland's economic difficulties.

During the Depression, unemployment was extremely high in Ulster, and Ulster Protestants organized to keep Protestants employed even while Catholics remained out of work. In 1933, the future prime minister of Ulster, Sir Basil Brooke, declared: "Many in the audience employ Cathoics, but I have not one about my place. Catholics are out to destroy Ulster with all their might and power. They want to nullify the Protestant vote, take all they can out of Ulster and then see it go to hell."

In addition to the economic disabilities suffered by Catholics, political power has been denied them. In Northern Ireland, Catholics are a permanent minority. Even under the most democratic election procedures, Catholics could not control the Stormont régime. Gerrymandering has helped to keep the Catholic vote from electing even the minority of the parliament that their numbers warrant. Those Catholics who have been elected have often refused to sit in the Stormont Parliament on the grounds that it is not a legitimate government. At local government levels, gerrymandering has often prevented a Catholic majority from gaining control of a local government. For their part, Catholic politicians have by and large refused to appeal to the Protestant vote and instead have used Catholic-Protestant differences to gain support. This, of course, reinforces the conviction of Protestants that Catholics must be kept from political power in Ulster.

Early in 1949, the Irish Free State broke its ties to the British Commonwealth and declared itself the Republic of Ireland (or Eire). Britain's subsequent recognition of the new title seemed to many Ulster Protestants to imply that Britain was recognizing Dublin's claim to all of Ireland. Northern Ireland pressed the British government for a specific guarantee of Ulster's place in Great Britain. The Westminster Parliament responded May 17, 1949 by passing legislation that declared Northern Ireland to be a part of the United Kingdom. The Ulster Protestants relied on this as a guarantee that Britain would never allow the uniting of both parts of Ireland under one government.

While partition has remained an important issue in Irish politics, by the late 1940s attitudes in the Republic had shifted sufficiently so that the Dublin government could begin to see areas of cooperation with the Ulster régime. Between 1950 and 1955, agreements were negotiated on a range of issues of mutual interest such as employment insurance, amalgamation of railroad and highway systems, and fishing rights. Northern Ireland in 1949 had revoked most sections of the Special Powers Act of 1922, which allowed the detention of suspects without charges or trial, and Stormont continued to dispense with them until a guerrilla raid in mid-June 1954. The Irish Republic began to explore proposals for the peaceful unification of the island. While the partition of Ireland was far from being settled, the 2 governments appeared to be heading for friendly relations and mutual cooperation by the mid 1950s.

Within Northern Ireland, however, the potential for trouble still remained. Many Catholics did not accept the partition of Ireland as permanent and did not recognize the legitimacy of the Stormont régime. The revolutionary tradition of the outlawed Irish Republican Army, moreover, had made violence an approved means of gaining political ends, and the reports of the IRA's death proved premature. The Protestants, for their part, remained convinced that Northern Ireland must remain Protestant and British, and many were ready to resort to force of arms to protect their position. Neither side expressed a willingness to compromise with the other, and the traditions of animosity between Catholics and Protestants remained alive.

Violence, rather than compromise and negotiation, had continually been used in the settling of disputes, and disagreements between Catholics and Protestants were widely held to be matters of physical survival. Neither side seemed willing to build a harmonious, multi-religious society under the existing political circumstances, and yet without such a society the future of Northern Ireland and peace between its peoples were regarded as problematical.

The material in this book is based largely on data published in FACTS ON FILE. As in all FACTS ON FILE books, great care was taken to keep this book as free of bias as possible.

RESURGENCE OF IRA TERRORISM: 1956 – 62

Early Guerrilla Incidents

Although greatly weakened by the de Valera government of the Irish Republic, the outlawed Irish Republican Army (the IRA) was not completely destroyed at the end of the 1940s. It apparently nursed its strength, reorganized and began preparations in the early 1950s for the initiation of a full-scale attack on the Northern Irish régime. Between 1950 and 1955, there occurred in Northern Ireland sporadic incidents that presaged the resumption of widespread terrorism in Dec. 1956.

A series of bombings aimed at the local police force took place in Belfast during 1950. Police barracks were bombed Mar. 8 and 10, and bombs were thrown at on-duty policemen Mar. 30 and Apr. 2. Although only minor injuries occurred, the Stormont régime was alarmed enough to reenact portions of the Special Powers Act. 10 men were subsequently arrested Apr. 6 by the police in Belfast's Falls Road area, a Catholic enclave.

King George VI of England May 30, 1951 canceled a trip to Belfast because of bomb attacks on British property and threats against his life by Irish revolutionaries there. His wife, Queen Elizabeth, and Princess Margaret visited Belfast June 1 without the king.

William Kelly, Republican member of Parliament (MP) for Mid-Tyrone in the Stormont Parliament, was sentenced Dec. 4, 1953 to 12 months in prison after having been found guilty on charges of sedition arising out of his speeches during the election campaign in Oct. 1952. In his speeches, Kelly had said that he would not swear allegiance "to a foreign queen of a bastard nation" and that he "believed in the use of force, the more the better, the sooner the better." Kelly had also said that "England does not understand what we mean by force, but we will make them understand by the strong-armed method." At his trial, he had said that he was "not prepared to compromise the sovereignty of the Irish people" and that the court was "an illegal assembly owing allegiance to the British Crown." Kelly stayed in prison until Aug. 19, 1954.

In 1954, the IRA began conducting raids for the purpose of capturing arms and ammunition. The IRA raided the Royal Irish Fusiliers' depot at Gough Barracks, Armagh June 12 and seized about 300 rifles and automatic weapons. In the wake of this attack, the Special Powers Act of 1922 was reenacted in its entirety. The IRA then attempted a raid on the armory of the Royal Inniskilling Fusiliers at Omagh, County Tyrone Oct. 17 but was repulsed after a short battle. 8 mem-

9

bers of the IRA were arrested and tried for the Oct. 17 attack. All were residents of the Irish Republic. They were sentenced to 10 to 12 years in prison, although they claimed to be prisoners of war and not criminals. IRA members Dec. 9 seized a small quantity of arms and ammunition in Liverpool, England.

The IRA Dec. 2, 1954 issued a pamphlet declaring that the raids in the North had been conducted solely to capture arms and not to generate propaganda. The IRA professed that it had no intention of initiating violence in the Irish Republic but denounced the Dublin régime for allowing "that greatest of all evils—the continued occupation of part of our country by the British Army."

The IRA had been denounced by both government and opposition leaders in the Irish Republic, who had decried the use of force to unite Ireland and had advocated peaceful means. The prime minister of Northern Ireland, Lord Brookeborough (Sir Basil Brooke), noted this reaction in the republic and declared Oct. 15, 1954: "I want to tell them . . . that nothing will accomplish the unity of Ireland." (Irish Prime Min. John Costello retorted Oct. 28: "There never was a political prophet more deceived.")

Philip Clarke and Thomas Mitchell, 2 of the men sentenced to prison for the Oct. 17, 1954 IRA raid, were nominated by the Sinn Fein Party of Northern Ireland to run in the May 26, 1955 election for the Westminster Parliament. Though both were serving sentences in prison, they were elected. Protestants challenged the validity of the elections. The British House of Commons July 18 ruled vacant the seat won by Mitchell. He was reelected at a special by-election Aug. 11, and a petition campaign was launched Aug. 16 to have the seat again declared vacant. An election petition court in Northern Ireland Oct. 7 awarded the seat to Charles Beattie, the Unionist candidate whom Mitchell had defeated in both elections. A Belfast court had ruled Sept. 2 that Philip Clarke's election was invalid and had awarded the seat to his defeated Unionist opponent, Col. Robert Grosvenor.

A British court sentenced 3 Irishmen to life imprisonment Oct. 5, 1955 for their part in a raid Aug. 13 on the British military depot at Arborfield, 40 miles west of London. The raiders, about 10 armed members of the IRA, got away with 68 weapons and 80,600 rounds of ammunition, most of which was recovered Aug. 16 by Scotland Yard detectives in an abandoned shop in central London. Other ammunition was recovered from a small truck soon after the raid, when the 3 Irishmen were seized.

The Royal Ulster Constabulary (RUC) barracks at Rosslea, County Fermanagh were raided shortly before dawn Nov. 26 by about a dozen armed men. The raiders, repulsed after an exchange of shots, fled across the border into the Republic. One constable was wounded in the raid, and it was subsequently learned that one of the raiders died of wounds.

Northern Irish Prime Min. Lord Brookeborough denounced the Irish Republic for not taking measures to prevent the IRA from conducting such raids. Irish Prime Min. Costello replied Nov. 30 that his government would use all means in its power to bring the terrorist activity to an end, but he asserted that the violence arose from actions of the British and Northern Ireland régimes. Costello Dec. 2 forbade newspapers in the Republic to carry items about the IRA or from purported IRA spokesmen.

IRA Terrorist Campaign

The IRA Dec. 12, 1956 initiated the most widespread series of raids against the Protestant-dominated régime in Northern Ireland since the 1920s. 11 separate incidents were reported in 5 of Ulster's 6 Protestant counties. The IRA operations included an attack on a police patrol near Torr Head, an explosion at a British Broadcasting Corp. station in Londonderry, an assault on the Gough Barracks at Armagh, the destruction of a courthouse at Magherafelt, County Londonderry, and the blowing up of a territorial army building at Enniskillen, County Fermanagh. In the course of the initial raids, most of which took place near the border between Protestant Ulster and the Irish Republic, 2 members of the Royal Ulster Constabulary (RUC) were killed and more than $200,000 in damage was done.

The IRA terrorist campaign begun in Dec. 1956 continued until Feb. 1962, when the "Irish Republican Publicity Bureau" announced the termination of the campaign as a result of the failure of the militantly anti-partition Sinn Fein ("Ourselves Alone") candidates in the Irish elections of Oct. 1961 and the imposition of tough measures to prevent IRA terrorism by the Irish government. Even as it announced the cessation of the 6-year campaign, however, the bureau declared that the "resistance movement renews its pledge of eternal resistance to the British forces of occupation in Ireland."

The IRA and allied groups attempted during the 6-year campaign to maintain the offensive against the RUC and continued attacks on public buildings. But there were long periods of comparative quiescence—notably during the summer months—and the massive security measures undertaken by both Stormont and Dublin made effective terrorist activity increasingly difficult.

The Northern Irish government, responding to the initial wave of IRA attacks, issued orders under the Special Powers Act providing for curfews and search and seizure without warrant and putting into effect regulations prohibiting the possession of certain articles or materials. 2 pro-Republican political parties believed connected to the terrorists were banned, as were their publications. In addition, British troops were sent to reinforce the permanent garrison in Northern Ireland. More than 30 suspected terrorists were detained. In the Republic, security forces were ordered to take measures to prevent illegal armed activities, and more than a dozen men were arrested.

Throughout Jan. 1957, and to a lesser extent in February, IRA terrorists continued their attacks on military and strategic objectives in Northern Ireland. Rail and road bridges were bombed, and the road between Belfast and Londonderry was cut Jan. 21 when the Ranagh Bridge at Fallagloon was bombed. RUC and army installations in Newry, Upperlands, Dungannon, Coleraine and elsewhere were attacked or bombed by the IRA. 4 electrical power installations were bombed, and IRA gunmen Mar. 2 hijacked a train just before it crossed from the Republic into Northern Ireland and sent the train at top speed into the Londonderry station. More than $60,000 worth of damage was done, but, because of a call from one of the crew of the hijacked train, casualties were avoided. In the Republic, the IRA raided weapons stocks and factories for explosives. Northern Ireland security forces discovered and seized several arms caches during January and February 1957 and arrested more than 50 suspects. The Royal Air Force provided spotter planes Feb. 14 to aid in the search for the IRA. Irish Prime Min. John Costello, together with Eamon de Valéra, leader of the Opposition, denounced the IRA activities on Jan. 6 as an attempt "to seize powers which belong to the Dáil [Eire's parliament] and the government and to impose upon us all the tyranny of a few," not a war of independence. The Republic's government proceeded in its campaign to round up IRA members involved in the incidents in Northern Ireland and succeeded in arresting and convicting many IRA suspects.

The IRA's 3d attack in 3 months on the RUC station in Derrylin, County Fermanagh was repulsed Mar. 7, 1957 after a brief engagement in which a constable was wounded. The main road between Rosslea and Fivemiletown was blocked Mar. 10 when a bridge was destroyed, thus almost completely isolating Rosslea from the rest of Northern Ireland. Most of the phone system in County Antrim was put out of order Mar. 22 by the bombing of an automatic phone exchange. In Apr. 1957 3 more bridges were blown up, and another phone exchange and 2 electrical transformers were seriously damaged by bomb blasts. A policeman was seriously wounded Apr. 21 by an IRA booby trap while he was attempting to remove an IRA flag from a water tower. A lodge owned by Sir Harry Mulholland, former speaker of the Northern Irish House of Commons, was burned down Apr. 23.

Terrorists attempted to take the lives of the inspector general of the RUC May 4 by planting a bomb on his motor boat. The port of Newry, 4th largest in Northern Ireland, was put out of operation for at least 2 months when terrorists May 13 destroyed gates on the canal that connected the port to the sea. Damage cost in excess of $150,000 and the loss of trade more than $280,000.

IRA attacks slackened with the 1957 summer months, but several serious incidents occurred nonetheless. One RUC constable was killed and another seriously wounded when an RUC patrol was ambushed by terrorists in County Armagh only 200 yards from the border with the Republic. Stormont's Prime Min. Lord Brookeborough asked the British government to take up the matter with the Dublin Government, since the ambushers had escaped into the Republic. In response, the Irish Republic July 8 revived the special powers available to the government under the Offences Against the State Act of 1940, which allowed internment of suspects without trial.

At the same time the Irish Army prepared the internment camp at the Curraugh training center for the reception of "a large influx of internees." This was preceded July 6–7 by a series of police raids in which 63 men were arrested, including 8 members of the executive council of Sinn Fein, the political party of the IRA. Among those apprehended was the president, Patrick McLogan. 60 of the men arrested were sent to Curraugh. Prior to this, 66 men had been arrested at an IRA training camp in May and June. IRA members arrested earlier in the year, and sentenced to short terms, were immediately rearrested on their release and interned at Curraugh. By the beginning of August, 114 men were being held at the camp.

IRA activity continued, however. Incidents in Newry Aug. 10 and 11 caused the government to order a curfew. 3 persons were injured by police batons in Newry Aug. 13 when policemen attempted to disperse crowds protesting the curfew. RUC Sgt. A. J. Ovens was killed Aug. 17 and 3 other policemen and 2 soldiers slightly injured when a booby trap exploded in a farmhouse at Brackville about 15 miles from the border with the Republic. Ovens had taken policemen and troops to the house after an anonymous phone caller reported that suspicious-looking men had entered the disused house. In the wake of this incident, British troops closed all but 19 major roads into the Republic Aug. 19–20.

The Stormont Parliament had taken action in June 1957 to provide full compensation for damages caused by IRA attacks, and it moved June 25 to prevent any members of illegal or anti-régime organizations from running for Parliament.

IRA terrorist attacks occurred at sporadic intervals during the remainder of 1957. Among the incidents: Sept. 30, the RUC barracks in Armagh City were bombed; Oct. 11, an RUC station at Rosslea was attacked; Oct. 16, an unsuccessful attempt was made to lure police into a booby-trap in the area in which Sgt. Ovens had been killed, and an RUC vehicle was attacked with automatic weapons in Londonderry; Dec. 1, an RUC patrol escaped injury when a land mine exploded near its vehicle in County Fermanagh. 5 men were killed Nov. 11, in an explosion near a cottage on the Republican side of the border near Dundalk. The men were believed to have been killed by their own land mine while setting out on a raid.

IRA activity in the first half of 1958 was generally low, except during January. Among other incidents, a special constable was injured Jan. 14 during a machine gun attack on an RUC barracks at Swatragh, and 2 bridges in County Londonderry and electricity transformers in County Antrim and County Tyrone were bombed. 2 large arms dumps were discovered subsequently in the Swatragh area. Raiders hit at a Northern Irish customs checkpoint Jan. 17. An attack on a customs post at Killeen Jan. 20 was beaten off by police, and as a result of the raid the main Newry-Omeath road was closed Jan. 28—the first time a major cross-border road was blocked—and it remained closed until June 1959.

Other customs posts were attacked or bombed Feb. 17, Apr. 7 and 10 and June 12. 2 policemen were injured Mar. 3 when their vehicle ran into an ambush near Rosslea. An explosion damaged a pilehole-boring apparatus in Coagh, where preliminary work was under way in the construction of an atomic power station. In England, IRA gunmen wounded a British soldier and escaped after an abortive attempt Feb. 16 to seize arms from a British Army camp at Blandford, Dorsetshire. An English soldier, a Cpl. Skuse, was later connected with the raid, and, after fleeing to the Republic, he was convicted there of IRA activities.

The IRA's campaign in 1958 reached a peak during the months of July, August and September, with only a few incidents afterwards. A member of a terrorist raiding party was killed by the RUC July 2, and another was seriously wounded; one man was killed July 15 and 2 were seriously injured inside the Republic when a bomb they were carrying exploded accidentally; an RUC member was mortally wounded in an ambush at Carrickbroad July 16; after an abortive attempt to blow up the Armagh police station July 17, 3 terrorists took refuge in the town's Catholic cathedral, where they were arrested. (In a subsequent search, police found that a room in the cathedral foundations had been used as a terrorist hideout.) The 3 men were sentenced to 14 years in prison.

An RUC patrol shot and killed a farmer, James Crossan, near Swalinbar Aug. 24, when he attempted to escape across the border after being challenged. (Crossan was a member of the Sinn Fein executive in County Cavan.) 3 RUC stations were attacked by raiders using machine guns between Aug. 30 and Sept. 2, and a bomb was discovered Sept. 5 in the Royal Irish Fusiliers depot in Armagh (4 Irish nationals in the Fusiliers were implicated in the latter incident). The Orange Hall at Kinawley was blown up Sept. 7, and the IRA Publicity Bureau alleged later that the hall had been used for training special constables.

During the remainder of 1958, there were few incidents: The Rosslea RUC station was attacked Oct. 9, the Strabane employment exchange was bombed Oct. 20, and an Ulster Transport Authority van and a Post Office van were burned Nov. 8 and Dec. 31, respectively.

The tempo of IRA activity slowed considerably after 1958. Few incidents of note occurred in 1959. Bombings damaged a phone exchange, a bridge and 2 electricity transformers in February and March. 4 members of the RUC were injured Mar. 13 in an ambush near Clogher. The next incident of note did not occur until Aug. 26, when 2 policemen were wounded in an ambush near Rosslea. The Rosslea and Clogher RUC stations were unsuccessfully attacked Oct. 19, and an attempted IRA ambush was similarly foiled Oct. 26. A police patrol surprised a raiding party near Cookstown Nov. 10 and arrested 3 men. 2 policemen were wounded in an ambush Nov. 20 near Crossmaglen, and 2 police facilities were attacked the following week.

The first half of 1960 produced few IRA operations. Waterworks and electrical installations were bombed, as were several customs posts and the Orange Hall at Clogher. Other than these bombings, IRA activity was limited to seizing a Royal Mail van near Augher Apr. 15 and making an unsuccessful grenade attack on a policeman near Keady. For the next 7 months there were no incidents at all in Northern Ireland. Then IRA terrorists fired Dec. 4 on a Northern Irish police station in Belleek, County Fermanagh from Irish Republican territory in County Donegal but were repulsed without causing casualties.

By 1961, the measures taken by the authorities in both parts of Ireland had succeeded in severely limiting the operations of the IRA. Northern Irish authorities Jan. 4 allowed Liam Kelly, leader of a group of dissident IRA terrorists, to emigrate to the U.S. During 1961, however, the IRA took the lives of 2 RUC members and injured several others; this was the highest toll in any year since the beginning of the terrorist campaign. A constable, Norman Anderson, was killed Jan. 27, at the border near Rosslea while returning from a visit to his fiancée, who lived in the Republic. Another constable was killed and 3 others were injured Nov. 12, when an RUC patrol was ambushed while checking traffic crossing the border at Jonesborough. 3 policemen were injured by a land mine near Jonesborough 2 weeks later. Other IRA activity in 1961 included the bombing of 8 bridges and 2 customs houses, and 2 buses and a mail van were seized and burned.

In early 1962, the IRA finally admitted defeat in its campaign to liberate Northern Ireland and decided to halt the terrorist attacks. The outlawed rebel organization announced Feb. 26 that it was abandoning its campaign of violence against the partition of Ireland. The announcement, published in Dublin newspapers Feb. 26, was made in a statement signed by James McGarrity, secretary of the IRA's publicity bureau. The statement said: The IRA had "ordered the termination of the campaign of resistance to British occupation [of Northern Ireland] launched on Dec. 12, 1956, and instructions issued to volunteers of the active service units and local units in the occupied area have now been carried out"; "all arms and other materials have been dumped and all full-time active service volunteers will be withdrawn"; "foremost amongst the factors motivating this course of action has been the attitude of the general public whose minds have been deliberately distracted from the supreme issue facing the Irish people—the unity and freedom of Ireland."

Irish Justice Min. Charles Haughey welcomed the IRA action as "good news" and said: "The partition of our country is deeply resented by the great majority of Irishmen, but the foolish resort to violence has been repeatedly condemned by all responsible people"; the government would consider releasing the 20 IRA men imprisoned in Ireland if they promised to obey the law. (About 50 IRA men were imprisoned in Northern Ireland.)

The IRA had caused an estimated $14 million worth of damage in Northern Ireland since it resumed violence in Dec. 1956. Fatalities during that period amounted to 15: 6 Northern Irish policemen; 9 IRA men.

Irish-English Relations

Throughout the period of the IRA campaign, the 3 governments concerned attempted to cooperate to end the violence but also sought their own different ends. The Stormont government complained that the Dublin régime was not taking sufficiently strong action against the IRA within the territory of the Republic. The British government tried to bring pressure on the Republic to increase its security activities, while at the same time it attempted to act as a diplomatic buffer between the 2 parts of Ireland. The Irish Republic, while taking measures against the terrorists, attempted to find a channel for the reunion of Ireland by peaceful means, using its avowed opposition to the violence of the IRA as a lever. The government in Northern Ireland rejected unification schemes but stated that it was amenable to cooperation with the Republic.

In 1957 and 1958, Prime Min. Éamon de Valéra of the Irish Republic conducted a vigorous diplomatic campaign to reopen discussion —dormant for years—on the reunification of Ireland. De Valéra told *N.Y. Times* correspondent Drew Middleton Nov. 25, 1957 that he would "welcome a conference" on Irish problems with British and Northern Irish leaders and would agree to the establishment of the Council of Ireland proposed in the 1920 act that partitioned Ireland between Britain and the Republic.

De Valéra went to London Mar. 16, 1958 for a St. Patrick's Day visit and told reporters there that "force is not the way to unity" for Ireland. 7 persons were arrested that day when 1,000 members of rival Irish factions clashed near a London church in which de Valéra attended mass. De Valéra told British newsmen Mar. 18 that he would favor the use of the U.S.' good offices to end the partition of Ireland. Back in Dublin later, the prime minister told visiting U.S. newsmen Apr. 28 that Ireland would consider some form of association with the British Commonwealth provided that partition of Ireland could be ended on terms acceptable to the anti-British minority in Northern Ireland.

Leaders in Northern Ireland betrayed no enthusiasm for de Valéra's various proposals. Viscount Brookeborough, the Stormont government's prime minister, appealed July 12, 1958—Orangeman's Day—for efforts to develop a "close friendship" with the Irish Republic. He insisted, however, that there could be no revision of Northern Ireland's British status.

Despite the intensified border security measures put into effect by the Dublin régime and the revival of internment in the Republic, Northern Irish leaders continued to criticize what they termed lack of adequate action in the Republic. Throughout the latter part of 1957 and up until mid-1958, IRA men were tried in the Republic and received short terms of imprisonment for a variety of offenses connected with IRA activity. In most cases, the accused men refused to recognize the legitimacy of the Irish Republic's courts and, on the completion of their sentences, were sent to the internment camp at Curraugh. In some other cases, especially in the latter half of 1958, suspects were not tried first but were sent directly to internment.

The Irish Republic's Civil Guard during this period took measures against the IRA by intensifying the border patrols and by making large numbers of arrests in the border areas after terrorist incidents in the 6 Counties. In addition, in Apr. 1958, they discovered and put out of service a clandestine IRA radio station in Dublin. Despite these measures, the British government, under pressure from Stormont, protested formally to the Irish Republic July 18, 1958 over the terrorist campaign. The protest noted that "these outrages were mounted from the territory of the Irish Republic" and reminded the Republic of its duty to prevent armed incursions from Republican soil.

The Curraugh internment camp in the Republic became a subject of contention among the 3 governments in late 1958 and early 1959 as the Dublin régime took steps to close it. A mass break-out from Curraugh Dec. 2, 1958, in which 14 prisoners escaped, caused considerable anxiety in Northern Ireland. De Valéra Jan. 12, 1959 rejected appeals for the release of the 110 IRA men still held in the camp, but he did initiate a program of periodic releases. 15 prisoners had been freed Dec. 23, 1958, and the releases continued during January and February 1959. British Prime Min. Harold Macmillan, speaking in Belfast Mar. 6, expressed concern at the program of releases from Curraugh and said that he had instructed the British ambassador in Dublin to issue a protest to the Irish Republic. De Valéra called Macmillan's statement "ill-advised and uncalled for" and said that the use of detention was "a matter for the Irish government alone."

The Curraugh internment camp was closed Mar. 11, 1959, when the last 12 detainees, among them Seán Cronin, editor and reputed IRA chief of staff, were released. Only 2 days after this, however, in the wake of an incident in Northern Ireland, de Valéra Mar. 13 repeated his government's strong opposition to the illegal activities of the IRA. He said: "Lest there should be any misunderstanding . . . , the release of those detained at Curraugh involves no change in the position of the government in regard to illegal groups or activities . . . .The government will . . . use every means at its disposal to prevent them."

The policy of the Irish Republic was restated by Seán F. Lemass after he succeeded de Valéra as Éire's prime minister in June 1959. At the same time, Lemass called for cooperation between the 2 parts of Ireland on economic matters as a practical step towards reunification. Lemass July 9 offered Northern Ireland the prospect of federation in a unified Irish state with the right to retain "a separate parliament with local powers." Lemass, in an interview in the *Belfast Telegraph*, proposed a meeting of the Irish Republican and Northern Ireland governments to seek improved economic cooperation.

Viscount Brookeborough, the Northern Irish prime minister, rejected Lemass' unity offer July 13 on the ground that it was a "takeover bid" and would require the abandonment of Northern Ireland's constitutional links with Britain. Brookeborough Aug. 12 further declared that the Stormont government "cannot follow any course which would have the effect of weakening our association with Great Britain," although he did not rule out "cooperative efforts with the Republic where mutual practical advantages can be demonstrated." Brookeborough cited as the most obvious field for cooperation "action to stamp out the illegal organizations who recruit and train in the Republic." Not to do this, he said, "destroys all the professions of goodwill and the desire to contribute to the welfare of Irishmen anywhere."

The Irish Republic pursued vigorous efforts against the IRA during the latter part of 1959, particularly after any terrorist incident in Northern Ireland. Lemass Aug. 28, again strongly condemned illegal activities, which, he said, were "directly inimical to every national interest and particularly to the aim of reuniting our people."

Lord Brookeborough, however, said that "in our view the situation will not be met by telling miscreants to behave themselves. . . . More drastic action is needed." A delegation of Ulster Unionist MPs met Nov. 24 with R. A. Butler, British home secretary, and requested that the British put pressure on the Dublin régime. During a visit to Northern Ireland in Dec. 1959, Butler stated that there had been contact with the Irish Republic but that there were "limits to the extent to which one can try to run someone else's country."

During 1960 the Dublin government continued to maintain vigorous police activity against terrorism suspects, and a number of known IRA members were arrested and imprisoned. Northern Ireland, however, renewed complaints against the alleged impunity with which the IRA was, nevertheless, able to operate in the Republic.

The killing of the 2 RUC constables during 1961 was met by Prime Min. Lemass with condemnation. He declared of Constable Anderson's death Jan. 27 that "the news of the brutal murder of this young Irishman will be received by all Irish people with horror and disgust." After the 2d slaying, in November, Lemass stated that "no sane person could think that such murderous activities serve any national purpose."

The British government protested to Dublin over the latter incident while Brookeborough asked for "strong and vigorous action to root out and destroy the IRA in the Republic." Northern Ireland Home Affairs

Min. Brian Faulkner called the Republic "a sanctum sanctorum for murderers" and the Republic's measures "futile"; in light of this, he declared, it was "hypocritical nonsense" to talk about cooperation between North and South.

To deal with the violence, Lemass Nov. 22 reconstituted the Special Criminal Court and authorized it to try offenses under the Offenses Against the State Act. Explaining that the regular courts could not give adequate sentences against terrorist or adequately curb them, Lemass said that this would demonstrate the government's determination to respond strongly to illegal activities. Lemass said that "because the persons concerned have constantly displayed their contempt for the fundamental principles of democracy, it would be undesirable to rely on trial by jury which might expose jurymen and witnesses to the danger of intimidation." The Special Court began operation Nov. 27, 1961 and subsequently levied heavy prison sentences on a number of men involved in illegal activities. The end of the terrorist campaign, in Feb. 1962, led to the repeal of the Offenses Against the State Act and the release of political prisoners Apr. 20, 1962 under a general amnesty. The Special Court was kept in existence, however, to handle any further IRA violence.

The last 4 IRA prisoners held in Northern Ireland were released Dec. 16, 1963, bringing the total of those set free over the preceding year to 34. All were serving sentences of 14 years, which none had completed.

VIOLENCE & FAILURE OF LIBERALIZATION: 1963 – 9

The failure of the IRA's terrorist campaign to rouse support among Protestant Ulster's Catholics and the resignation of Lord Brookeborough from Northern Ireland's prime ministership in 1963 seemed to close an era of mutual Protestant-Catholic distrust in Ulster during which Catholics were allowed no part in Northern Ireland's government. The new prime minister, Capt. Terence Marne O'Neill, appeared to be by background and inclination disposed towards ending the antagonisms among the people of Northern Ireland and building a régime that would have the support of both religious communities. O'Neill attempted to liberalize the Stormont government's approach to Catholics, to initiate economic policies that would benefit all and to establish a rapprochement with the Irish Republic.

Initially, O'Neill's policies met with some success. Elements within his own Unionist Party and in the Protestant community, however, mobilized to oppose what they criticized as a dangerous flirtation with "popery." The most vocal spokesman of those with such views was the Rev. Ian Paisley, later moderator of the Free Presbyterian Church (founded in 1966), who quickly became the leader of the opposition to O'Neill and the Catholics.

At the same time, Catholic leaders began to organize groups to guarantee the civil rights of Catholics in Northern Ireland. The Catholic civil rights movement was modeled by its leaders on the Negro civil rights movement in the U.S., and it employed many of the same non-violent tactics. Asserting that Catholics had proved their loyalty to Stormont by refusing to support the IRA terrorist campaign, members of the civil rights movement pressed for reforms in areas of job and housing discrimination; later, demands for an end to political discrimination were also articulated.

O'Neill was caught between extremes; he did not move fast enough for Catholic militants, and any move at all towards liberalization was attacked by Protestant militants. Civil rights demonstrations by Catholics led to communal violence in Oct. 1968, and O'Neill proved unable to prevent the clashes. He was forced to resign by the right-wing opposition within his party in 1969 as the level of Protestant-Catholic violence increased.

O'Neill Attempts Liberalization

Lord Brookeborough (Basil Brooke) Mar. 25, 1963 announced his resignation at the age of 74 after 20 years as prime minister of Northern

Ireland. He had undergone a hernia operation Mar. 3 and cited his health as the reason for his retirement.

In a statement following the submission of his resignation, Lord Brookeborough said: "All through my long term of public office my aim has been to safeguard the constitution of Northern Ireland, to maintain the same level of social services as in Great Britain, to create a flourishing agricultural industry and to ease our heavy burden of unemployment. I feel it is only in this last task that, in spite of the real successes achieved in attracting new industries, I did not attain my ambition to secure a major reduction in the number of unemployed. . . ."

Brookeborough was succeeded as prime minister by Terence M. O'Neill, 48. O'Neill was descended from both Plantation aristocracy and the legendary O'Neills of Gaelic Ulster. He was too young to have experienced the troubles at the time of the division of Ireland. Educated entirely in England, he had served in the British Army outside of the 6 Protestant counties of Ulster. O'Neill had been the Belfast government's finance minister since 1956 and had entered the Stormont Parliament in 1946. O'Neill's cabinet was virtually the same as Brookeborough's; it included (Arthur) Brian Deane Faulkner as minister for both home affairs and commerce. O'Neill appointed William Craig to the Ministry of Home Affairs Apr. 29, 1963, retaining Faulkner as commerce minister. Craig, who had been Unionist chief whip in the Stormont Parliament, was succeeded in that post by Maj. James Chichester-Clark.

O'Neill indicated that he viewed the economy as a primary concern for the government. Unemployment in Northern Ireland was unusually high, even for that generally depressed area. In 1963, 7½% of the labor force was jobless in the 6 Protestant counties and the situation appeared to be worsening

In 1962, a committee led by Sir Robert Hall, the economic adviser to the British government, had predicted that unemployment would rise in Northern Ireland because of the decline in older industries and in agriculture. In response to prediction, O'Neill appointed Prof. Thomas Wilson of Glasgow University to prepare a report on the prospects for economic development in the 6 counties. Other reports followed. On the basis of these findings, O'Neill initiated policies aimed at bringing new industry into Ulster and opening up employment opportunities.

A variety of indices suggest that in economic terms, O'Neill's policies were successful. By June 1968, the number of workers employed had increased 22,000 over June 1963; the number of houses built rose from 8,842 in 1963 to 12,120 in 1968; and the index of money wages increased from 118 in 1963 to 173 in 1968. Unemployment, however, remained relatively stable at 7.2% in 1968, a decline of only 3/10 of a percentage point from 1963.

While O'Neill's policies served to strengthen the economy some-what, the economic situation was still poor when compared with Great Britain as a whole. Unemployment remained almost twice as high as in other areas of the United Kingdom, and welfare expenditures increased as more welfare measures were passed by the Westminster Parliament. The British Treasury was forced to underwrite welfare costs in North-ern Ireland, and the province remained an economic liability at a time when the rest of Britain was not very prosperous. More significantly for Stormont's problems, the Catholic unemployment rate was much higher than the over-all unemployment rate in the entire 9 counties of Ulster. Much of the new industry was located in areas with small Cath-olic populations, while the predominantly Catholic counties in the west of Ulster received little new industry.

What was regarded as the boldest of O'Neill's initiatives was to re-open direct contacts with the Irish Republic. O'Neill apparently hoped to find areas for cooperation with the Republic and to build friendly relations that would take the partition issue out of Ulster politics.

O'Neill and Republican Irish Prime Min. Seán F. Lemass conferred Jan. 14, 1965 in Belfast, Northern Ireland. This was the first time that the prime ministers of the 2 states had met since Ireland was parti-tioned. The conference took place as the result of an invitation ex-tended by O'Neill. O'Neill and Lemass said in a joint communiqué is-sued after *their* meeting: "We have discussed matters in which there may prove to be a degree of common interest and have agreed to ex-plore further what specific measures may be possible or desirable by way of practical consultation and cooperation. Our talks—which did not touch on constitutional or political questions—have been con-ducted in a most amicable way, and we look forward to a further dis-cussion in Dublin."

The planned meeting between the 2 had been kept a close secret beforehand. After the meeting, Lemass said that it was of "tremen-dous significance. . . . The problems which we are concerned with are Irish problems which can best be dealt with in Ireland by Irishmen. . . . Things can never be the same again so far as North-South relations are concerned." O'Neill stressed the mutual benefits of closer ties be-tween the 2 parts of Ireland, but noted that Northern Ireland's inde-pendence was not a question for discussion. He praised Lemass for the "symbolic act" of visiting, and thus implicitly recognizing, the govern-ment of Northern Ireland. (This was in line with an earlier statement by Lemass in July 1963 in the port town of Tralee [County Kerry, Republic of Ireland]. Lemass said then that his government recognized that the Stormont government "exists with the support of the majority in the Northern Ireland area, artificial though that area is.")

Reaction in both North and South seemed favorable to the meetings. The 2 prime ministers met again Feb. 9, 1965 in Dublin and continued their discussion of cooperation. The official communiqué stated that "there was a general review of the scope for mutually beneficial cooperation on matters of common interest" and that arrangements were made "to continue to explore specific possibilities in further meetings at both ministerial and official levels."

John Lynch (Seán Ó Loinsigh) later succeeded Lemass as the Republican Irish *taoiseach* (prime minister), and O'Neill held similar meetings with him in Belfast and Dublin. The first Lynch–O'Neill meeting took place Dec. 11, 1967 and the 2d Jan. 8, 1968. According to the official communiqués after each meeting, practical areas of mutual cooperation were discussed, particularly the prevention of the spread of hoof-and-mouth disease from Britain.

The result of these meetings was that both governments attempted to cooperate when incidents occurred. For instance, fishing trawlers from the Republic of Ireland and Northern Ireland clashed Jan. 3, 1966, off Ireland's southeastern coast. (A 1960 decision by the Irish Republic's government had permitted trawlers from Northern Ireland to fish in Southern territorial waters.) Capt. William McKee of the Northern Irish trawler *Victory* claimed that Southern crews had ripped the nets of his ship and of 8 other Northern trawlers and had thrown coal and lead at the Northern vessels. McKee had sent out a distress signal after a Southern trawler had rammed his ship, and the Irish republic's corvette *Macha* had fired warning shots over the bows of 5 Republican vessels. Capt. Michael Orpen of the Southern trawler *Ardent* was arrested later Jan. 3 and charged with the ramming. The Dublin High Court Jan. 10 issued an injunction forbidding members of the South East Coast Fishermen's Association to interfere with trawlers from Northern Ireland.

Within the Republic, however, there was still resentment toward Britain and Northern Ireland. An explosion at Ballocolla in County Laoighis Jan. 7, 1965 had rocked houses in a wide area, including the Abbeyleix Manor House, where British Princess Margaret and her husband, the Earl of Snowdon, were vacationing (they were unharmed). Electric wires and trees in the explosion area were reported down and roads strewn with debris. Police said that saboteurs apparently had caused a short circuit that touched off the explosion in a transformer station.

(10 men were arrested after a 20-mile police chase Jan. 8 in connection with the explosion. They were said to be members or followers of the outlawed IRA, which had protested Princess Margaret's visit as improper while Northern Ireland remained part of the United Kingdom instead of being united with the Republic. Spectators and defendants clashed with policemen at a preliminary hearing for 9 of the defendants in Tramore, County Waterford Jan. 12. The defendants were charged with unlawful assembly and "unlawfully and maliciously damaging 2 trees" by felling them across a road to impede police pursuit. Justice William Sweetman in Port Laoighise Jan. 22 gave 4-month jail sentences to each of the 10 men accused of participating in the explosion. The prisoners, who were convicted of malicious damage to property, had refused to give the judge their word that they would not cause trouble again for 2 years.)

Dublin's Nelson Column, a granite monument to British Adm. Horatio Nelson, was severely damaged by an explosion at 1:30 a.m. Mar. 8, 1966. The blast destroyed about 60 feet of the 104-foot column and the 20-foot statue of Nelson at its top. 8 men were arrested for questioning later Mar. 8 in connection with the bombing but were released Mar. 9. Police attributed the explosion to a faction of the outlawed IRA. What remained of the monument was dynamited by the Irish Army early Mar. 14 to the cheers of watching crowds. (Dublin's City Council on several occasions had called for the demolition of the column but had never been able to raise the estimated $112,000 cost of demolition. Dublin's mayor was reported Jan. 3, 1964 to have rejected a suggestion to put a statue of the late John F. Kennedy in its place.)

Within Northern Ireland, Prime Min. O'Neill's economic policies and his tolerance for Catholics received a mixed response from both Catholics and Protestants. Generally speaking, Catholics mistrusted the Stormont government and even a prime minister such as O'Neill. For instance, in 1962 before O'Neill came to power, the British Parliament had amended certain laws concerning the compulsory purchase powers of the government so as to bring Northern Ireland into line with the rest of Britain for the administration of welfare projects. An extension of previous Stormont powers, it permitted the purchase of property for housing or slum clearance projects; previously, only projects involving roads or public utilities could warrant the use of eminent domain purchase. The Roman Catholic primate of all Ireland, John Cardinal D'Alton, issued a statement Feb. 11, 1962 on behalf of the 6 counties' Catholic bishops in which he asserted that the bill was "open to abuse." The Catholic hierarchy apparently feared that the measure would be used by Stormont to take Church land arbitrarily.

The Lockwood Report on higher education in Northern Ireland recommended Feb. 9, 1965 that a new university be built in Coleraine, County Londonderry, and that Magee University College in Londonderry be closed. Catholics opposed this inasmuch as Magee was largely Catholic in its student body and was readily accessible to the Catholic population of Londonderry. A university at Coleraine appeared to them to be further discrimination against Catholics.

Protestants were upset by O'Neill's visits to Catholic organizations and his refusal to brand all Catholics as potential traitors. In 1966, Protestant militants protested when a new bridge across the River Lagan in Belfast was not named Carson Bridge, after the co-founder of the régime. Instead, its proposed name was changed to the Queen Elizabeth II Bridge. Protestant militants indicated a feeling that this name was patriotic enough, although it could hardly be called pro-Catholic. (When the queen and Prince Philip came to dedicate the bridge, the car in which they were riding in Belfast was damaged July 4 by a 30-pound concrete block, dropped 4 floors from a nearby building. No one was injured in the incident, which occurred on the first day of a 2-day trip by Elizabeth and Philip to Northern Ireland. Police arrested John Francis Morgan, 17, and charged him with attempting to injure the queen. Several minutes before the incident, police had arrested Miss Iris Carruthers, 44, accused of throwing a bottle at the car carrying the royal couple. RUC Inspector Gen. Sir Albert Kennedy said that the incidents seemed to have no political motive.)

O'Neill's policies eventually gained mild support among certain Catholic leaders. The 2 main opposition parties in the 6 counties were the Nationalists, whose strength was drawn almost totally from Catholics, and the Northern Ireland Labor Party, whose strength was also predominantly from Catholic votes. The Nationalists, the stronger of the 2, had consistently refused to accept the title of Loyal Opposition in the Stormont Parliament. In 1965, however, under Edward McAteer the Nationalist Party did agree to become the Loyal Opposition, thus taking half a step towards cooperation with the prevailing Unionists.

Despite his—for Ulster—liberal bent, O'Neill took no steps in the political area to ameliorate the conditions of Catholics. His measures were all "nonpartisan" and held out no promise of reducing the political disabilities placed on Catholics. For instance, by 1966 there were only 9 Catholics among the 102 members of statutory committees and boards. The gerrymandering of local areas still remained unchanged, particularly in Londonderry (which Catholics called Derry, its earlier name), where the borough government was controlled by Protestants although the population was predominantly Catholic. Perhaps an even more important point to Catholics involved voting qualifications. In Northern Ireland, a citizen had to own property to vote. Since Catholics were disproportionately renters, this qualification disfranchised more Catholics than Protestants. O'Neill never indicated having considered changing the system.

Growth of Protestant Extremism

The first challenge to Prime Min. O'Neill came from Protestants within his own party. O'Neill's economic policies were enacted with the obvious hope that, in improving the economic welfare of Northern Ireland's residents, they would blunt the cutting edge of the Catholic-Protestant differences. This seemed threatening to some Unionists and Orangemen, who perceived their political control to be based precisely on such differences. Criticism of O'Neill within his own cabinet resulted in an extensive reorganization of the cabinet July 23, 1964 and again Apr. 2, 1965. Finally, O'Neill called for a general election in Nov. 1965 to vindicate his policies. The Unionist Party won an overwhelming victory and picked up several more seats in Stormont.

Protestant militants increased their activities against the O'Neill government, and the Rev. Ian Paisley emerged as the leader of these extremists. Paisley had associated himself with a group called the "Ulster Volunteer Force" (UVF). This was a militant group dedicated to maintaining Protestant hegemony by whatever means necessary. The Stormont government declared the organization illegal June 28, 1966 after a series of incidents alleged to have been caused by UVF members.

During the first half of 1966, there had been a series of bombings of Catholic buildings in Belfast and a few bombings of Presbyterian chapels (Paisley had broken from the regular Presbyterian Church over the Catholic-Protestant issue). 2 Catholics were murdered in the streets of Belfast May 27 and June 26; another woman died of injuries sustained from a Molotov cocktail thrown through the window of her home, apparently mistaken for the Catholic pub next door. 8 men were arrested in Belfast and tried June 28 for these incidents and others. One defendant, Hugh McClean, charged with one of the murders, said to police: "I am terribly sorry about this. I am ashamed of myself. I am sorry I ever heard tell of that man Paisley or decided to follow him."

After the UVF was outlawed, Paisley dissociated himself completely from the organization but continued his attacks on the Presbyterian Church and on O'Neill's government. He was denounced by the leader of the Orange Order, Sir George Clark, on Orangeman's Day (July 12). Clark said: "The right of free speech is one of the liberties we have all fought to maintain. . . . Mr. Paisley has been given the fullest police protection on numerous occasions so that he can exercise this right to the full, but I think it is entirely wrong that brother Orangemen should lend their platforms to a man who used it to mount a continuous attack on a member of the Order. In this case it is a member who is not only a distinguished brother but the prime minister recently elected by an overwhelming majority to lead the country. . . ."

Paisley was convicted July 10 by a Belfast court on unlawful assembly charges arising from disturbances June 6 at Belfast's Assembly Hall. The June 6 demonstration, led by Paisley, had been directed against the Presbyterian Church of Ireland, which had disowned Paisley's sect. Paisley told 1,000 of his followers July 19 that he would serve a 3-month jail sentence rather than pay the £30 fine imposed by the court. He went on to declare that there was one law for "O'Neill-ites and papists" and another for "people who protest against Romanist tendencies in a Protestant country." He added that "the day is coming when I will be in the [British] House of Commons." He called the Stormont government "a ruling junta of Lundies." (The term "Lundy" has been synonymous with "traitor" among Protestant militants in Northern Ireland ever since the deposition of a mayor named Lundy by the Protestants of Derry in 1689 for proposing that the beleaguered city surrender to the Jacobite forces besieging it.)

Paisley was released from Belfast Prison Oct. 19 after serving his 3-month sentence. He told supporters that he would hold a prohibited "real good Protestant rally" the following morning, but later he abandoned the plan.

The government July 25, 1966 banned all marches in Belfast for a 3-month period. This had the effect of forestalling a number of demonstrations planned by Paisley's followers. The ban followed serious disorders that had occurred during the weekend of July 23-24. In the disturbances police had fought running battles with Paisleyite supporters. O'Neill met with British Prime Min. Harold Wilson Aug. 5 at Wilson's official residence, 10 Downing St., London, and discussed the problem of the militant Paisleyites.

O'Neill, back Sept. 23, 1966 from a short vacation in England, found an open revolt within his own party at Stormont. He said: "On returning from a very brief holiday, during which I carried out several official engagements, I find that a conspiracy has been mounted against me in my absence. I have only this to say—I will fight this out. I believe that my policies represent the best safeguard to our constitution position and our best hopes for prosperity. I believe, too, that the people of Ulster support them. I do not intend to desert all those who have backed me. I fought for my country in time of war. I have fought to maintain our constitution in time of peace. There will be no surrender now."

Some of the Unionist Party backbenchers had been circulating a petition calling for O'Neill's dismissal. This action was decried by the Unionist chief whip, James Chichester-Clark, who implied that it was of Paisleyite origin. O'Neill received a spontaneous vote of confidence Sept. 24 from some 200 Unionist delegates in Belfast. In a BBC interview that evening, O'Neill said: "I do not think any prime minister worth his salt would give in on hearing that certain backbenchers had been alleged to have taken certain actions. . . . In addition, and perhaps more important, had I assented to those suggestions it would have given encouragement to a certain gentleman who has been carrying such suggestions on his banners [Paisley]. Whoever succeeded me would have been open to blackmail in the future on the grounds of 'Remember what happened to O'Neill; we will do it to you now unless you carry out our policies.' For these reasons I decided that the only responsible action was to fight this issue to a finish, and this is what I intend to do."

O'Neill won a unanimous vote of confidence Sept. 27 from his Parliamentary Unionist Party, whose right wing had criticized O'Neill's policies of tolerance towards the Catholic minority and of rapprochement with the Irish Republic.

O'Neill strengthened his position Oct. 7 by making minor shifts within the government. His chief rival within the party, Commerce Min. Brian Faulkner, 45, was removed as House of Commons leader. Ex-Development Min. William Craig, 42, under attack by rightists, was again appointed home affairs minister (responsible for preserving order against extremist threats). Craig succeeded (Robert William) Brian McConnell, 44, who was appointed state minister of education.

But discontent continued within Unionist ranks. O'Neill dismissed Agriculture Min. Harry West from his post Apr. 26, 1967 after West refused to resign. West was dismissed on account of conflict-of-interest charges in accordance with a code established for cabinet ministers in June 1963.

Despite the code, the dismissal of West was used by Unionists opposed to O'Neill to mount another campaign against his leadership. Commerce Min. Faulkner, whose attitude towards O'Neill's policies was noncommittial, refused to attack O'Neill and promised his support, although he did declare that West was "certainly absolutely blameless."

West charged O'Neill in Stormont May 2 with having damaged his
reputation by quoting letters out of context and using privileged information. In a vote May 2, the Unionist Party narrowly passed a resolution supporting O'Neill's actions, but the members also acquitted West
of any dishonesty.

Growth of Catholic Civil Rights Movement

The first Catholic civil rights activity appeared at almost the same
time as the accession of Capt. Terence O'Neill to power in Stormont.
Action was sparked by a single incident in Dungannon, County Tyrone.
In 1963, Mrs. Patricia McCluskey, a doctor's wife, took action against
the Protestant-dominated town council's refusal to move Catholics
from overcrowded housing to some empty postwar utility homes generally considered superior to the current housing.   Mrs. McCluskey
organized the Homeless Citizens League in Dungannon and protested at
Stormont Castle and in Dungannon, using the "sit-in" technique in the
Tyrone County town. The families were finally moved to the better
housing.

Following this victory, Mrs. McCluskey and her husband, Dr. Conn
McCluskey, founded the Campaign for Social Justice in Jan. 1964 to
collect and disseminate information on cases of injustice in Northern
Ireland. While not widely recognized in Ulster, the literature and information distribution by the Campaign reached a wide audience in
Britain. Successful contacts were made with a number of British Labor
Party members who later became MPs. Although the Campaign was
intended to be apolitical—but not to refuse cooperation with groups or
individuals who would support its cause—the McCluskeys became
involved in anti-Unionist affairs in the Mid-Ulster riding (electoral
district), and in 1965 their organization affiliated with the National
Conference for Civil Liberties (NCCL) in London. With the help of the
NCCL, the Northern Ireland Civil Rights Associated was formed
in 1967.

The incident that sparked the beginning of civil rights demonstrations was deliberately undertaken by Austin Currie, a young Nationalist
MP from County Tyrone in the Stormont Parliament. Currie was frustrated by the refusal of Unionists to help him get public housing in
Caledon for a Catholic family living in poverty. The house in question,
it had been decided by the local Protestant-dominated council, was to
be given to an unmarried 19-year old Protestant secretary of a Unionist
politician. The Stormont government refused to intervene in the case,

contending that housing was a local matter over which it had no jurisdiction. Currie decided, according to his own account, that "if I waited a thousand years, I'd never get a better case than this one." Currie organized a "squat-in" at the house June 20, 1968. The publicity that this action drew led to a civil rights demonstration Aug. 24 in nearby Dungannon. The civil rights march was peaceful, so it was decided to schedule a civil rights march and demonstration in Londonderry for Oct. 5, 1968.

Londonderry Demonstrations

The police in Londonderry Oct. 5, 1968 broke up a demonstration organized by a local committee of the Northern Ireland Civil Rights Association in protest against electoral, housing and job discrimination against Catholics. The demonstrators had planned a march through the central Protestant area of the city, but the march had been banned Oct. 3 by Home Affairs Min. William Craig, after one of the Protestant Apprentice Boys' clubs declared that it intended to parade along the same route. Craig declared that if the Civil Rights Association wanted to demonstrate, "there is plenty of space and opportunity for them to do so." "If they don't, it will bear out what many people have thought, that they want to create a situation."

The demonstrators, led by Edward McAteer, head of the Nationalist Party in Stormont, Gerard Fitt, Republican Labor MP for West Belfast in the British Parliament, Patrick (Paddy) Devlin, chairman of the Northern Ireland Labor Party, and Ivan Cooper, secretary of the Derry City Labor Party, defied the ban and marched from Waterside railway station along Duke Street towards Craigavon Bridge, intending to cross the River Foyle into the center of the city. At the end of Duke Street the demonstrators were confronted by police with clubs who demanded that the crowd disperse. In the ensuing violence, MP Fitt was struck and taken to a hospital. Despite appeals for calm, some of the demonstrators attempted to breach the police barricade, and a mêlée erupted. Further disturbances took place Oct. 6, and by the end of the week 25 people had been arrested and more than 30 people had been treated in hospitals.

Home Affairs Min. Craig thanked the RUC Oct. 6 for the "efficient and discreet manner in which they prevented this happening" and rejected all allegations of police brutality. Explaining why he had banned the march, Craig declared: "There are certain areas in every town in Ulster in which Orange and Green respect each other's rights.

The procession was a direct provocation of that tradition. I know they say they are nonpolitical and nonsectarian, but all their activities indicate that they are definitely a Republican front."

Capt. Terence O'Neill explained the government's position Oct. 7. He said: "The police are the experts and the Ministry of Home Affairs backed them up." "No Republican parade has ever marched down this road in the history of Northern Ireland or, indeed, under British rule, and it could only have led to bloodshed." "I was hoping that the policies I have been trying to adopt in the last few years were beginning to break these things down. That is why I deplore what happened on Saturday, because I'm afraid it will have an effect on the more friendly relations which were beginning to grow up between the 2 sections of the community."

The Stormont ·cabinet Oct. 8 heard a full report of the Londonderry riots from Craig and declared that it was "satisfied that the action of the police was timely and prevented an extremely dangerous situation from developing."

About 1,500 Roman Catholic students of Queens University in Belfast staged a street sit-in Oct. 9 in protest against alleged police brutality in the Londonderry riots. The demonstration took place within sight of a hostile Protestant group, but a police roadblock set up between the opposing factions prevented violence.

The Rev. Ian Paisley, leader of Northern Ireland's Protestants, accused Prime Min. Terence O'Neill Oct. 9 of being soft on Catholic demands for Northern Ireland's secession from the United Kingdom and for its union with the Irish Republic.

In the 2d half of October and in Nov. 1968 Londonderry was the scene of more demonstrations, most of them organized by the Citizen's Action Committee (a Catholic civil rights group) but in one case by an extremist Unionist group. About 3,500 people took part in a sit-down demonstration Oct. 19 within the ancient walls of the city in protest against housing conditions, the local government's limitations on the franchise and alleged employment discrimination against Catholics. About 2,000 Catholic demonstrators marched in Londonderry Nov. 2 and read the UN Declaration of Human Rights. As the marchers approached one of the gates in the old city walls, members of the Loyal Citizens of Ulster, a Protestant extremist group associated with Ian Paisley, attempted to block the line of march but were restrained by police. There was no violence.

While Paisley was addressing the Ulster Constitution Defense Committee Nov. 9, however, a crowd of about 100 teenagers tried to force their way through police cordons and, when unsuccessful, threw stones and slightly injured one policeman. The upshot was that Home Affairs Min. Craig announced that all demonstrations, parades and meetings within the city walls of Londonderry were banned for a month, from Nov. 13 to Dec. 14. He said this action was taken "because of the atmosphere of tension prevailing" in the city.

More than 10,000 Catholics staged a protest march in Londonderry Nov. 16. At least 3,000 of the demonstrators, defying a government ban, marched into the inner city while the police made no effort to intervene. The demonstrators later clashed with rock-throwing Protestants.

The Northern Ireland Civil Rights Association congratulated the people of Londonderry and the Citizens' Action Committee for defying Craig and establishing their "right to march in any part of their own city." The group called on O'Neill to dismiss Craig, who, it alleged, was "leading the province along the path of intercommunal strife."

Catholic demonstrators fought with police on the steps of Londonderry's City Hall Nov. 18. The clash followed a court hearing on charges against 46 demonstrators accused of breaking the Public Order Act in the Oct. 5 demonstration. The leader of that demonstration, Nationalist Party leader Edward McAteer, did not appear in court to answer his summons. McAteer had announced Nov. 17 that the Nationalist Party would launch a civil disobedience campaign to support its demands for government reforms. The principal object of the drive, he said, was to abolish the Special Powers Act, which permitted the government to ban political demonstrations.

About 3,000 Catholics held a march in Armagh Nov. 30 while about 1,000 Protestants staged a counterdemonstration. Scuffles developed despite police efforts to keep the 2 groups apart. 6 policemen and 2 demonstrators were injured. Police Dec. 3 served a summons on Paisley for contributing to the Armagh disturbances.

Paisley and Maj. Ronald Bunting, another prominent Protestant militant, were sentenced to 3 months in prison Jan. 27, 1969 for participating in an unlawful assembly during the disturbances in Londonderry Nov. 30, 1968. Both men left the court before the sentences were passed and after scuffles had broken out in the room between police and about 30 Paisley supporters. Both men began serving their sentences Jan. 29, but Paisley was released the next day after signing a 14-day bond.

Paisley led 7,000 Protestant demonstrators in Belfast Feb. 1, 1969 in a march demanding O'Neill's dismissal. Bunting was freed on bail Feb. 4. Both appealed their 3-month sentences. They both lost their appeals, and Judge Rory Conaghan imposed additional 3-month prison terms after Paisley and Bunting refused a court order to put up a $600 bond guaranteeing a promise to desist from public disorders for 2 years. Both began to serve their 6-month sentences Mar. 25.

Stormont & British Parliaments' Debates

The Stormont House of Commons Oct. 15–16, 1968 debated the Londonderry events. Capt. O'Neill took the position that allegations of discrimination against Catholics had been exaggerated. Employment problems in Ulster were largely the consequence of economic difficulties in Britain as a whole, he declared. Similarly, allegations of discrimination in housing and local government were, he contended, unsubstantiated and unfair.

The House Oct. 16 passed a government resolution deploring the behavior of the Londonderry marchers and supporting the government's firm action. Home Affairs Min. Craig contended that the Civil Rights Association was not nonpolitical or nonsectarian and that it included members of the James Connolly Association, the Republican Party, the IRA, the Young Socialists and the Communist Party. In addition, Craig asserted, the police in Londonderry had taken no action until they had been attacked, and subsequently the minor nature of most of the injuries suffered by demonstrators belied charges of police brutality. He concluded by asserting that the government would not be intimidated and would uphold the rule of law.

The debates were boycotted by the Nationalist members of the Stormont Parliament, who decided to give up the rôle of official Opposition that they had held there since 1965. The Nationalists declared Oct. 15: "We earnestly enjoin continued restraint upon all sections of the people in the present situation, which has not been of their making. The prime minister's statement of today is not enough. While it offers some consideration in the area of housing, it is noticeably and regrettably silent in relation to the franchise and other vital matters."

In London Oct. 10, 3 Labor MPs, Russell Kerr, Mrs. Anne Kerr (his wife) and John Ryan, who had observed the Londonderry march at the invitation of the Northern Ireland Civil Rights Association, submitted a report to L. James Callaghan, the British home secretary. In it they declared that the parade consisted "of people of all religions and of none, and seemingly every shade of opinion in Northern Ireland was represented, with the exception of the Unionist Party." They also reported that the actions of the police had made it impossible for the marchers to retreat, as the police had positioned themselves well behind the marchers after the initial skirmish.

Lord Gardiner, the Lord Chancellor, had declared Oct. 7 in the House of Lords that under the Government of Ireland Act, 1920, the maintenance of law and order in Northern Ireland was in the hands of the government of Northern Ireland and that it would not "accord with the constitutional relationships" for the British government to institute an inquiry into the Londonderry events, unless the British Parliament amended the Act—an initiative that he indicated he considered injudicious.

During the (annual) debate on the "queen's speech" Nov. 4, several MPs commented on the Northern Irish situation. J. Jeremy Thorpe, the Liberal Party leader, declared that he would like to see the 1920 Act replaced to provide "even better" government in the 6 counties. Gerard Fitt declared that violence would result if no steps were taken to eliminate discrimination in Northern Ireland. He asserted that working-class Protestants as well as Catholics had been subjected to the "jackboot" of the Unionist Party. MP James Chichester-Clark (who was also Stormont's Unionist member for Londonderry) responded that MP Fitt held "Republican and extremist views" and had achieved the "high point of political hypocrisy" in "almost, but not quite" announcing his support for Capt. O'Neill's policies.

Irish Leaders Visit London

Prime Min. John Lynch of the Irish Republic paid a semi-official visit to London Oct. 29–Nov. 1, 1968 and raised the issue of partition. At a luncheon of the Anglo-Irish Parliamentary Group Oct. 30, he declared: "It has been the aim of my government and its predecessors to promote the reunification of Ireland by fostering a spirit of brotherhood among all sections of the Irish people. The clashes in the streets of Derry are an expression of the evils which partition has brought in its train."

Later Oct. 30 Lynch joined British Prime Min. Harold Wilson for a discussion of the Londonderry disturbances. He told the press afterwards that the ending of partition would be "a just and inevitable solution to the problems of Northern Ireland."

Capt. O'Neill responded Oct. 30 by deploring Lynch's "quite unwarranted intervention into our domestic affairs." "This cannot do other than make the future development of a friendly relationship on a basis of mutual respect more difficult," he declared. O'Neill concluded: "A policy of 'Ulster's difficulty is Éire's opportunity' may make sense in the Republic's domestic politics, but in the long term it can only have a negative effect both on cross-border relations and upon community relationships within Northern Ireland."

O'Neill declared Oct. 31: "I want to affirm that there is no member of the Unionist Party, let alone of the Unionist government, who wants to have anything to do with changing the constitutional position of Northern Ireland. Mr. Lynch knows that I have always refused to discuss Ulster's constitution, but let me also make it plain that there are many people in Northern Ireland, who are not all members of the Unionist Party, who are determined to maintain Ulster's heritage and defend their constitution against anyone who threatens it."

O'Neill, accompanied by William Craig and Brian Faulkner, visited London Nov. 4 and conferred with Prime Min. Wilson, Home Secy. James Callaghan and Alice Bacon, minister of state for education and science. In a joint statement, the 2 prime ministers declared that they had discussed local government franchise, housing, the Special Powers Act of 1922, the events in Londonderry and the appointment of a parliamentary commissioner for administration in Northern Ireland. On partition, Prime Min. Wilson had reaffirmed ex-Prime Min. Clement Attlee's pledge of Oct. 28, 1948 that "no changes should be made in the constitutional status of Northern Ireland without Northern Ireland's free agreement."

Speaking at a meeting of the Commonwealth Parliamentary Association later Nov. 4, O'Neill recalled that the Attlee government had provided certain assurances to Northern Ireland. Section 1, Paragraph 2 of the Ireland Act, passed May 17, 1949, stated that Northern Ireland "remains part of his majesty's dominions and of the United Kingdom, and it is hereby affirmed that in no event will Northern Ireland or any part thereof cease to be part of his majesty's dominions and of the United Kingdom without the consent of the Parliament of Northern Ireland." In addition, Attlee Oct. 28, 1948 had guaranteed Northern Ireland's "right to constitutional self-determination," with the "clear inference" that "there ought not to be any major change in constitutional arrangements affecting Northern Ireland which would be unacceptable to it," O'Neill contended. He declared: "If the UK government and Parliament were to make a declaration tomorrow in favor of a United Ireland, it would achieve nothing really practical within Ireland. The choice must clearly be between a union by coercion, which is even more unthinkable now than it was in 1912; a union by consent, and let there be no doubt that we in Ulster do not consent to it; or an acceptance of the position as it actually exists. . . . What we ask in Northern Ireland is to be allowed to make up our own minds about our own destiny. That is enough. That is all we seek . . . . Leave us in peace and there will be peace, in which the governments in Ireland, North and South, may get on with the things which really matter. . . ."

Prime Min. Wilson answered Parliamentary questions about his talks with O'Neill by noting Nov. 5 that, in his view, a reform of the Northern Irish local government franchise to ensure "one-man one-vote" should be undertaken immediately. He added that he would send O'Neill the report of the 3 MPs (Mr. and Mrs. Kerr and John Ryan) who had observed the Londonderry disturbances. Referring to O'Neill, Wilson observed: "Many have paid tribute to the reforming liberalism, so far as it goes, of Capt. O'Neill, and that ought to be encouraged to continue. But we cannot get into a position where his vulnerability to pressure from the extremists can be used as an occasion for blackmail and as an occasion where we fail to press for reforms we think are necessary. Certainly, if he were to be overthrown . . . by extremists, we would need to consider a fundamental reappraisal of our relations with Northern Ireland. Meanwhile, he should be encouraged to push on with reform as soon as he can."

O'Neill Announces Reforms

The Protestant-dominated government of Northern Ireland announced a series of political, social and economic reforms in Nov. 1968 to satisfy the grievances of Roman Catholics, who had charged they were discriminated against in housing, voting and employment. As was noted, reforms in these spheres had been requested by British Prime Min. Harold Wilson.

Northern Ireland Prime Min. Terence O'Neill Nov. 18 announced plans for the construction of 9,600 new houses in Londonderry and for the creation of 12,000 new jobs in the city by 1981. The Londonderry mayor was stripped of his power to allocate public housing. A 3-man committee, consisting of one Catholic and 2 Protestants, was established instead to allocate housing on an impartial point system. O'Neill appealed for public calm in Londonderry and elsewhere while government officials discussed implementation of the plan.

O'Neill Nov. 22 announced (a) the extension of the point system for housing to other parts of Northern Ireland, (b) the appointment of an ombudsman to hear grievances against the Belfast government and (c) the withdrawal as soon as possible of the government's powers of detention without trial. The government Nov. 25 announced the replacement of Londonderry's mayor and governing council by an appointed commission that would be impartial in the administration and development of the city.

Despite the announced reforms, the Catholics' principal demand for "one-man one-vote" was rejected. Since eligibility for voting in

Northern Ireland's parliamentary elections continued to be confined to home owners and their wives, Catholics, who were largely renters or lodgers, remained disfranchised.

O'Neill's political and social reforms of November were assailed by the Northern Ireland Labor Party Dec. 23 as too weak. The party urged O'Neill to rid the Unionists of extremists and to recognize the integrity of the Catholics' civil rights movement.

In a move to mitigate political and religious tensions, the government Dec. 16 had declared a virtual amnesty for arrested civil rights demonstrators. The announcement was made at the trial of 60 demonstrators seized during the October riots in Londonderry. The government prosecutor asked for a postponement of the hearings until May 1969, and it was indicated that the charges would be dropped then.

Further Catholic Protests Lead to Violence

Roman Catholic students marching in a civil-rights protest from Belfast to Londonderry Jan. 1-4, 1969 were frequently harassed and attacked by Protestant counterdemonstrators. Most of the paraders were members of People's Democracy, a Queen's University (Belfast) student group.

The 73-mile march, aimed at emphasizing the Catholics' charges of discrimination in housing, voting and employment, first precipitated serious violence Jan. 2 in Maghera, County Londonderry, 40 miles from Belfast. After about 90 students marched through, Protestants and Catholics brawled in the town. Police quelled the rioting, and 5 policemen were injured. The marchers had clashed earlier with members of the Protestant Loyal Ulster Organization on the outskirts of Randalstown and Toome, both in County Antrim. A bomb exploded near Toome Bridge. Catholics Jan. 3 besieged Londonderry's City Hall, where 1,000 Protestants were meeting. Police used water hoses to disperse the crowd. About 30 persons were injured.

The worst violence erupted Jan. 4 on the last leg of the march to Londonderry. 111 persons, including 12 policemen, were injured. As about 100 marchers approached the Bruntollet Bridge, about 7 miles from Londonderry, they were charged by 200 Protestant extremists, who hurled rocks, sticks and other missiles. Some of the marchers were chased into the fields and beaten. The Catholic students, whose ranks were swelled by about 2,000 sympathizers, were attacked again by Protestant extremists and stoned on the outskirts of Londonderry. The demonstrators marched into the city and to Guildhall Square, where

5,000 civil-rights supporters were holding a rally. A strong police force was posted between the demonstrators and a roving group of 1,000 Protestant extremists to prevent violence.

About 5,000 civil-rights marchers, most of them Catholics, staged a violent demonstration Jan. 11 in Newry, a town straddling Counties Armagh and Down 33 miles south-southwest of Belfast. Defying a ban on the march, the demonstrators rampaged through the town, clashing with police, setting fire to 7 police trucks and causing widespread damage. 24 demonstrators were arrested. 28 persons, including 10 policemen, were injured. A force of more than 400 police had been called into Newry to block routes that would bring the Catholic paraders into possible conflict with Protestant extremists. Northern Irish Home Min. William Long had been authorized by the cabinet Jan. 6 to reinforce the police. He received this authority following a public warning Jan. 5 by Prime Min. O'Neill that the government would strengthen its powers to maintain public order.

A new anti-riot law, aimed at curbing clashes between Protestants and Catholics, was announced by the Stormont government Jan. 28. The proposed measure, subject to approval by Ulster's Parliament, barred sit-downs in the streets or illegal occupation of public buildings, banned quasi-military organizations, made it a crime to carry offensive weapons in public and prohibited the molesting of peaceful demonstrators.

Unionist Dissension Spurs Cabinet Changes

In a radio-TV address Dec. 9, 1968, Prime Min. O'Neill had asserted that Protestant extremists had taken Northern Ireland to "the brink of chaos." O'Neill singled out the "bully-boy tactics" employed by Paisley's followers in the Armagh disturbances Nov. 30. "They incur for us the contempt of Britain and the world," he said. But warning Catholics as well that his government would not tolerate violence, O'Neill appealed for a "swift end to the growing civil disorder" in the country. The communal strife threatened the loss of British subsidies that supported Northern Ireland's economy, he warned.

O'Neill Dec. 11 dismissed Home Affairs Min. William Craig, who was opposed to the prime minister's policy of moderation in the Catholic-Protestant dispute. Capt. William Long, a moderate, was appointed acting home affairs minister. Craig's ouster came after he had delivered a speech earlier Dec. 11. In the speech, Craig had challenged O'Neill's views on Britain's role in Northern Irish affairs. In a letter handed to Craig, O'Neill said: "Your idea of an Ulster which can go it alone is a delusion. Clearly you cannot propound such views and remain a member of the government."

In reply, Craig said that if British Prime Min. Wilson "or anyone else should threaten to interfere in the exercise of our proper jurisdiction, it is your duty and that of every Unionist [Party member] to resist."

A Unionist Party caucus was called Dec. 12 on the heels of O'Neill's dismissal of Craig. The party members in Parliament voted 28-4 to retain O'Neill as prime minister and to support his moderate stand in the communal strife. 4 party members abstained and 2 left the emergency meeting. Craig was one of the 2 Unionists who left the meeting.

But O'Neill's policies continued to meet with increasing opposition within his own cabinet. Northern Irish Deputy Prime Min. Brian Faulkner resigned Jan. 24, 1969 in a dispute over the government's decision to establish an independent commission to investigate Ulster's civil rights disturbances. In his letter of resignation to O'Neill, Faulkner called the proposed probe "a political maneuver and to some extent an abdication of authority." Faulkner said the commission was being set up "to do a job which the government should be able to do itself—introduce the one-man one-vote principle in local government elections."

William Morgan resigned as Northern Irish health and social services minister Jan. 26. Morgan said he was leaving the cabinet in protest against the dispute within the Unionist Party over the government's handling of the civil-rights controversy.

O'Neill's handling of the civil rights dispute was approved by a voice vote in Parliament Jan. 29. The indorsement of the motion followed the defeat, by 31-3 vote, of an amendment criticizing O'Neill's leadership. Specifically, the approved motion outlined Northern Ireland's constitutional relationship with Britain.

O'Neill Remains As Government Head

Prime Min. O'Neill announced Feb. 3, 1969 that general Parliamentary elections would be held Feb. 24. Parliament was dissolved Feb. 4 in preparation for the nationwide balloting. O'Neill said he had decided to call the elections in an effort to win a mandate for his moderate reform program aimed at meeting the civil-rights demands of the Catholic minority. O'Neill said Feb. 5 that, if he failed to receive a clear mandate, he would resign. The Unionists lost one seat in the Feb. 24 election, but O'Neill stayed on as prime minister after defeating the Rev. Ian Paisley in a County Antrim rural constituency for a contested seat in parliament. (O'Neill was reelected from Bannside. He defeated Paisley, the Protestant extremist leader, by 7,745 votes to 6,631. A 3d candidate, Michael Farrell, leader of a militant leftwing student group, People's Democracy, polled 2,310.)

A group of 10 dissidents of the ruling Unionist Party parliamentary members opposed to O'Neill's leadership had objected to the elections in a statement issued Feb. 3. They warned that the elections would "widen the divisions" among the Unionists and "could lead to further riots and disorders." The statement said that the dissidents were not against the government's policies but that the Unionist Party under O'Neill's leadership "has seen a steady decline in the unity of the party in each year of his administration—an alarming fact, particularly in the present hazardous situation." 13 Unionist dissidents had formally called Jan. 30 for O'Neill's resignation as party leader.

Although he had failed to win a decisive victory in the Feb. 24 elections, O'Neill said Feb. 25 that he would not resign even though he had not received the mandate he sought for a civil-rights reform program. O'Neill's ruling Unionist Party had won 36 of the 52 seats in Northern Ireland's House of Commons, a loss of one seat from the 37 it had held in the previous House. 3 seats were taken by pro-O'Neill Unionist candidates who ran outside the party. 11 of the 36 newly-elected Unionists were opposed to O'Neill's leadership, and 4 others were inclined to oppose him. This still gave O'Neill a 21-15 margin in his own party. In the previous House, 14 Unionists had lined up against O'Neill. The strength of the opposition parties in the new House of Commons as a result of the elections: 6 Nationalists (Catholic), a loss of 3 seats; 2 Republican Laborites; 2 North Ireland Laborites; 3 independents. Party leader Edward McAteer was among the 3 Nationalists defeated.

(A Unionist election manifesto issued Feb. 14 had pledged to settle the dispute between the Catholics and Protestants. It said it would consider reviewing election rules to meet the grievances of Catholics who charged that they were deprived of full voting rights in local elections. The manifesto affirmed the right of all citizens to equal treatment under the law, to full social benefits and to protection against injustice.)

The Unionists voted confidence in O'Neill's leadership and reform policies at a party caucus Feb. 28. The vote was 23 to one, with one abstention. 10 dissident party members opposed to O'Neill's leadership had walked out of the caucus before the vote. The lone dissenting ballot was cast by William Craig, considered the leader of the Unionist rebels.

O'Neill announced these cabinet changes Mar. 12: William Long became development minister to replace Ivan Neill, who had been elected speaker of the Ulster House of Commons. Robert Porter succeeded Long as home affairs minister. William Fitzsimmons of the Education Ministry replaced Porter as minister of health and social services. Phelim O'Neill was appointed education minister. Nat Minford was named minister of state in the Development Ministry.

British Troops on Guard Duty

British troops began to guard public utilities, public service and government installations in Northern Ireland Apr. 21, 1969 on the heels of violent clashes between Protestants and Catholics and 3 weeks after the outbreak of what became widespread sabotage. About 500 of the 3,500 British troops regularly stationed in Northern Ireland were assigned to guard duty. The troops had been requested by the Belfast government Apr. 20 when it appeared that the Ulster constabulary force was unable to cope with the sabotage attacks.

A power station had been blown up Mar. 30 in Castlereagh, to the south of Belfast. Police contended that the blast was the work of a subversive organization seeking to disrupt Ulster's economic life. The government Mar. 31 mobilized more than 1,000 part-time policemen, members of the Ulster special constabulary, to guard key installations against possible further sabotage.

The worst outbreak of sabotage occurred in Belfast Apr. 20. 9 post offices and a bus station came under gasoline bomb attacks, and one of the city's main reservoirs was heavily damaged by an explosion, leaving parts of Belfast without water. The fires were quickly extinguished, and no injuries were reported. A power pylon was blasted at Kilmore, southwest of Belfast, but service was interrupted only temporarily.

Northern Irish police officials claimed Apr. 21 that members of the outlawed Irish Republican Army (IRA) were responsible for the Belfast explosions. The attacks, they said, were "part of a pattern" designed to exploit unrest in Ulster. An IRA spokesman in Dublin charged Apr. 21 that the Royal Ulster Constabulary, a predominantly Protestant force, and other police units had carried out the explosions "at the behest" of the Northern Ireland government. "This is a last ditch effort" by Prime Min. Terrence O'Neill "to reunify" his ruling Unionist Party, the spokesman said. Some Ulster Catholics believed the bombings had carried out by right-wing Protestants.

In a further move to increase security measures, Northern Irish

Home Affairs Min. Robert Porter announced Apr. 24 that British helicopters would be used to assist in guarding water mains and power lines against terrorist attacks and that there would be a further call-up of the constabulary. The further mobilization of the constabulary was assailed Apr. 24 by Austin Currie, a Nationalist member of the Stormont Parliament. He called the decision "absolute insanity" that could only increase tensions.

Another water main supplying Belfast was blown up Apr. 25. The incident occurred at an installation 27 miles south of the city. The blast prompted police to set up roadblocks in 3 counties and in Belfast. A water main unguarded by British troops had been blown up near Clady Apr. 24. The blast had cut off water to north Belfast.

Prime Min. Harold Wilson Apr. 25 authorized the use of 550 more British troops to guard public utilities in Northern Ireland. The additional force was requested by the Ulster government to cope with possible fresh sabotage. The new troops increased to 4,000 the number of British soldiers stationed in Northern Ireland. A British Defense Ministry statement said that the extra troops "are necessary if undue strain is not to be placed on those already there."

Members of People's Democracy, a student group supporting Catholic civil rights, had clashed with police Apr. 4 in Lurgan, an Armagh County borough 19 miles west-southwest of Belfast, during an Easter protest march from Belfast to Dublin, Ireland. 16 persons were arrested. The fighting broke out when about 400 demonstrators attempted to march on the town square in defiance of a police order to stay away. A large group of Protestant supporters of the Rev. Ian Paisley were congregating in the square but they did not become involved with the marchers. Attending the civil-rights march were students from London, Manchester, Glasgow and Wales.

In complying with Ulster's request for more troops, the British Defense Ministry made clear Apr. 20 that soldiers would be used only "for guard duty at key public utility installations." The ministry insisted that "there is no question of the use of troops to control crowds or demonstrations." (Under the 1920 act that made the 6 counties of Northern Ireland a largely self-governing state under the British Crown, Britain retained the right to intervene in Ulster in case of emergencies.)

The worst outbreak of crowd violence had occurred in Londonderry Apr. 19 after the government barred Catholic demonstrators from conducting a civil-rights protest march to Burntollet, 12 miles away. About 1,000 of the demonstrators staged a sit-down in the center of the city. A group of 200 Protestant extremists later appeared on the scene. Police, attempting to keep the 2 groups apart, were attacked by the Catholics with stones, bricks and gasoline bombs. The Protestant extremists then attacked the Catholics. Police dispersed the crowds with water hoses. The incident was followed quickly by 2 more disturbances. The Catholic protesters attacked a Londonderry police station, breaking doors and windows, and later entered the city's Bogside residential section and set up roadblocks. Police tore down the barriers, fired shots into the air and dispersed the crowd. The day's fighting resulted in injury to 209 policemen and 79 civilians.

British Parliament Debates Crisis

The British House of Commons began an emergency debate of the Ulster crisis Apr. 21, 1969. Commenting on the use of British troops in Northern Ireland Home Secy. James Callaghan said that, "clearly, our primary aim is to avert civil war, from which no one could benefit, and indeed, I do not think for a moment this is a probability." Callaghan assured Commons that the troops would not be "used actively against any element in Northern Ireland. What they will be required to do will be to repel any criminal or terrorist attack upon installations that are essential to maintain the life of the community." As for Britains's long-range interest, Callaghan said that "one must maintain the proper constitutional progress to see that [Northern Ireland's Catholic] grievances are removed and reforms introduced. If guarding the essential installations, maintaining the life of the community, by British soldiers can help to this end, I believe everyone will support it."

Catholic grievances were outlined sharply in Commons debate Apr. 22 by Bernadette Devlin, 21, who had won her seat in a by-election Apr. 18 in the Northern Irish district of Mid-Ulster. (Running as an independent Unity candidate, Miss Devlin, a Catholic civil-rights leader, had defeated Mrs. Anna Forrest, widow of the Unionist whose recent death had resulted in the by-election.)

In her maiden speech to the house, Miss Devlin charged that the ruling Unionists had sought to stir up Protestant working people against Catholics so they would not rebel against their poverty. Miss Devlin declared: "There is no place for us, the ordinary peasant, in Northern Ireland. It is a society of landlords, who by ancient charter of Charles II, still hold the rights of ordinary people in Northern Ireland over such things as fishing and paying ridiculous and exorbitant ground rents." Miss Devlin warned against a British military intervention in the affairs of the 6 counties. She said that "the one common point among all Ulstermen is that they don't like Englishmen telling them what to do."

New disorders broke out in Belfast Apr. 22 when Catholics in the Falls Road District stoned shops and buses. Police moving in to seal off the neighborhood were pelted with rocks and firebombs; 12 persons were hurt.

Meanwhile Irish Republican Foreign Min. Frank Aiken told UN Secy. Gen. U Thant Apr. 21 that the situation in Northern Ireland was "deteriorating very rapidly." Aiken expressed his concern on instructions from the Irish Republican cabinet, which had discussed the Ulster crisis at an emergency meeting in Dublin earlier Apr. 21.

Chichester-Clark Succeeds O'Neill

Capt. Terence M. O'Neill resigned Apr. 30, 1969 as prime minister of Northern Ireland. He had quit as head of Protestant Ulster's ruling and Protestant-dominated Unionist Party. Apr. 28 in the natural order of procedure before relinquishing control of the government. O'Neill was succeeded in both posts May 1 by Maj. James D. Chichester-Clark, 46, a Unionist moderate.

O'Neill was led to resign by his party's failure to give firm support to his efforts to meet the economic, political and social grievances of Northern Ireland's Roman Catholic minority. In a key test of his policy Apr. 24, Unionist members of the Ulster Senate and the House of Commons had upheld by only a narrow 28-22 vote O'Neill's proposed legislation to grant equal electoral rights to Catholics by abolishing property qualifications for municipal voting. Chichester-Clark then had resigned in protest as agriculture minister and as leader of the House. He asserted that instituting a one-man one-vote system at that time would not satisfy Catholic civil-rights demonstrators and might provoke further Protestant violence.

O'Neill, in announcing his decision to retire, had said Apr. 28 that he was stepping down in the hope that a new leader might stand a better chance of carrying out his reform program "unhampered by personal animosities." (Frank Gogarty, chairman of the Northern Ireland Civil Rights Association, a Catholic group, said Apr. 28 that O'Neill's resignation "makes no difference to us. We will continue the pressure for our demands.")

The Unionist Party's members in the Stormont House of Commons elected Chichester-Clark May 1 by 17-16 vote. He defeated Brian Faulkner, former commerce minister, who had been nominated by the party's right wing. Chichester-Clark's election was later made unanimous on the motion of 2 of Faulkner's supporters. Backed by the O'Neill faction, Chichester-Clark declared after his election that "in broad terms I agree with Capt. O'Neill." But, he said, "I'm not going to try to create a personality cult."

Prime Min. Chichester-Clark retained 6 of O'Neill's ministers and shifted 2 others in his new cabinet, announced May 3. 3 O'Neill foes received cabinet positions: John Dobson, 40, became chief whip and leader of the House of Commons; Capt. John Brooke was chosen as parliamentary secretary at the Commerce Ministry in charge of tourist development; John Taylor, 30, was assigned as Parliamentary secretary at the Home Affairs Ministry. Faulkner was appointed development minister.

Chichester-Clark's Initial Reforms

Prime Min. Chichester-Clark May 6, 1969 declared an amnesty for 133 persons, including some in jail and others awaiting trial for offenses stemming from 8 months of rioting and clashes between Catholics and Protestants. Chichester-Clark announced the decision in the 6 counties' parliament, calling it "a bid to wipe the slate clean." Among those affected by the amnesty was the Rev. Ian Paisley, extremist Protestant leader, who was freed from Belfast jail after serving 2 months of a 6-month sentence. Another public figure affected by the amnesty was Bernadette Devlin, the young Catholic civil-rights leader who had been elected to the British Parliament in April. A breach-of-the-peace charge against her was dropped.

Chichester-Clark won a unanimous vote of confidence from the Ulster Parliament May 7 after pledging universal suffrage in local elections. Voting was currently based on property holdings. Chichester-Clark said that "our immediate aim must be to produce, not later than the autumn of this year, our positive proposals for the basis" of universal suffrage. The standing committee of the ruling Unionist Party unanimously approved Chichester-Clark's appointment as prime minister at a meeting May 9. It also indorsed his pledge to seek voting reforms. The resolution, introduced by Lord Brookeborough, a former prime minister, committed the Unionists "to create a united and prosperous community on a basis of equality and justice."

Chichester-Clark announced May 15 that legislation would be introduced to establish an ombudsman "to consider citizens' grievances against public bodies or authorities outside the field of central government." The ombudsman, to be known officially as the "Parliamentary commissioner for administration," "would hear complaints of alleged religious discrimination and other grievances.

A group campaigning for government changes, the Ulster Civil Rights Association, warned Chichester-Clark's régime May 18 that if it did not produce a time-table for reforms within 6 weeks, there would be a renewal of street demonstrations and other civil disobedience. In response to the association's demand, Chichester-Clark said May 20 that his government would "not contemplate yielding to threats of duress or anything in the nature of an ultimatum from any quarter."

Northern Ireland's local elections, scheduled for 1970, were postponed until Oct. 1971, Home Affairs Min. Robert Porter announced in Parliament in Belfast May 20, 1969. Porter said that the balloting would be held on the basis of universal franchise under terms of legislation yet to be introduced.

The system of "one man one vote," as demanded by Catholic civil-rights protesters, was one of several reforms that Chichester-Clark discussed with British Prime Min. Harold Wilson in London May 21. Reporting to the British House of Commons on the meeting, Wilson said May 22 that he was "reasonably satisfied" with Protestant Ulster's reform program. Wilson said that he had urged the elimination, as soon as possible, of the 1922 Special Powers Act, which he described as "this source of embarrassment." The act permitted arbitrary arrest and detention in the interest of public order.

Chichester-Clark told the Stormont Parliament May 22 that Wilson had accepted Northern Ireland's reform program as "a sustained momentum of social reform." He said that a greater reduction of unemployment and improved housing remained Northern Ireland's greatest needs. British troops, sent to Ulster in April to prevent sabotage attacks against public utilities, would remain "until the nature of any continuing threat had been morefully assessed," Chichester-Clark said.

Protestant Celebrations Spark Riots

Northern Ireland was swept by a fresh outbreak of clashes between Protestants and Catholics July 12-16, 1969. The most serious disturbances centered in Londonderry and Belfast. Officials blamed the violence on hooligans rather than religious or political demonstrators.

The communal strife was precipitated by Protestant celebrations marking the 279th anniversary of the Battle of Boyne (a river near Dublin), in which a Protestant force led by King William II defeated the deposed Catholic king, James II. The occasion was marked with parades staged throughout Ulster July 12 by about 100,000 followers of the Protestant Orange Order. Most of the marches were peaceful but clashes broke out in Londonderry and Lurgan. 20 policemen were injured and 40 rioters were arrested in Londonderry, where the violence continued through July 13. At least 40 gasoline bombs were hurled at police attempting to halt the fighting and looting in the city.

Police were pelted with bricks and bottles July 14 when they tried to break up a mêlée between Protestants and Catholics in Belfast. More than 1,500 British troops moved from the Belfast area to a military base in Londonderry July 14 to guard key installations and tighten security. They were not to be used to quell the rioting, a Northern Irish government spokesman said. At the same time, the government warned after an emergency cabinet meeting July 14 that it would use tougher measures to enforce the peace. Home Affairs Min. Robert Porter announced that the police would be strengthened immediately by several hundred members of the special constabulary and auxiliary force known locally as the "B-Specials." A government statement said Northern Ireland "would not be held ransom by irresponsible and antisocial elements."

Prime Min. Chichester-Clark had cut short a vacation in England to return to Belfast July 13. He called the situation "disturbing." Bernadette Devlin, the young Catholic Northern Irish member of the British Parliament, ascribed the violence to "drink" and "oppression."

BRITISH ARMY INTERVENES: AUG. 1969—APR. 1970 PHASE

With the resumption of communal violence in Protestant Ulster in Aug. 1969, the British government altered the rôle of the British army in Ulster from one of protecting public facilities to that of direct interposition between the opposing groups. During this period, the internal security forces in Northern Ireland proved incapable of halting the continued strife.

Initially, Roman Catholics welcomed the army's intervention, viewing it as a shield to protect them from the Protestant-dominated Royal Ulster police. This view changed by mid-1970, however, as the British army allegedly began to behave as an arm of the Stormont government. In contrast, many Protestants who had seen the army's initial intervention as pro-Catholic began to revise their views, apparently perceiving the army as a means of maintaining the political and social status quo.

Belfast & Londonderry Riots; British Intervene

The worst communal rioting in more than 30 years took place in Belfast Aug. 2–4, 1969. Battles were fought between police and rival mobs of Catholics and Protestants. Some of the heaviest fighting centered in Shankhill Road, a predominantly Protestant district. Damage to 200 shops in the area, looted and burned by the rioters, was estimated at $750,000.

The Stormont cabinet announced Aug. 5 that it had drawn up emergency plans to cope with any further rioting in Belfast. The plans, which were not disclosed, were to be initiated only if the police lost control of the situation. The Northern Ireland Command disclosed Aug. 5, however, that some British troops in Ulster had been alerted to assist the police if violence intensified.

The clashes were precipitated Aug. 2 by a march of junior members of the Protestant Orange Order down Shankhill Road. As the paraders passed a group of houses occupied by Catholics, stones were thrown at the marchers, and fighting ensued. 97 persons, including 17 policemen, were injured in the more than 16 hours of subsequent violence. 35 persons were arrested. Clubwielding police charged both Protestant and Catholic groups to keep them apart.

In the rioting Aug. 3, more than 2,000 Protestants attempting to march into the Catholic residential districts of Belfast clashed again with police. The rioters built street barricades of old cars and set them ablaze. They stoned police and firemen who tried to remove the bar-

49

riers. The barricades were finally dismantled after armored cars were dispersed into side streets. 10 policemen were injured when cans of burning paint were thrown at their vehicles. The Aug. 3 rioting broke out only hours after the cabinet, in an emergency meeting, had appealed to the public to stay off the streets.

The Aug. 4 violence occurred in a predominantly Catholic section in the western part of Belfast. More than 30 gasoline bombs were thrown at police and firemen as they sought to clear a path through a barricade to reach 2 shops and a house set afire by the rioters. Policemen, using water cannons, charged into 1,000 rioters and made their way to the flaming wreckage. The Catholic and Protestant factions pelted each other with bricks, stones and bottles.

Following a 2-hour emergency meeting shortly before the fighting broke out again Aug. 4, Prime Min. Chichester-Clark had announced that he had "no intention of introducing a curfew, and I am reluctant to call in British troops" to help the Royal Ulster Constabulary (RUC) maintain the peace. Later in the day, Chichester-Clark and Catholic political leaders issued a joint statement appealing "to the community to to resist all forms of provocation and assist in the restoration of law and order."

A Belfast court Aug. 4 sentenced 21 rioters to prison terms ranging from one to 6 months. 33 persons were fined a total of $3,200.

Britain openly intervened militarily in the Protestant-Catholic dispute in Northern Ireland by dispatching troops to quell new clashes between the rival communities Aug. 12-16. 8 persons, most of them Catholics, were killed, and 532 civilians and 226 policemen were wounded. The strife was marked by savage gunfights and gasoline-bomb and fire attacks waged by the 2 opposing forces in Londonderry, Belfast and other Northern Irish cities. Property damage was heavy in Belfast and Londonderry. Northern Irish officials estimated Aug. 19 that the fires started in the Aug. 12-16 riots had destroyed more than 400 homes, 15 factories and warehouses and hundreds of small shops. More than 5,000 persons had left their homes in Belfast because of the destruction or out of fear.

The deadly outbreak of violence had erupted in Londonderry Aug. 12 as more than 1,000 RUC men fought with Catholics using sticks and gasoline bombs. The police had intervened after Catholic youths had swarmed out of their Bogside slum area and stoned marchers representing a Protestant fraternal order, the Apprentice Boys of Derry (Irish Catholic name for Londonderry). The day's fighting resulted in injury to 80 policemen and 12 civilians. The fighting continued in Londonderry Aug. 13 and spread to Dungiven, Newry and

Armagh, where crowds attacked police stations. Policemen in Lurgan separated Catholic and Protestant mobs.

As the violence mounted in intensity, the Stormont government called on Britain Aug. 14 to assist in its suppression. In response to the appeal, 300 British soldiers moved into the center of Londonderry Naval Base to reinforce the police battling Catholic mobs. The troops sealed off the Bogside area, separating the Catholics from the Protestant mobs. Heretofore, British troops in Northern Ireland had been assigned almost entirely to guard utilities against sabotage attacks. The troop intervention marked the first use of British soldiers for riot control in the British Isles since the 1916 Easter rebellion in Dublin. Britain began airlifting reinforcements from England to Northern Ireland Aug. 15, and by Aug. 17 the British force there totaled about 4,200 men.

The Belfast government Aug. 15 mobilized the 8,000-member Special B Constabulary, the part-time police force, to augment the 3,000-man RUC. The B-Specials had been depicted by the Catholics as Protestant extremists and denounced as a bigoted anti-Catholic force. It had been formed after the 1921 partition of Ireland to help the RUC combat the terrorist attacks of the outlawed Irish Republican Army (IRA), which was pledged to the reunification of Ireland. The last time they had been used previously was for patrol duty during IRA raids in the late 1950s.

As the rioting in Londonderry was brought under control, violence intensified Aug. 15 in Belfast, where 3 persons were shot to death. Sniper fire was reported from tenement windows, apartment roofs and barricades in the Catholic areas. Protestant and Catholic youths fought in the Protestant area of Shankhill Road, hurling stones and bottles. General calm was restored in Belfast by British troops Aug. 16, although a few shooting incidents were reported. During the previous 24 hours, police reported 236 persons, including 4 policemen, had been injured. Of these, 66 had been shot.

Prime Min. Chichester-Clark called a meeting of 20 Protestant and Catholic civic leaders Aug. 18 to discuss ways of restoring peace and understanding between the 2 religious communities. The leaders agreed to the formation of a reconciliation committee of representatives from the churches, industry, universities and the legal profession in an effort to re-establish "peace and confidence."

Pope Paul VI Aug. 17 had expressed "immense sadness because of the bitter riots and repressions" in Northern Ireland. The pope supported Catholic demands for equal rights but cautioned that such rights must not be achieved "by means of violence or riots."

British Army's New Rôle Formalized

The British Army assumed control of all security in Northern Ireland Aug. 19, 1969 as a result of the bloody clashes between Protestants and Catholics. The British action, agreed to at a meeting held in London Aug. 19 by British Prime Min. Harold Wilson and Northern Irish Prime Min. James Chichester-Clark, was denounced by Protestant political leaders in Ulster and by the Irish government in Dublin.

According to a joint declaration issued by Wilson and Chichester-Clark, the British Army in Ulster, led by Lt. Gen. Ian H. Freeland, would be in command of the 8,400-member Special B Constabulary, the emergency police force, and of that part of the regular 3,000 man RUC assigned to riot duty. The Wilson-Chichester-Clark declaration also said:

● Britain would establish a "political presence" in Northern Ireland by sending 2 senior civil servants to Belfast to seek a long-term solution of the Protestant-Catholic dispute. The 2 British officials would be permanently stationed there. (Appointed to the posts Aug. 22 were J. Oliver Wright, deputy undersecretary of state in the Foreign & Commonwealth Office, assigned to Chichester-Clark's office, and A. S. Baker, assistant secretary at the Home Affairs Office, assigned to the home affairs minister.)

● All citizens in Northern Ireland should be "treated with the same freedom, the same equality before the law and the same freedom from discrimination in all matters."

● Britain reaffirmed that the latest violence in Ulster did not detract from previous British pledges "that Northern Ireland should not cease to be a part of the United Kingdom without the consent of Northern Ireland." The border between Ireland and Northern Ireland "is not an issue" in the current dispute.

● Northern Ireland agreed to establish an impartial investigation of the recent violence and to urge the public to surrender unauthorized weapons under an amnesty.

● "In order that British troops can be withdrawn from the internal security rôle at the earliest possible moment, the 2 governments will discuss . . . the future of the civilian security services of Northern Ireland which will take over when those troops withdraw."

In a TV report later Aug. 19, Wilson said that London expected Ulster's government to proceed with "full momentum in putting into effect civil rights programs dealing with housing, jobs and local voting." He added: "There is no good sending troops if the cause of riots are not dealt with." Wilson said that his government "believes the B-Specials should be phased out of riot control. Their disarming will be a matter for Gen. Freeland to decide."

Chichester-Clark said after the meeting that the decision to give the British Army control of all forces in Ulster was his proposal.

In a move to calm Catholic fears, the British Army Aug. 22 called on the B-Specials to turn in their weapons. They had been permitted to keep their issued arms at home. Freeland emphasized, however, that under his order the B-Specials were "not being disarmed. Their weapons are being brought under control." Freeland also announced that an additional 500 British troops would be flown to Ulster Aug. 23, raising his force there to about 6,600 men. Some Catholic political leaders denounced Freeland's directive as doing too little to curb the B-Specials, whom they blamed for most of the violence in mid-July and August.

Some of the B-Specials began turning in their weapons Aug. 23. An announcement made by an underground radio calling itself Radio Free Belfast said, howevèr, that Catholic streets in Ulster would remain barricaded until the B-Specials were disbanded and the Ulster government was taken over by London. The announcement assailed the B-Specials as "Protestant thugs with a license to kill."

A spokesman for the Royal Ulster Constabulary (RUC) reported Aug. 25 that a 21-member platoon of the B-Specials at Ballynahinch, 15 miles south of Belfast, had resigned Aug. 23 and turned in their uniforms and weapons in protest against the order to turn in their arms. A petition submitted to Ulster's government authorities Aug. 25 and signed by many RUC members deplored what it called British Prime Min. Wilson's implication "that the RUC is not an impartial force." "We are greatly perturbed at the ever-increasing amount of antipolice propaganda and demand that steps be immediately taken by the appropriate authorities to insure that the truth be propagated to the public," the statement said.

The Belfast government Sept. 2 announced a 3-week amnesty under which people could turn in arms and ammunition without being prosecuted. The Belfast government Aug. 21 had announced the formation of an advisory board to reorganize Protestant Ulster's police and to re-examine the role of the B-Specials. 2 Britons were named to the board: Sir James Robertson, the chief constable of Glasgow, and Robert Mark, deputy commissioner of the London Metropolitan Police Force. Northern Irish Development Min. Brian Faulkner had declared Aug. 20 that despite the agreement granting Britain a greater role in Ulster's internal affairs, "there is absolutely no diminution in the pow-

ers of the Northern Ireland government." Faulkner vowed that the
Special B Constabulary would be neither disarmed nor dissolved.

Catholic leaders in Ulster Aug. 20 had hailed the Wilson-
Chichester-Clark agreement as a victory for them. The Rev. Ian Paisley,
the militant Protestant leader, said that the Ulster government had
"capitulated to the Roman Catholic Church."

Irish Republic Takes a Stand

The Northern Irish civil strife assumed an international character
for the first time when the government of the Irish Republic, sympathetic to Ulster's Catholics, renewed its controversy with Britain over
the 1921 partition of Ireland, which had separated 6 Ulster counties
from the other 26 of Ireland. The Irish Republican government expressed its concern by mobilizing 2,000 reservists Aug. 15, 1969 for
possible use in a Dublin-proposed British-Irish or UN peace-keeping
force in Northern Ireland and by moving its regular forces closer to the
Protestant Ulster frontier. Following London's rejection Aug. 15 of
Dublin's proposal for a joint British-Irish peace team, Ireland asked the
UN Security Council Aug. 17 to call a meeting to consider the dispatch
of a UN force to Ulster.

In a statement accompanying the announcement of the mobilization of 2,000 Irish army reservists, Prime Min. John Lynch called
Aug. 15 for a permanent solution to the partition of Ireland. He appealed for "a period of restraint so as to create an interim situation of
non-violence, during which every possible channel may be explored so
as to arrive at an acceptable solution of the immediate problems and
eventually reach a permanent solution of the basic issues involved."

In addition to mobilizing reservists, the Irish Republican government moved about 120 regular troops to the Ulster border near Cavan.
The announced purpose of the move was to defend 5 field hospitals
established to treat Catholic victims of the Northern Ireland fighting
who might refuse to be treated in Protestant Ulster hospitals. The Irish
army also set up 2 refugee centers at Finner Camp in County Donegal,
Ireland's northern-most county, and at Gormanston, about 20 miles
north of Dublin. About 1,000 Ulster Catholics were said to have fled
to the Irish Republic.

Prime Min. Lynch Aug. 20 expressed dissatisfaction with the decision to turn over Northern Ireland's security to British forces. Lynch
reiterated that British troops should be withdrawn from Ulster and replaced with a UN force. An Irish Republican government statement
Aug. 21 predicted that the Ulster-British accord would do little to solve

"the political, social and economic injustices from which the [Catholic] minority in the 6 counties [of Northern Ireland] have suffered so grievously and for so long." The statement repeated Dublin's call for a UN peace-keeping force or "other appropriate United Nations involvement" in Northern Ireland. The statement reaffirmed Ireland's claim to Northern Ireland and said that Dublin rejected London's assertion that responsibility for Protestant Ulster was an internal British affair.

Lynch Aug. 14 had first proposed the dispatch of a UN force to quell the disorders in Northern Ireland, then at their height. He said that British troops would be unable to maintain order there. Lynch also called on London to open talks with Dublin to review the constitutional position of Northern Ireland, which, he claimed, was at the root of the problem.

The British Foreign & Commonwealth Office Aug. 15 rejected both of Lynch's proposals. It insisted that no decision would be made on Northern Ireland's status without the consent of the Stormont Parliament. The introduction of a UN force in Northern Ireland, part of the United Kingdom, would be interference in Britain's internal affairs, the statement said.

Britain Aug. 15 also rejected Ireland's suggestion for a joint Irish-British peace-keeping force in Ulster. In spurning the proposal, Lord Chalfont, minister of state for foreign and commonwealth affairs, who had just met with Irish External Affairs Min. Patrick J. Hillery in London, reiterated the British view that events in Northern Ireland were an internal matter for the British government.

Ireland's request for a UN Security Council meeting on the Ulster crisis was formally presented to Security Council Pres. Jaime de Pinies of Spain Aug. 17. External Affairs Min. Hillery conferred with UN Secy. Gen. U Thant in New York Aug. 18. Thant said later that they had discussed "the possibility of a United Nations contribution toward easing the situation in Northern Ireland."

The UN Security Council Aug. 20 rejected Ireland's appeal to place the Ulster dispute on its agenda. The Council adjourned without a vote. In presenting Dublin's case, External Affairs Min. Hillery took issue with Britain's argument that the question of Ulster was an internal British matter. Hillery held that Article 2 of the UN Charter did not apply in this case because Ireland had never recognized the partition of Ireland, making the 6 northeastern counties a part of the United Kingdom.

Before departing for Dublin Aug. 21, Hillery said that the Council's refusal to take up the Northern Ireland dispute did not represent a defeat for his country. The Council's adjournment without debate "left the question open," Hillery said. He added: "I have opened with U Thant and the United Nations the whole question of trying to do something about the situation."

Northern Irish Prime Min. James Chichester-Clark had declared in the Belfast House of Commons Aug. 15 the communal violence in the 6 counties had been fomented by a "conspiracy of forces" attempting to overthrow his politically young government. "Those who cry loudly for British intervention see it as a halfway house for the long-sought goal" of a unified Irish Republic, he said. Chichester-Clark also said that Britain had given Protestant Ulster's government "complete and unqualified assurance that the position of Northern Ireland as an integral part of the United Kingdom is not now in question, nor will it be brought into question."

Prime Min. Chichester-Clark Aug. 15 denounced Irish Prime Min. Lynch's proposal of a UN peace-keeping force as a "clumsy and intolerable intrusion into our internal affairs." Asserting that he would oppose any outside force in Northern Ireland, Chichester-Clark said he would hold Lynch "personally responsible for any worsening of feeling which these inflammatory and ill-considered remarks may cause."

Chichester-Clark charged Aug. 17 that Ireland's leaders were "behaving like hooligans" in ordering the mobilization of reserves and sending troops to the Northern Irish border. He said these moves had badly damaged relations between the 2 countries. He repeated his charge that "sinister and irresponsible" elements sympathetic to the Irish Republic had been responsible for the current violence, which, he claimed, was aimed at ending the 1921 partition. Chichester-Clark ruled out any possibility of including Protestant Ulster's Catholics in a coalition government on the ground that the opposition Catholics in the Stormont Parliament were "opposed to the very existence of this state itself." He said, however, that he would continue to press for reforms to meet the grievances of the Catholic minority, the underlying cause of the current unrest.

IRA Resumes Activities in Ulster

The outlawed Irish Republican Army (IRA) in Dublin appealed Aug. 15 for arms, funds and volunteers to cross the border into Northern Ireland to join their fighting fellow Catholics. The appeal followed a meeting of the 12 commandants of the IRA's executive committee.

The IRA announced in Dublin Aug. 18 that "a number of fully equipped" IRA units had crossed into Northern Ireland to assist the embattled Catholics there. The statement, signed by IRA chief of staff

Cathal Goulding, said his men were being employed only in a defensive capacity where Catholics had been "terrorized by. . . mobs backed by armed B-Specials." The statement said that British troops must "take the consequences" if they permit themselves "to be used to suppress the legitimate attempts of the people to defend themselves against the B-Specials and the sectarian Orange [Protestant] murder gangs." The IRA warned the British troops that until Britain "disarms and disbands the B-Specials, legislates for all [Catholic] civil-rights demands and indeed removes you from the country altogether, you are in a very perilous situation."

Goulding said that the IRA had taken part in fighting in Londonderry and Belfast. He called on the Irish government to "immediately use the Irish army to defend the persecuted people of the 6 counties."

Irish Prime Min. Lynch Aug. 19 assailed IRA interference in the strife in Northern Ireland. The Irish government, he said, would "not tolerate any usurpation of its powers by any group whatsoever." As for the Aug. 18 statement "purporting to come from the Irish Republican Army," Lynch said: "I wish to assert on behalf of the government and people of Ireland that no group has authority whatever to speak or act for the Irish people."

Both Sides Seek U.S. Support

Bernadette Devlin, Northern Irish Catholic civil-rights activist and member of the British House of Commons, arrived in the U.S. Aug. 21 on a mission to raise $1 million for the more than 500 Catholic families made homeless by the Ulster rioting and to rally public opinion to her cause.

Miss Devlin, landing in New York, said that the British Army must remain in Northern Ireland because if it were withdrawn, "the underlying problems will again raise their heads." The Catholics' "short-term demand is that the British must disarm and disband the constabulary and the special police, which are instruments of the Unionist Party that dominates the 6 northern counties," Miss Devlin said. The final solution to the problem, she held, was a united free Ireland. But Miss Devlin contended that it must not be based on the Irish Republic, which, she said, was economically too weak to absorb industrially depressed Northern Ireland.

Speaking at a New York street rally Aug. 22, Miss Devlin called for a boycott of British Overseas Airways Corp. and of British goods. She said Ulster Catholics wanted the Protestant Unionist government replaced by direct British rule until an all-Irish plebiscite could be held to consider reunification of Ireland.

In an interview published Aug. 17 in London's *Sunday Mirror*, Miss Devlin had called for an end to Protestant rule in Ulster. She said that "the barricades of Northern Ireland can never be taken down while the police are controlled by the Unionist Party and work to serve the ends of that party." Miss Devlin warned that if these Catholic demands were not met, "we would have a right to ask for help from any quarter." This was an apparent allusion to the Irish Republic.

Miss Devlin returned to Belfast Sept. 3, 4 days ahead of schedule. She said that she had cut short her visit "because the fund is going well and I have business in Northern Ireland."

Miss Devlin had conferred with Secy. Gen. U Thant at UN headquarters in New York Aug. 26. She said afterwards that he had expressed sympathy with her complaint that the Special B Constabulary had not been disbanded.

2 leaders of the ruling Unionist Party, acting as a self-styled "truth squad," had arrived in the U.S. Aug. 29 to counteract what they called Miss Devlin's propaganda campaign on behalf of Ulster's Catholics. They were Robert Bailie, a member of the Stormont Parliament, and W. Stratton Mills, a member of the British House of Commons. Both men charged on arriving in New York that Miss Devlin had been "wildly irresponsible and totally inaccurate" in presenting her assessment of the Ulster crisis to the American public. Mills said Miss Devlin was a "female Castro in a miniskirt" who "must be put into true perspective, and that is what we hope to do." Bailie described Miss Devlin's speeches as "a campaign for the destruction of Northern Ireland."

The money that Miss Devlin had collected in the U.S. was the subject of a New York TV debate between Miss Devlin and Mills Sept. 2. Mills questioned whether the funds would be used for Catholic relief, as Miss Devlin said it would, or for further violence. Miss Devlin replied that the $200,000 in contributions she had received in the previous 10 days would be administered by the Northern Ireland Civil Rights Association for the benefit of the riot victims.

Bailie and Mills called on the Irish embassy in Washington Sept. 3 and inquired whether Dublin was behind Miss Devlin's visit to the U.S. They specifically asked whether her efforts had the support of the Irish Tourist Board, Irish International Airlines or the Irish consulate in New York.

Reforms Proposed

A civil-rights program aimed at ending discrimination against Catholics in Northern Ireland and at eliminating the causes of the Protestant-Catholic strife was proposed in a joint communiqué issued by the British and Ulster governments Aug. 29, 1969. The plan had been drawn up in talks held by British Home Secy. James Callaghan with Prime Min. Chichester-Clark and other Northern Irish officials in Belfast Aug. 27-29.

The Parliamentary delegation of the ruling Unionist Party unanimously approved the reform proposals Sept. 2. The proposals, some of which had been advanced previously by the Northern Irish government, dealt with abolishing bias in jobs and housing and local voting rights. The communiqué also said:

• A community relations board, composed of Protestants and Catholics should be formed "to promote good relations between all sections of the community."

• The Belfast government would introduce legislation "to establish machinery for the investigation of citizens' grievances against local or public authorities, with ultimate recourse to the courts." This would be in addition to the already-approved Parliamentary commissioner, who would carry out similar functions.

• Britain would provide $600,000 in relief money for the victims of the summer disorders.

• Britain noted with satisfaction Northern Ireland's formation of a Tribunal of Inquiry to investigate the disorders and the creation of an advisory board to study the revamping of Protestant Ulster's police force.

Callaghan, who had visited the riot-torn areas, said that he had found people "badly shocked and frightened." He said: "If these reforms are carried out with energy and sincerity, this day could be the beginning of a new era in the creation of confidence between the 2 communities." Callaghan said that in view of the latest reform proposals, the barricades that had been installed in Belfast and Londonderry after the fighting of Aug. 14-15 should be removed, but he said they would not be dismantled forcibly.

Chichester-Clark called Aug. 30 for the removal of the barriers in Londonderry and Belfast. He said: "Let the barricades come down now—whether they be street barricades or barricades of the mind. . . . Give peace a chance."

William Cardinal Conway, Roman Catholic primate of Ireland, expressed confidence in the reform program Aug. 30 and urged Catholics to give the government time to implement it. After delivering his statement, the cardinal for the first time attended a meeting of the Belfast government's Protestant-Catholic reconciliation committee. Government officials welcomed his attendance as a sign of "greater participation" by the Catholic Church in the Protestant régime's efforts to find a solution to the controversy.

The Rev. Ian Paisley, militant Protestant leader, denounced the reform proposals Aug. 30. He charged that Callaghan had given the Catholics "a charter for revolution and violence" and that Chichester-Clark had been "coerced, cajoled and bullied."

Barricades in Londonderry & Belfast

Catholics in Londonderry and Belfast defied appeals to remove their street barricades and were reported Aug. 31 to be strengthening them instead. Protestants built barricades of their own in those 2 cities as a protest against the failure of the British Army and the police to remove the Catholic barriers.

In Londonderry, the 20-member executive committee of the Catholics' Derry Citizen's Defense Association said Aug. 31 that it would maintain the street obstructions in the Bogside area pending "concrete evidence" that the British-Protestant Ulster reform program announced Aug. 29 would be carried out. The association said, however, that "in the interest of peace and the convenience of citizens," it was prepared to discuss the eventual removal of the barricades with British military authorities. Bogside Catholic leaders Aug. 31 rejected a British request to station military police there to stop an outbreak of thefts. The leaders said they would prefer to use their own volunteer force to patrol the area.

An illegal extremist Protestant group, the Ulster Volunteer Force, demanded Sept. 1 that Catholics remove the barriers in Londonderry and Belfast. The group warned that its "battalions" were ready for counteraction. The threat was conveyed in a letter delivered to the Belfast office of the British Broadcasting Corp. and signed by a "Capt. Stevens, chief of staff of the Ulster Volunteer Force.

About 200 British troops Aug. 24 had occupied Dungannon, 40 miles west of Belfast, following repeated warnings by Catholic civil-rights leaders that new violence with Protestants was imminent. Dungannon, a town of 6,500 was predominantly Catholic.

A joint statement issued by Northern Ireland's 5 Catholic bishops Aug. 24 charged that Protestant militants were to blame for the previous week's violence. The bishops asserted that Catholic districts in Belfast had been "invaded" Aug. 21-22 by "mobs equipped with machine guns and other firearms." "We reject entirely the hypothesis that the origin of last week's tragedy was an armed insurrection," the 5 bishops said. Prime Min. Chichester-Clark took issue with the bishops' statement but said he would not go into details in order to avoid an unnecessary "exchange of recriminations." He said that "no section of the community has a monopoly of either the victims or the guilty."

Catholics in Londonderry's Bogside district Sept. 22 dismantled the street barricades that had stood since Aug. 12 as a defense in the fighting against rival Protestants. The Catholics replaced the barriers with a white line and continued to warn that their area remained off-limits to police and British army troops.

Catholic refusal to remove the Belfast barricades had provoked a series of incidents involving British troops in the city Sept. 4-14 and further heightened tensions between Catholics and Protestants. *Among the major developments in Belfast*:

● Protestant extremists Sept. 4 attempted to build barricades in the southern half of the city in protest against Catholic refusal to remove theirs. They overturned trucks and cars to set up the obstacles.

● British troops Sept. 6, with Catholic consent, tore down the Albert Street barricade, permitting a resumption of traffic for the first time in 3 weeks through the Catholics' Falls Road area. Earlier Sept. 6, Protestant crowds had marched on a mixed Catholic-Protestant district in East Belfast despite attempts by a group of clergymen to stop them by linking arms across a road. The Rev. Ian Paisley, the Protestant extremist leader, was carried out by the police to calm his followers. He persuaded the crowd to disperse. Paisley's intervention had prevented a similar Protestant outburst in Belfast the previous day.

● British troops Sept. 7 used tear gas for the first time to disperse about 3,000 Catholic and Protestant extremists confronting each other across a barricade on a street that joined the Catholics' Falls Road with the Protestants' Shankill Road.

● One person was killed Sept. 8 during a night of violence in which 8 buildings were set on fire by gangs of Protestants and Catholics. Police said the dead man, a member of a Protestant "peace patrol," was shot from a passing car in the Protestant area of West Belfast as a store was being looted.

● Protestant mobs attacked 3 British Army trucks Sept. 12 when troops intervened to prevent a clash between a group of Protestants and Catholics.

● 2 British soldiers were shot to death in separate incidents Sept. 14. One soldier was slain while guarding an arms depot near Ballynahinch, 10 miles south of Belfast. One report suggested that the death was accidental, but an Army spokesman said later that "no conclusions have been drawn." The other soldier was shot and killed while on duty at an Army camp north of Belfast. Police said no foul play had been involved.

Lt. Gen. Sir Ian H. Freeland, the commander of British forces in Northern Ireland, had requested Sept. 10 that 600 more British troops be sent to Ulster to increase the strength of his garrison to about 7,500 men. The first elements of the reinforcements, 100 soldiers, were flown into Northern Ireland Sept. 12.

British authorities in London Sept. 15 issued a new demand that all barricades in Ulster be removed, and they rejected Catholic conditions for their dismantling. Home Secy. James Callaghan issued the demand following a meeting with Prime Min. Harold Wilson, Defense Secy. Sir Geoffrey Baker and Gen. Freeland. Protestant Ulster's Central Defense Committee, which claimed to represent 75,000 Catholics, issued a statement Sept. 15 listing these conditions for the removal of the barricades: adequate military protection; suspension of the Special Powers Act, which permitted detention without trial; and assurance that Britain would act if the Northern Irish government failed to implement promised reforms.

British forces Sept. 15 had just completed the building of a "peace line" in Belfast to separate the warring religious factions. The barrier was a 7-foot-high iron-railing fence erected between the Protestant Shankhill Road district and the Catholic Falls Road area. The decision to replace the street barricades in Belfast with the "peace line" had been announced Sept. 9 by Prime Min. James Chichester-Clark. He said that the "best way for these barricades to be brought down is willingly, . . . by those who erected them." But, he insisted, "come down they must because law and order must be assured."

But Catholics in Belfast a week later began rebuilding street barricades in their area after having dismantled them Sept. 16 in reponse to British army orders. The new obstructions were put up in the wake of a fresh outbreak of shooting and arson during the weekend of Sept. 10-21.

Irish Republic Proposes Federation

Irish Republican Prime Min. John Lynch Aug. 28, 1969 renewed his call for an end to "the unnatural and unjustifiable" partition of Ireland. He proposed negotiations with Britain to merge the Irish Republic and Northern Ireland into a single federal state. Although he did not provide details about the plan, it was said that Lynch envisaged the continuance of the parliaments of both states but subject to a Council of Ireland that would have supreme authority over the entire country. Lynch said he "recognized that there are social and economic problems" standing in the way of the creation of a federal state, but he asserted that they were not "insurmountable."

Northern Irish Prime Min. Chichester-Clark Aug. 28 rejected

Lynch's proposed merger. He said Northern Ireland's affairs were not Lynch's concern. Chichester-Clark reaffirmed Belfast's view that "the constitutional position of Northern Ireland as an intergral part of the United Kingdom . . . was conclusively and unequivocally asserted" in the joint Ulster-British declaration of Aug. 19.

Ireland was reported Aug. 20 to have launched a worldwide propaganda campaign to gain international support for an end to partition. 20,000 copies of a pamphlet charging "savage treatment" of Catholics by the Royal Ulster Constabulary were to be distributed by Irish embassies and consulates before the UN General Assembly opened its 24th annual session in New York in mid-September. The pamphlet, entitled "The Story in Pictures of the North's Distress," showed photos of British troops in Ulster but mentioned only briefly that they had been requested by the Belfast government.

Riot Report Supports Catholic Charges

Catholic charges of government discrimination and police misconduct were upheld in a report made public Sept. 11, 1969 on the Londonderry riots between Oct. 1968 and Jan. 1969. The inquiry, ordered by the Northern Irish government in March, had been conducted by a 3-member commission headed by Lord Cameron, a Scottish High Court judge. Its 2 other members were Sir John Biggart and James J. Campbell, both faculty members of Queen's University, Belfast.

The report "disagree[d] profoundly" with Protestant contentions that the Catholic civil-rights movement, supported by some liberal Protestants, was "a mere pretext for other and more subversive activities." The report praised the moderate Northern Ireland Civil Rights Association but was critical of People's Democracy, a more radical group that had been formed at Queen's University after the first Londonderry violence in Oct. 1968. People's Democracy, the commission charged, was "dedicated to extreme left-wing political objectives" and was "prepared to break the constitutional links between Northern Ireland and Britain."

The report singled out British Parliament Member Bernadette Devlin, a leader of People's Democracy, as one who "would not rule out the use of force to achieve her own purposes if other methods of political persuasion had, in her judgment, failed." Alluding to the Rev. Ian Paisley, Protestant extremist leader, the commission assailed those who "by their appeal to sectarian prejudices and bigotry have assisted to inflame passions and keep alive ancient hatreds." It also criticized right-wing Protestants for their "vicious" assaults on a Belfast-London-derry march held by People's Democracy Jan. 4.

The commission held that some policemen were "guilty of assault and malicious damage to property" in the Catholics' Bogside district in Londonderry. The inquiry condemned the police for using batons and water cannons "indiscriminately" in suppressing a peaceful civil rights march in Londonderry in Oct. 1968.

The report listed 6 areas in Ulster where Catholics were in the majority but were under Unionist Party control because of gerry-mandering of election districts and franchise restrictions. "All these Unionist-controlled councils have used and use their power to make appointments which benefited Protestants," the statement said. It agreed with Catholic contentions that the Ulster régime favored Protestants in government jobs and "manipulated" public housing in favor of Protestants. But the commission praised the Unionist government for pledging reforms to correct these deficiencies. Noting that the Unionist Party had been in power since Northern Ireland was formed after the partition of Ireland in 1921, the report said: "A party in power, which can never in foreseeable circumstances by turned out, tends to be complacent and insensitive to criticism or acceptance of any need to reform."

Reaction to the Cameron Commission's findings was mixed. The Northern Irish government Sept. 11 lauded the report "for widespread public study and reflection." Miss Devlin asserted Sept. 12 that the commission report "fails to deal with basic social problems of housing, low-wages, unemployment and self-interested government."

Report on Police Reforms Stirs New Riots

A report Oct. 10, 1969, recommending widespread reform of Northern Ireland's police forces, precipitated intense Protestant riots in Belfast the night of Oct. 11–12. The disturbances caused the deaths of 3 persons, including one policeman. 56 people were injured and 69 arrested.

The report, submitted by a 3-member commission headed by Lord Hunt, suggested that the Royal Ulster Constabulary (RUC,) the regular 3,000-man police force, be disarmed and relieved of all military duties and that the B-Specials, the part-time 8,500-member force that assisted the constabulary, be gradually disbanded and replaced by a 4,000-man locally recruited, part-time police force under the control of the commanding officer of the British troops in Ulster. The commission urged that more Catholics be recruited for the constabulary "to achieve a better proportion in relation to the population." It noted that "the present imbalance lies deep and reflects the long-standing divisions in the community." The commission said the projected new police force should not only enforce the law but should create "a new attitude of friendship between its members and the public." The revamped constabulary should serve as "a civil police force, which will be in principle and in normal practice an unarmed force, having the advantage of closer relationships with other police forces in Britain," the report said.

Prime Min. Chichester-Clark immediately accepted the recommendations "in principle." The report prompted the resignation of Anthony Peacocke, inspector general of the constabulary. He was replaced by Sir Arthur Young, police commissioner in London's City (the financial district).

The Hunt Report was published in a joint communiqué issued by the Northern Irish government and British Home Secy. James Callaghan at the end of a 2-day visit by Callaghan to Ulster. The communiqué also announced a $2.4 million work program to relieve Northern Ireland's unemployment, under which the government was to provide 2,500 new jobs in the coming winter. The communiqué further announced the appointment of a minister of community relations and the introduction of a Parliamentary bill to establish a commission for complaints to consider charges of discrimination in public employment.

Militant Protestants, led by the Rev. Ian Paisley, denounced the proposal of police reforms as a "complete and absolute sellout to the Roman Catholic civil-rights movement." The Catholics had long complained that the RUC and the Special B Constabulary were violently anti-Catholic and had demanded that their powers be curbed.

The British Army reported that the rioting had started shortly before midnight Oct. 11 when a crowd of about 1,500 Protestants marched down Shankill Road in an attempt to storm a Catholic apartment house, the scene of previous communal clashes. A line of police vehicles and a combined force of policemen and British troops stopped the advance a quarter of a mile away, while other troops cordoned off the apartment house and kept civilians away. The Protestants opened the attack with guns and gasoline bombs. The police retaliated with tear gas, and the troops opened fire. The battle continued until 5 a.m. Oct. 12. Shankill Road was littered with wrecked cars and broken glass from the windows of shops that had been looted. A contingent of 600 British soldiers was flown into Belfast from England Oct. 12 to join the 8,000-man force already in Ulster. About 100 soldiers raided Protestant homes in the Shankill Road section and seized gasoline bombs, ammunition and a radio transmitter.

The outbreak in Belfast had been preceded by a series of violent incidents in the city Sept. 28–Oct. 5. A Protestant mob Sept. 28 charged through the barbed wire "peace line" that divided the Catholic and Protestant areas and set fire to 5 Catholic homes before they were dispersed with tear gas by the soldiers. Soldiers were attacked by gasoline bombs thrown from roofs during the 5-hour clash. The troops again came under attack later Sept. 28 as they moved Catholic families from their charred homes. 20 persons, including 8 soldiers, were injured during the day's fighting. Catholics in the Falls Road area built 6 new street barricades Sept. 28 following residents' complaints that they had not been sufficiently protected by British troops. The barriers went up as 600 more troops arrived from England to bolster the British force. Belfast was swept by 5 hours of street fighting the night of Oct. 4–5, marking the first anniversary of the communal fighting that further split the Catholic and Protestant communities.

Catholics dismantled at least 12 barricades in Belfast Oct. 7 after receiving further assurances from the British Army that they would be protected from militant Protestants. Catholics had begun removing barricades in the Bogside area of Londonderry Sept. 22 but fighting broke out with Protestants Sept. 24. One person was killed and 6 were wounded, police said. British troops separated the warring factions and set up a 50-yard no-man's land on the edge of Bogside. Police said that the fighting began when 5 Catholic youths chased a Paisley supporter.

Some of the Hunt Report's recommendations were implemented in early Nov. 1969. The formation of an Ulster Defense Regiment to assist the regular British Army in Northern Ireland was announced in a White Paper issued in London Nov. 12. The new force, to come into existence Jan. 1, 1970, was to take over all paramilitary duties from the B-Specials Apr. 1. The 6,000-man regiment was to aid British troops in protecting the border with Ireland and in guarding key installations. (The regiment actually became operational in Apr. 1970.) A White Paper issued by the Northern Irish Home Affairs Ministry Nov. 12 announced the creation of a new Royal Ulster Constabulary Reserve (RUCR), which was to become operational Apr. 1, 1970. The RUCR's projected initial force of 1,500 men was to assist the regular police but would not receive firearms and would not support the regular RUC.

Violence in Early 1970

Violent clashes between Protestants and Catholics resumed in Northern Ireland in Jan. 1970. British troops on guard duty fought with the demonstrators in quelling the disturbances.

The first outbreak occurred Jan. 4, when stones and bottles were thrown at soldiers and military police dispersing a Protestant crowd in the Catholic Bogside district of Londonderry. British troops were alerted in Belfast Jan. 20 following a 5th night of demonstrations by Protestant extremists in the city. A policeman had been struck and seriously wounded by a rock Jan. 19 as 300 Protestant extremists made an unsuccessful attempt to break through the British army's "peace line" dividing the Protestant and Catholic areas. Communal clashes in Londonderry Jan. 24 prompted British troops to erect barbed-wire barricades in the main streets. 400 soldiers fought with mobs throwing stones and bottles. Several arrests were made.

As a safety precaution, the Northern Irish government Jan. 29 ordered the closing of all bars 1½ hours earlier than usual for the following 2 days and a ban on parades and demonstrations until Feb. 15.

A new Public Order Act went into effect Feb. 5 in Northern Ireland and was quickly defied by Catholic groups, who charged that the bill was aimed at suppressing their civil-rights movement. The enactment of the measure was followed by further disturbances. The Catholics had largely opposed the act's provisions barring sit-ins and the occupation of public buildings, the requirement for 3 days' notice of demonstrations and the home secretary's right to ban marches. The act also barred counterdemonstrations and broadened curbs against weapons.

More activity by the Rev. Ian Paisley, the Protestant extremist leader, precipitated a riot by Catholics in Londonderry Feb. 6. The violence erupted when British troops tried to disperse 300 persons who had gathered outside the Guildhall, where Paisley was addressing a crowd of 1,300 supporters. The fighting spread to other parts of the city, where Catholics set up barricades, smashed store windows and hurled bottles and rocks at the troops. 9 persons were arrested.

The Public Order Act was openly defied Feb. 7 by civil-rights marchers in Belfast and in 9 provincial towns. They sat down in the streets and disrupted traffic for short periods. Small groups of Protestant extremists staged counterdemonstrations, but there was little violence.

Sheelagh Murnagham, a Liberal member of Protestant Ulster's Parliament, appealed to all sides to abide by the new law. She made the plea in a speech Feb. 7, and her home in Belfast was heavily damaged by a bomb blast Feb. 9. Miss Murnagham was not home at the time.

Violence erupted in Londonderry Mar. 7 when protesters hurled rocks and other missiles at police and soldiers during and after a parade of about 4,000 supporters of the Catholic Civil Rights Association demonstrating against unemployment. Similar protests were held in other towns in Northern Ireland. (In Londonderry, 17% of the male population was jobless.)

Reorganizing the Police

Prime Min. James D. Chichester-Clark announced at the opening session of a new Parliament Feb. 11, 1970 that the police force would be increased from 3,500 to 4,940 men and that 300 more men could be recruited for the force in the current fiscal year.

The Northern Irish lower house a week later began debate on whether to approve a 2d reading of the Police Bill (3 readings were necessary for passage). The bill had already been passed by the British Parliament and provisionally assented to by Queen Elizabeth II. The bill, aimed at implementing the Hunt Report's recommendations, also included provisions implementing the Belfast government's proposal that a Royal Ulster Constabulary Reserve (RUCR) of 1,500 personnel be created to replace the B-Specials. The Belfast House of Commons approved the 2d reading by 27-to-one vote Feb. 19, with ex-Home Affairs Min. William Craig and ex-Agriculture Min. Harry West abstaining.

After the bill had returned to committee and prior to a 3d reading, Craig Feb. 26 moved an amendment designed to subject the Police Authority, the projected new organ of responsibility for all Northern Irish police, to the direction of the Home Affairs Ministry. It was defeated by 37-5 vote; the opposition voted with the government. West moved an amendment that would permit the new police forces to go "armed" but later removed it after assurances from Home Affairs Min. Robert Porter that the police would receive arms when essential to the performance of their duty.

The bill was reported out for a 3d reading Mar. 3, 1970. West moved another amendment, this one requiring all police stations to carry a permanent store of ammunition and firearms and to train all policemen in how to use them. The government and opposition members present, voting together, defeated the amendment by 35-5 vote. The bill then received an unopposed 3d reading in the House. The Northern Irish Senate passed the bill Mar. 23, and the queen gave it her assent Mar. 26, making it law.

While the bill was still in committee before the 3d reading, the government forces and 5 Unionist right-wing MPs had joined in voting down 3 opposition-sponsored amendments: (a) to have the government consult all opposition MPs and senators beforehand on all appointments to the Police Authority (27 votes to 9); (b) to forbid any member of the police force to "be a member of a secret sectarian society" (29 votes to 10—moved by MP Gerard Fitt); and (c) to exempt all British policemen lent to the RUC from the obligation of enforcing or executing any provisions of the 1922 Special Powers Act or the 1954 Northern Irish Flags & Emblems Display Act (27 votes to 10—also moved by MP Fitt).

Official Bias Charged

Sir Arthur Young, inspector general of the Royal Ulster Constabulary, Jan. 20, 1970 dismissed charges of misconduct against 16 policemen in connection with the Londonderry riots in the fall of 1969. Young said that only one of the 157 persons who had filed complaints could make a positive identification of policemen involved. John Hume, a pro-Catholic independent member of the Stormont Parliament, called Young's action "a scandalous decision" that would "undermine the people's trust in the police force."

A jury in Belfast Feb. 20 acquitted 5 Protestants of conspiring to blow up a water pipeline at Dunadry, County Antrim Apr. 24, 1969 in protest against the jailing of the Rev. Ian Paisley. The defendants were freed despite their implication by the main prosecution witness, Samuel Stevenson, who had been sentenced to 12 years imprisonment in Nov. 1969 after pleading guilty to taking part in the plot. The jury's decision was deplored by many of Protestant Ulster's moderates, who contended that it would arouse the suspicion of Catholics. Gerard Fitt, also a Protestant Ulster member of the British Parliament, said that "the outcome of the case, the dropping of disciplinary charges against 16 policemen who went on the rampage in Londonderry a year ago, and a number of other issues have made Roman Catholics and even moderates despair."

The Belfast trial had been briefly adjourned in its 2d day Feb. 18 when an explosion tore a hole in the wall of a corridor leading to the courtroom. Damage was slight and there were no injuries.

3 U.S. Congressmen Criticize Stormont

3 members of the U.S. House of Representatives Mar. 17 and 18, 1970 deplored developments in Northern Ireland, criticizing in particular what they alleged to be discrimination against the Catholic minority in the country.

Rep. Allard K. Lowenstein (D., N.Y.) inveighed against the British reliance on the Special Powers Act of 1922, which allowed the authorities to suspend *habeas corpus*. He also asserted that the British government had a particular responsibility for the events in protestant Ulster. Lowenstein said:

What I do want to emphasize is the responsibility of the government of Great Britain for bringing justice and peace to the people of Northern Ireland. Constitutionally, Northern Ireland has a character unlike any other part of the United Kingdom, and the problems of making the writ of the central government run in a province with wide powers of self-government is not unknown to Americans. Indeed, our own difficulties in implementing federal law throughout the Union make it clear how unfair it would be to blame Westminster for injustice and violence in Northern Ireland.

But despite constitutional problems nothing can excuse the failure of the British government to do much more, much sooner. That government bears a large measure of responsibility for allowing the injustices inflicted on the Catholic minority to have festered for so long.

In the past few months, following the recommendations of various commissions, the British government has exerted pressure on the government of Northern Ireland to institute some reforms and to attempt to redress some of the major grievances of the Catholic minority. A major problem arises, not with the theory of these reforms, but with their actual implementation in the face of dogged opposition from those who are determined to maintain the *status quo* with all that that implies. . . .

Lowenstein suggested that civil rights in the 6 counties could best be restored by repealing the 1922 Special Powers Act and the 1970 Public Order Act, proclaiming a bill of rights, outlawing discrimination, ending electoral gerrymandering and calling early elections.

Rep. Thomas P. O'Neill Jr. (D., Mass.) took a similar stand, demanding the repeal of what he termed "repressive laws that have kept the Catholic minority oppressed for 50 years." He said:

If the government of Northern Ireland was sincerely interested in according to all its citizens equal protection and equal rights under the law, its first act would be to repeal the Special Powers Act. This law, which allows the Parliament to suspend all civil liberties, including those most precious—freedom of speech, access to the courts, freedom of the press and the right of privacy—is as powerful today as it was in 1920 [*sic*], when it was first enacted. With this law hanging over the heads of every dissenter, there can be no real freedom for anyone opposed to the present policy and present system of government.

Unfortunately, what I said on June 25 [1969] is still true; and that is intolerance and discrimination are encouraged by, and rooted in, the laws of Northern Ireland. Individual prejudice is tragic and destructive in itself, but when discrimination is founded in law, which is the case in Northern Ireland, intolerance is nourished and must spread. Only by assuring the same rights to all citizens can a government ever hope to be truly democratic, and only by ending government-sanctioned discrimination can a people hope to end private and personal intolerance.

Lowenstein and O'Neill were followed Mar. 18 by Rep. Edward P. Boland (D., Mass.) in criticizing Britain's administration of Ulster.

Boland said that for 50 years "Great Britain has remained stonily aloof to Northern Irish politics despite the grievances of that state's Catholic citizens." He praised the British for reforms but argued that "they do not go far enough" and that what the 6 counties most needed was "a sweeping reform program that outlaws discrimination and guarantees civil liberties."

Paisley Wins Stormont Parliament Seat

The Rev. Ian Paisley's growing popularity among militant Protestants resulted in his election to the Stormont Parliament in Apr. 1970.

Paisley and a follower, the Rev. William Beattie, won by-elections Apr. 16 to fill seats in Northern Ireland's parliament. Both men ran on the Protestant Unionist ticket, defeating candidates of the ruling moderate Unionist Party of Prime Min. James Chichester-Clark. Paisley defeated Dr. Bolton Minford in the rural constituency of Bannside. Beattie won in South Antrim.

The results were a setback for the Unionist Party, which had given strong backing to Minford in an effort to deprive Paisley of a Parliamentary forum. Paisley had campaigned against the government's policy of granting political concessions to Ulster's Roman Catholic minority.

At a news conference Apr. 17, Paisley called for the resignation of Chichester-Clark. "If not," he said, "I will make it so hot for him that he will want to retire."

BRITISH ARMY INTERVENES: APR. 1970 – AUG. 1971 PHASE

In Apr. 1970, Lt. Gen. Sir Ian Freeland, commanding British forces in Northern Ireland, began pursuing a tougher policy to prevent further clashes between Protestants and Catholics. Instead of merely keeping the opposing groups separate, the Army began to intervene more vigorously, patrolling and searching Catholic strongholds. Thus, as the London Sunday Times of Nov. 21, 1971 observed: "By a compound of political misjudgments and ancient suspicions, the rôle of the British Army was changed—from Aug. 1969, when it was sent in to protect the burning Catholic ghettoes, to Aug. 1970, when it found itself facing a hostile Catholic population." The increasing vigor with which the British Army carried out the security measures in Northern Ireland began before the ousting of the Labor government of Harold Wilson in the British general election of June 18, 1970 and its replacement by the Conservative government of Prime Min. Edward Heath. The Conservative majority depended in part on Unionist MPs from Northern Ireland.

Rioters 'Are Liable To Be Shot Dead'

British troops used tear gas to quell a new upsurge of Catholic and Protestant rioting in Northern Ireland Mar. 29–Apr. 4, 1970. Most of the disturbances were carried out by Catholics, who continued to press their demands for equal rights. Gen. Freeland announced Apr. 3 that rioters who threw gasoline bombs "are liable to be shot dead" if they ignored officers' warnings.

The fresh violence erupted Mar. 29 during parades marking the anniversary of the 1916 Dublin Easter rebellion, which eventually led to the establishment of the Irish Free State in 1921. 30 persons were arrested in clashes in Belfast, Londonderry, Lurgan and other cities, and many were injured. 24 of those seized were Catholics who tried to tear down the British flag at a police station in Londonderry.

20 British troops were wounded in a fierce battle with Catholics in Belfast Apr. 1. A defiant crowd of nearly 400 hurled bricks, bottles and fire bombs at the soldiers before they were forced back by tear gas and armored cars. At least 56 persons were arrested. The British troops resorted to tear gas again in a clash with Belfast Catholics Apr. 2. At least 8 shots were fired in a 4-hour clash involving 1,000 troops and 600 rioters. Again, several soldiers were injured, none seriously, by youths hurling fire bombs, bottles and paving stones.

British troops once more used tear gas, this time on a crowd of several hundred Protestants who twice attempted to march on a Catholic district in Belfast Apr. 4. 500 more troops were flown into Northern Ireland Apr. 4, raising the British force there to 7,000.

A spokesman for the outlawed Irish Republican Army in Belfast, responding to Gen. Freeland's "get-tough" policy, warned Apr. 5 that if civilians were killed by British troops, the IRA would shoot British troops in reprisal.

27 British soldiers were wounded May 10 while breaking up 16 hours of rioting between Catholics and Protestants in Belfast.

British Troops' Stay Called Indefinite

British Prime Min. Harold Wilson pledged Apr. 7 that British troops would remain in Northern Ireland as long as they were needed to keep the peace. Wilson made the statement in the House of Commons in response to expressions of fear aroused by a warning Apr. 6 by Gen. Freeland of a possible withdrawal of his troops. Freeland had said that the Army might not be able to remain long enough in Northern Ireland unless it received more cooperation from the people. He also said that "time will run out" and that he was "not optimistic." Freeland warned the IRA against exchanging fire with British troops in Protestant Ulster. He asserted that his troops had the firepower to win.

Freeland's statements were assailed by 2 Northern Irish members in the British House of Commons debate Apr. 7. Stratton Mills, a Unionist, said that "the credibility of Gen. Freeland has been destroyed." Gerard Fitt, the Republican Labor member, described Freeland's warnings as an "unpopular and arrogant attitude" and "disastrous." Fitt said that the withdrawal of British troops would produce "an absolute massacre."

The growing crisis in Northern Ireland had already been reflected in a British House of Commons session Mar. 24. House member Bernadette Devlin, the militant Catholic leader from Mid-Ulster, demanded a new inquiry into the death of Samuel Devenney, who had died of a heart attack July 1969 in Londonderry, 3 months after a police charge. Her demand was supported by 6 British Laborites. Miss Devlin claimed that renewed Protestant-Catholic clashes in Londonderry the past 3 nights were caused by dissatisfaction with the police handling of the Devenney case. The house turned down Miss Devlin's request for an emergency debate. The chamber was thrown into an uproar when Capt. Lawrence Orr, a Protestant member from Northern Ireland, accused Miss Devlin of "seeking to stir up violence." Orr and 5 sympathizers walked out after Laborites accused him of trying to stifle free debate. Miss Devlin had staged an all-night sit-down in front of 10

Downing Street the night before in an unsuccessful effort to meet with Prime Min. Wilson. Wilson told her in Commons debate Mar. 24 that she could have arranged for the meeting by just asking for it.

Orangemen's Parades Heighten Tensions

The British government, preoccupied with forthcoming general elections and noting the relative quiescence of Ulster during the first 5 months of 1970, discounted the possibility of further serious violence when Orangemen were slated to begin their "season" of Protestant parades in June. British Home Secy. James Callaghan turned down a report suggesting a significant revamping of Belfast's 1922 Special Powers Act, although some observers took the view that this could have gained much Catholic support in Ulster while at the same time not alienating the Protestant majority. Rather than introduce these changes, Callaghan reportedly indicated that it would be better "to let the old act fall into disuse." The Labor government appeared to some to proceed on the assumption that its problems in Ulster were solved, or nearly so.

The calm of early 1970 seemed to have induced a euphoric optimism among British officials. When Oliver Wright, Harold Wilson's representative in Northern Ireland, ended his tour of duty there in March, he announced at a press conference: "Cheer up. Things are better than you think." But Wright's successor, Ronald Burroughs, expressed foreboding at the new series of Protestant marches due to start in June.

One of the first Protestant marches, held June 3, 1970 in Belfast, sparked violent confrontations between the opposing groups. A gunman fired into the crowd during one of the clashes, wounding 2 persons. 2 soldiers and a policeman were injured and 10 people arrested during the violence. The Protestant march was on a route fraught with a high probability of violence; it lay along a boundary of a Catholic ghetto whose residents were highly militant. After a local British officer tried to divert the march from the Catholic area, 2 days of rioting ensued.

Further incidents occurred later in June. Police protecting a parade of 2,000 Protestants in Dungiven, Londonderry June 14 were the targets of stone-throwing Catholics. Police in Strabane and Londonderry June 21 dispersed crowds of Catholics and Protestants after being pelted by stones and bottles. The Catholics were celebrating the reelection to the British Parliament of Bernadette Devlin when they ran into the opposition group.

The Joint Security Committee met at Stormont June 24 to consider the Protestant marches slated for Belfast on June 27 and 28. The routes of these marches were past several trouble spots, but the routes were difficult to change because they were based on long tradition. Burroughs and Arthur Young of the RUC argued that the marches ought to be banned. Both had been warned by their contacts in the Catholic community that, if the Protestants were allowed to march over the ground of their previous "victories," there would be Catholic attempts to stop them. Prime Min. Chichester-Clark, however, argued that a ban would destroy his political position in the Unionist Party. Gen. Freeland argued that the Protestants would march whether or not the marches were banned and that a legal march would be easier to control. The London *Sunday Times* commented: "Freeland's attitude was that, in the end, the Army must show who was boss. . . . If the Catholics don't like it, they must lump it."

Burroughs was warned by a Catholic leader June 25 that the IRA would be present to defend Catholics in the event of the Protestant march. Burroughs called British Prime Min. Heath and asked him to ban the marches, as bloodshed was otherwise inevitable. Heath consulted with his new home secretary, Reginald Maudling, and decided to do nothing.

Wilson Ousted in Election

Voters in the British Isles June 18, 1970 turned Prime Min. Harold Wilson and his Labor Party government out of power and assigned the country's direction to the Conservatives, headed by Edward Heath.

Of the 12 Northern Irish seats in the Westminster Parliament, the Ulster Unionists lost 2 and kept 8; the Rev. Ian Paisley won the seat from Antrim North as a Protestant Unionist, and Frank McManus won the South Tyrone seat as a Unity Party candidate, joining Bernadette Devlin, reelected as the Unity Party's candidate from Mid-Ulster. Gerard Fitt was reelected as the Republican Labor Party's candidate from Belfast West. Since the Ulster Unionists generally voted as Conservatives on all major issues in the British Parliament, the Heath government's voting majority came to 31 seats.

Both major British parties had taken explicit campaign stands on the Northern Irish problem. The Conservatives declared in their party's manifesto, "A Better Tomorrow": "We reaffirm that no change will be made in the constitutional status of Northern Ireland without the free consent of the Parliament of Northern Ireland. We support the N[orthern] I[rish] government in its program of legislative and executive action to ensure equal opportunity for all citizens in that part of the United Kingdom. We will provide the military and other aid necessary to support the Royal Ulster Constabulary in keeping the peace and ensuring freedom under the law, with the Ulster Defense Regiment as a strong efficient reserve force capable of playing a significant rôle in maintaining peace and security."

The British Labor Party's manifesto expressed the view that: "Northern Ireland presents major problems. 50 years of one-party Tory rule has led to social tensions and lack of opportunities which erupted into major disorders last summer. The government has helped stabilize the situation and has insisted on reforms being carried out in Northern Ireland based on the practice and principle of nondiscrimination. In particular, it has been agreed that the reform of local government in Ulster shall proceed and that a Central Housing Authority shall be set up. British troops will remain in Northern Ireland so long as they are needed. . . ."

Britain's 3d party, the Liberals, made no direct mention of the problem in their preelection manifesto and referred instead to "Scotland and Wales" as "distinct national entities within the United Kingdom" entitled to "their own parliaments for Scottish and Welsh affairs, united with England by a federal parliament. . . ." Such a step would strengthen the Stormont government's claims to traditionality and legitimacy, some observers held. The Liberals also proposed "12 regional assemblies in England, exercising many of the powers now exercised at the center [London]." The Liberals lost 7 of their 13 Parliament seats in the June 18 election.

IRA Split Creates 'Provisional' Wing

In the interval between the 1956–62 terrorist campaign and the recurrence of sectarian violence in 1968, the IRA underwent basic changes. The failure of the earlier campaign had resulted in considerable soul-searching among IRA leaders, for, despite great efforts in the 6 counties, they had not been able to kindle the fire of revolution among Protestant Ulster's Catholics, without whose direct support and participation the freeing of all Ulster from British rule could not be achieved. Since 1920 the IRA had existed for one basic reason—the reunion of the 2 Irelands into one political unit under an independent government by whatever force necessary.

The IRA in Ulster—and especially in Belfast—had developed a different character from the IRA leadership in Dublin. The Belfast IRA, because of the long isolation of the Catholic population in ghettoes, was said to have come to think of itself largely within the limits of the self-defense of Catholic areas from Protestant militants' incursions. For this reason, in previous IRA activities, Belfast had notably been absent as a theater of operations: the Catholic community was too exposed to Protestant reprisals. The Belfast IRA, it was reported, saw itself, and largely functioned, as defender of the Catholic minority from what came to be viewed as an ever-present threat from Protestant militants.

The IRA leaders in Dublin, on the other hand, began to explore new methods for achieving their end soon after the failure of their terrorist campaign of the late 1950s and early 1960s. Starting with a simple dedication to a 32-county republic, they moved to a more sophisticated participation in the civil-rights movement and then to an optimistic brand of socialism. As the Dublin leaders shifted towards a political position well on the left, many old-time leaders in Belfast were bewildered by the change. The Dublin IRA's support for the civil-rights movement (an effort in which it bolstered its demands by calling attention to the rights of British citizens) and for the election of Bernadette Devlin to the Westminister Parliament suggested to some IRA members in Belfast a tacit recognition of a permanent division of Ireland.

The opposition within the movement led to a split between members of the IRA and to the emergence of 2 groups: (1) the "Official" IRA, Marxist and left-wing, led from Dublin, involved in political activism, and (2) the "Provisional" IRA, old-line, with no clear political aim other than the liberating of Ulster by force, and opposed to any and all activities that might even hint at any recognition of British legitimacy in Ulster.

The initial split between the 2 groups came in 1964 in Belfast out of a dispute over the leadership of the one IRA "battalion"—in reality said to number fewer than 100 diehards—in the city. Its commander, William McKee, was overthrown, and he left the IRA with a group of followers to set up a rival IRA. 4 of the men who walked out with McKee became the top leadership of what later became "the Provisionals": Joseph Cahill, the ex-chief of staff; Seamus Toomey, the current chief of staff; William Kelly, leader of the 3d Belfast Battalion; and Seán MacNally, quartermaster general.

The IRA's "Official" wing in Dublin decided in 1968 to sell its weapons to the Free Wales Army to raise money to maintain the IRA newspaper, *United Irishman,* in the hope that weapons were no longer necessary. As the violence in Belfast and Ulster increased in the summer of 1969, however, resentment against this sale grew, and some Ulster IRA veterans began to take "precautions." These involved rearmament, but on a miniscule scale—considered far from adequate to defend the Catholic enclaves in Belfast from Protestant attacks.

When old IRA fears came true and Protestants did attack Catholic areas in Belfast in Aug. 1969, some observers asserted that the inability of the "Officials" to defend the Catholic inhabitants all but completely discredited them. The "Provisionals" thereafter maintained that the IRA leadership in Dublin had actually planned that Belfast Catholics should be left unarmed before the Protestant attack. According to this theory, the Dublin leadership had reasoned that there would be a terrible massacre of Belfast Catholics that would both eliminate the IRA dissidents and bring down the Stormont régime.

In Sept. 1969, the IRA leadership in Belfast announced its independence from the Dublin IRA after a meeting in which such veterans as McKee pressured the group to take the step. The formal split in Belfast occurred in December when some of the leaders there decided to return to the official Dublin-led IRA while the others formed themselves into the provisional IRA. Between August and December 1969 the Belfast IRA had grown from about 150 members to more than 600, but of these only 80 or so were trained activists. The Provisionals won about 400 men at the time of the split in December, but only about 30 of these had urban guerrilla training.

The provisional leadership held, however, that urban guerrilla warfare required a nucleus of no more than 50 men. The Catholic enclaves in Belfast were divided between the Provisionals and the Officials, with one or 2 areas remaining neutral. The Lower Falls area was the only one that remained firmly in the Officials' camp; the Official leader, James Sullivan, had managed to produce 3 Thompson submachine guns for the defense of Lower Falls in Aug. 1969.

The relative quiescence of IRA activity in Ulster until 1970, thus resulted from the Dublin leadership's turn away from terrorism as a political instrument and the disarming of Protestant Ulster's IRA. During the first half of 1970, the 2 groups in Belfast were occupied in regrouping and reforming themselves. The Provisionals were considered not strong enough to challenge British troops in Northern Ireland, then, and there is some debate over whether or not they wanted to. The British Army's relations with the Catholic community were good up to the middle of 1970, apparently because its relations with the Protestants were bad.

The Provisionals were described as unhappy over this state of affairs and were said to have sought to spread discontent among Catholics where they could. Until the summer of 1970, however, there were only 2 incidents for which the Provisionals are definitely responsible.

When a Protestant crowd was trying to storm an isolated Catholic housing block in the center of Belfast Sept. 28, 1969, a Provisional attempted to frighten off the Protestants with a burst of submachine-gun fire. The Provisionals Jan. 27, 1970 blew a hole in the wall of an old police barracks in Belfast. Even in the first clash between British troops and Catholics in Ballymurphy in western Belfast Apr. 1-3, 1970, it appeared that the Provisionals attempted to stop the rioting, forming vigilante squads to round up Catholic troublemakers.

Events in the summer of 1970, however, altered the Provisionals' (as well as the Catholic community's) view of the British Army. With the outbreak of violence in Belfast in late June, the Provisionals became involved in the defense by force of Catholic areas; curfews imposed by the new British Conservative government, the imposition of the Criminal Justice Act in mid-1970 and British Army raids into Catholic areas for arms seemed to opponents of the Protestants to place the British Army firmly in the structure of Unionist supremacy.

The ranks of the Provisionals swelled greatly in the 2d half of 1970, and by the end of 1970, the Provisionals were in the position of being the acknowledged leaders of the Belfast Catholics without really having control over events. During this period the Officials and the Provisionals began to war with each other. 2 men were shot to death by an unidentified gunman Nov. 16, 1970 in Belfast. Belfast police indicated that they believed the slayings to be linked to the dispute between the rival IRA factions. Shortly before the spring of 1971, matters had escalated into gun battles between the 2 groups.

The 2 rival factions engaged Mar. 8-9, 1971 in gun battles for control of Belfast's Catholic areas. Provisionals, armed with machine guns and shotguns, invaded the Official IRA headquarters Mar. 8; one Provisional was killed, and 2 men were wounded Mar. 9.

The Provisionals, in a statement Mar. 10, accused the Officials of beatings and torture and said that these tactics were "aimed at diverting the Republican movement from . . . the fight against British imperialism in Ireland." The *Washington Post* cited Belfast sources for a report Mar. 10 that at least 30 Northern Irish suspected of being traitors to the IRA had been assassinated.

Bernadette Devlin Jailed, New Violence Follows

5 persons were shot to death and 240 seriously wounded in a new outbreak of clashes between Catholics and Protestants in Northern Ireland June 26-28, 1970. The violence was precipitated by the jailing June 26 of Bernadette Devlin for her rôle in the Londonderry communal rioting in Aug. 1969.

Miss Devlin began serving a 6-month prison term after her request for permission to appeal to the British House of Lords was denied by the Appeals Court June 26. A previous appeal had been rejected by the Northern Ireland High Court June 22. Appearing before a committee of inquiry on the riots Oct. 29, 1969, Miss Devlin had acknowledged that she had organized the throwing of stones and a gasoline bomb at police during the Londonderry unrest. But she insisted that she had never thrown a bomb. She was found guilty by a Londonderry Magistrate's Court on 3 counts of inciting to riot and one count of riotous behavior. 9 other charges were dismissed. Miss Devlin was sentenced by the court Dec. 22, 1969, to 6 months' imprisonment, and she was released on $600 bail, pending the appeal. Miss Devlin was released from Armagh prison Oct. 21, 1970 after serving 4 months of her sentence, which was reduced for good behavior.

The first outbreak in the 2d summer of violence occurred June 26 when more than 1,000 youths in Londonderry's Catholic Bogside district fought with the British garrison. The demonstrators threw stones and gasoline bombs at the soldiers, injuring 20 of them. Fighting also broke out in Belfast, where the disturbances were touched off by a march of members of the Protestant Orange Order as it passed a Catholic neighborhood. Catholic youths threw rocks and bottles at the Protestants.

Rioting broke out again in Belfast June 27 when Catholics disrupted a parade of the Orange Order. As the fighting intensified throughout the day, shops, automobiles and buses were set afire, and a police station was wrecked. Civilian sniping and firing by the British in 2 areas of the city resulted in the deaths of 3 persons. Troops hurled tear gas in separating rival crowds. Protestants laid seige to St. Matthew's Church in eastern Belfast. This prompted the first entry of gunmen of the IRA Provisionals into organized action.

In Londonderry, Catholics attacked soldiers and policemen with stones, bottles and gasoline bombs June 27. The violence abated in the early morning hours of June 28 but was resumed that night. British troops fired tear gas to dispel a Catholic mob in the Bogside district. The troop action was followed by bombs igniting shops and houses in the area. The Army sealed off the areas to all but military traffic. The Protestants continued their parades, and no further incidents occurred.

The 8,000-man British garrison in Northern Ireland was reinforced by 450 troops flown in June 28.

Stormont's Prime Min. James D. Chichester-Clark said June 28 that any civilians carrying firearms were liable to be shot without warning. He also warned of automatic imprisonment for rioters and of the possible imposition of a curfew on much of Belfast. Chichester-Clark asserted that "there is clear evidence that there are people who want to destroy Northern Ireland." Deputy Prime Min. Brian Faulkner June 28 described the new violence as "planned arson" and "gunmen active against the Army." He said that the disturbances were unlike the rioting Aug. 1969 when the Catholics thought they were defending their homes.

About 1,500 persons demonstrated in London June 28 against the jailing of Miss Devlin. 28 persons were arrested during scuffles with police.

Anti-Riot Laws

After the British Labor government was swept from power in the June 1970 election, the responsibility for Northern Ireland shifted from Labor's Home Secy. James Callaghan to the Conservative Reginald Maudling. It was reported that Callaghan had been planning to institute direct rule of the 6 counties from London, but this plan was aborted by the Labor Party's election defeat.

During a visit to Northern Ireland June 30–July 1, Maudling called for a restoration of law and order. 3 Catholic members of the Stormont Parliament walked out of meetings with Maudling June 20, complaining that he made no mention of the reforms promised to Catholics. They also accused him of failing to provide sufficient assurances against use of the Special Powers Act to imprison suspects without trial.

The Northern Irish Parliament July 1 approved 2 bills to deal with rioters. Stormont's Prime Min. Chichester-Clark had described both measures June 28 as "exceptional legislation" that would "stay in force only so long as the situation requires it." One measure, the Criminal Justice Bill, provided mandatory jail terms of one to 5 years for various riot offenses, such as throwing Molotov cocktails. The other, the Prevention of Incitement to Hatred Bill, provided severe penalties for false statements or publications that inflamed sectarian feelings.

The Criminal Justice Bill "provide[d] for the imposition of minimum sentences of imprisonment on persons convicted of certain offenses committed during the period of present emergency and for related purposes." A number of existing laws were amended so that anyone convicted of an offense during the "present emergency" would be liable to imprisonment, "notwithstanding anything to the contrary in the various acts." Persons convicted under the Malicious Damage, Explosive Substances, Public Order and Firearms Acts were made liable to prison terms of from 6 months to 5 years. The "period of present emergency" was to extend from June 30, 1970 to any day determined as its expiration date by Northern Irish Gov. Lord Grey through an Order-in-Council.

The Prevention of Incitement to Hatred Bill made it illegal (a) to use threatening, abusive or insulting language to incite or foment ill-will toward or arouse the fear of any section of the community on account of religious belief, color, race or ethnic or national origin; (b) to publish spurious statements or reports known to be false with intent to provoke a breach of the peace likely to stir up hatred or fear on the basis of religion or race. The maximum penalties for both offenses would be 6 months' imprisonment or a £200 ($480) fine or both if convicted without trial, and 2 years' imprisonment or a £1,000 ($2,400) fine or both when convicted on indictment.

The Criminal Justice Bill remained in force between July 1 and Dec. 17, 1970, when it was repealed. Under its provisions, 269 people were charged with riotous or disorderly behavior, and 109 were tried and convicted. The London *Sunday Times* of Nov. 21, 1971 observed: "Inevitably, the Criminal Justice Temporary Provisions Act 1970 came in Catholic eyes to rank, after the Special Powers Act, as the 2d most repressive piece of legislation at Stormont's command. And the Army was Stormont's instrument for enforcing it. The stage was set for the emergence, at last, of the Provisionals."

Arms Searches & Violence

The British Army began to move into Catholic areas to search for arms in the beginning of July 1970, further reinforcing Catholic mistrust of British intentions. These arms searches led to violence between Catholics and the Army. 5 persons were killed and more than 200 were injured in fighting July 3–4 between armed Catholics and British soldiers in the Falls Road district of Belfast. Among the injured were 15 soldiers struck by shrapnel and gunfire. The dead included 2 snipers shot by soldiers and 2 other civilians slain by non-Army gunfire. More than 300 people were arrested.

The violence followed arms raids in which the Royal Irish Constabulary joined the British Army. The incident that immediately led to the fighting was a grenade attack on British troops trying to disperse a crowd of Catholics in the Falls Road district. 5 soldiers were injured. The troops then opened fire on part of the crowd that was hurling stones, bricks and gasoline bombs. The violence quickly spread and mounted in intensity, with the Catholics reported to be using sniper fire and explosive charges. The troops finally suppressed the attacks and brought the area under control.

A rigid curfew imposed on the Falls Road district was lifted July 5. A house-to-house search by troops in the area July 4–5 had resulted in the seizure of 20,000 rounds of ammunition, more than 100 guns and rifles, 25 pounds of explosives, about 100 incendiary devices and an unspecified number of grenades. Stormont's Prime Min. Chichester-Clark had said July 4 that the seized arms were "ample evidence that the measures being taken are fully justified." He expressed his "determination to rid Northern Ireland of the terrorists in its midst."

Nearly 100,000 persons marched in the Orange Order parades throughout Protestant Ulster Monday, July 13, 1970 without incident. The parades marked the 280th anniversary of a Protestant victory over Catholics in the battle of the Boyne. But in a move aimed at easing tensions between Catholics and Protestants, the government July 23 banned public parades for 6 months. Chichester-Clark said that the ban was necessary because "the security forces needed a period of calm and stability." (About 2,000 Protestants marched July 26 through Kilskeery, 15 miles west-southwest of Finton, in County Tyrone, in defiance of the ban against parades. The police chief ruled that the demonstration was "not a parade in the accepted sense.")

31 persons had been injured, 9 seriously, in an explosion July 16 in a bank in downtown Belfast; this was the 55th explosion in Northern Ireland since Jan. 1. Despite the incident, 2,000 British troops left Belfast that day as part of a scheduled withdrawal, reducing the British force to about 9,000 men.

Bombs exploded July 25 and 26 in Belfast at the homes of the Rev. Martyn Smyth, a leader of the Protestant Orange Order, and Judge Lord Chief Justice Lancelot Curran, who had sentenced Bernadette Devlin to prison June 26. No one was injured.

Catholic rioters, throwing fire bombs, fought with British troops in Belfast July 31–Aug. 1. The soldiers used tear gas and nausea gas grenades and water cannon to quell the disturbances. A demonstrator, Daniel O'Hagan, 19, was shot to death by an Army trooper July 31. An Army spokesman said the youth was fired on after he ignored a warning not to throw a fire bomb. After receiving anonymous threats of reprisals against soldiers for O'Hagan's death, the British Army Aug. 1 announced new security measures for its forces. Soldiers were forbidden to travel alone and were prohibited from entering certain troubled areas of the city. Extra guards were placed on patrol vehicles.

A crowd of 3,000 marched through Belfast at O'Hagan's funeral Aug. 3 without incident. Rioting erupted later that night in the Ballymurphy section of the city, where a crowd of about 150 demonstrators threw bottles and stones at troops guarding a housing project. The soldiers responded by firing tear gas at the crowd.

In subsequent incidents:

● 2 Northern Irish policemen died of injuries suffered Aug. 11 in a bomb explosion in Armagh County near the border with Ireland. The explosion occurred when the door of a stolen car was opened.
● British soldiers fought with Protestants and Catholics in Londonderry Aug. 12 but managed to contain the violence. The disturbances followed a rally of about 2,000 Protestants in a field 2 miles from the center of the city. 2,000 British soldiers and 500 Northern Irish policemen sealed off the Bogside district and other Catholic areas and prevented large-scale encounters between the rival factions.
● An explosion in Northern Ireland Aug. 18 heavily damaged a British naval recruiting station in Belfast, near the city hall. 2 persons were injured.

Hillery's Secret Visit to Belfast

A secret visit to the riot-torn area of Belfast July 6, 1970 by Irish External Affairs Min. Patrick J. Hillery was assailed by the Stormont and British governments. Hillery disclosed on his return to Dublin later July 6 that Irish Prime Min. John Lynch had asked him to make the visit "for the purpose of relaxing tensions in Northern Ireland and to let the people in the Falls feel that they were not so isolated so far as the government in Dublin was concerned."

Hillery said nothing had occurred in the Falls Road district for months that justified a British move to "invade" the area. The weapons discovered were old rifles, and the total seized would not provide more than one gun for every 500 of the residents in the district, he asserted. Hillery said he had advised the Catholics with whom he had spoken to adhere to the Dublin government's moderate policy and "not to follow" the outlawed IRA militants. He reported that his government's grave apprehension" about the scheduled parades of militant Protestant groups in Ulster had prompted Lynch to have him express these fears to several foreign ambassadors in Dublin who were "friendly" to both the Irish and British governments.

Northern Irish Prime Min. Chichester-Clark July 6 deplored Hillery's secret trip to Belfast, asserting that "I am astounded that the foreign minister of any state should show such a lack of courtesy as to visit Northern Ireland without reference to me or the Northern Ireland government, the more so in the present very dangerous situation." British Foreign Secy. Sir Alec Douglas-Home July 7 termed Hillery's failure "to have consulted" the London government in advance of his trip "a serious diplomatic discourtesy." Hillery's visit,

Douglas-Home said, "magnified the difficulties of those who are working so hard for peace and harmony in Northern Ireland."

Hillery rejected the British criticism of his visit to Belfast after discussing the mission with Douglas-Home in London July 8. Hillery said at a news conference later that "I represent a sovereign state and will not be rebuked by anyone else." He insisted that "I speak" for Northern Ireland's 500,000 Roman Catholics. "At any time that minority needs to speak, I am available to them." Hillery said that he had urged Douglas-Home to have the Protestant Orange Order parades, scheduled for June 13, rerouted so they would not pass through sensitive Catholic areas in Ulster. He said Catholics objected to the annual marches because they were "aggressive" and "insulting" and reminded "them of their subjection."

British MPs Tear-Gassed in Commons

The British House of Commons was thrown into an uproar July 23, 1970 when an Ulster Catholic demonstrator in the visitors' gallery hurled 2 canisters of tear gas to the floor. The bombs filled the chamber with thick white smoke, forcing the evacuation of the hall. The session was resumed later in the day. After the incident, police arrested James Anthony Roach, 26, and accused him of violating the Firearms Act. Bowes Egan, an adviser to Parliament Member Bernadette Devlin, was arrested July 28 on charges of conspiring with Roach. Egan was formally charged in court July 29.

Large caches of bombs and explosives believed destined for use by a dissident Irish Republican Army faction in Northern Ireland and England were uncovered by British police in raids in London Aug. 13–14. 8 men were arrested in connection with the bombs' seizure, and 6 of them were charged by London police Aug. 16. They were accused under the Explosive Substances Act of 1883 of "conspiring to cause by an explosive an explosion of a nature likely to endanger life or to cause serious injury to property." The London *Daily Express* had reported Aug. 15 that one of the planned targets was a factory in Surrey that manufactured CS (tear and nausea) gas used by the British Army and Northern Ireland's riot control in Northern Ireland.

British police Aug. 26 carried out 50 simultaneous raids in the London area and throughout England and seized machine guns, other firearms and explosives. An initial announcement said that the raids were connected with tracking down IRA units and left-wing extremists, but police later denied that the seizures had any political significance.

Security Chiefs Resign Posts in Ulster

Lt. Gen. Sir Ian Freeland, commander of British forces in Northern Ireland, and Sir Arthur Young, head of the Royal Ulster Constabulary, were reported Sept. 24, 1970 to be leaving their posts at their own requests. Freeland was replaced by Maj. Gen. Vernon Erskine-Crum, chief Army instructor at the Imperial Defense College. Young, who planned to resume his duties as commissioner of London police, was replaced by Graham Shillington, his current deputy in Belfast.

The British government named Maj. Gen. Harry Tuzo to command security operations in Northern Ireland, it was reported Feb. 19, 1971. He replaced Lt. Gen. Erskine-Crum, who had suffered a heart attack Feb. 16, less than 2 weeks after assuming the post, and who died Mar. 17 at the age of 52.

Communist Countries Comment

Radio Tirana of Albania condemned the British government July 6, 1970 for using "terrorist" methods to suppress Catholics in Northern Ireland. "Bourgeois propaganda had always interpreted the various revolts of the population of Northern Ireland as religious strife between the 2 religious groups, as strife between the Catholics and the Protestants," the Tirana radio spokesman said. "But the true causes of this revolt have their roots in the 700-year-old, ruthless colonial oppression of the Irish people by the English colonialists. This is also proved by previous events, the continuous struggle of the fighters for freedom against colonialism, which have made clear the objectives of their war." Radio Tirana concluded by charging that the "exploitation and oppression of the working class is continuing, the colonialist policy of divide and rule continues to be followed in a more brutal way. As a result, even today Northern Ireland is the most backward part of Great Britain. Its economy suffers from continuous . . . crisis and almost complete paralysis."

The Polish Communist Youth League's newspaper, *Sztandar Mlodych*, observed Aug. 17 in a commentary entitled "Hot Irish Summer": "The bitter disappointment, frustration and despair of the Catholic communities find justification in the conduct of both the Protestants and the British forces. The main cause breeding these feelings is the fact that no request of the Catholic minority and no pledge of the Chichester-Clark government has been fulfilled. The only thing that has been achieved so far was the disarmament of Protestant police squads, the so-called 'B-Specials,' notorious for their uncommonly cruel assaults on Catholics. This, however, has not been followed up by any changes in the economic, social and political situation of the Catholic minority, which sees no end to its miseries. Tension in Ireland, the division between the Catholics, the stubborness of the Protestants and the incompetence of the British military command have [had this result] : . . . The 'hot summer' has already . . . begun in the streets of Belfast, Londonderry and elsewhere."

Communist China's New China News Agency (Hsinhua) commented Jan. 18, 1971 on the renewed violence in Belfast and Londonderry. The text did not mention Catholic-Protestant differences but rather characterized- the events as part of the "heroic resistance among the people of Northern Ireland" to the "savage suppression by British imperialist troops." Describing the events of Jan. 11-13 in the Ballymurphy district of Belfast, Hsinhua noted that "the struggle of the people's masses in the city . . . threw the reactionary authorities into panic." Hsinhua asserted that "this is the first wave of the struggle [against British imperialism] in that region in 1971." Commenting on the deployment Jan. 14 of new British forces in Belfast, the NCNA dispatch said: "Far from being able to intimidate them . . . the savage suppression aroused bigger indignation and fiercer resistance among the masses."

Radio Prague of Czechoslovakia commented Feb. 9 that "the presence of British troops appears to sharpen the conflict in the country" and that the violence "is not the product of sectarian differences." Radio Prague said: "The British government is now attempting to describe the events in Belfast and other cities as an expression of religious unrest and the rôle of the British troops as that of keeping order and preventing clashes between the Protestant majority and the Catholic minority. It is, however, a class-motivated social and political struggle of the oppressed Catholics against the Protestant majority. The unrest in Northern Ireland at the same time, however, gives expression to the colonialist policy of the British government, because the monopolies can hire a cheap labor force there. The long autocracy of the Unionist Party under the auspices of the government in London is now bringing its bitter fruit. . . ."

U.S. Congressman Deplores British Behavior

Rep. Richard L. Ottinger (D., N.Y.) declared Aug. 14, 1970 that the Special Powers Act exemplified the political truism that "the road to tyranny is paved with repressive measures." Ottinger, a candidate for the U.S. Senate seat held until his death by Robert F. Kennedy, called for the repeal of the 1922 legislation and the restoration of civil rights in Northern Ireland. Ottinger asserted: ". . . Northern Ireland in 1970 is [itself] a divided country, as it has been through most of its brief history. It is clear that the differences between Protestant and Catholic, between those loyal to England and those who want Irish re-unification, are exacerbated by the repression of civil rights under the Special Powers Act. The cure has become part of the malady. To keep such a lid clamped on the cauldron that is Northern Ireland can only intensify the pressures already straining the bonds of national unity. Thus the emergency continues and will not abate until the civil liberties of all the citizens of Ulster are restored. Charges of disenfranchisement, discrimination in housing, prejudice in obtaining and holding employment cannot be answered with further deprivation of rights."

Ottinger read into the *Congressional Record* Sept. 14 the text of a petition submitted to the UN by Paul O'Dwyer, a U.S. Senate candidate from New York State in 1968. The petition traced an alleged pattern of discrimination against Catholics in Northern Ireland in housing, employment, education, the right to assemble, enforcement of the law and social services and urged the imposition of sanctions against Great Britain until full civil liberties were restored in Protestant Ulster. The petition read in part: "Wherefore, your petitioner prays that the Subcommission on Prevention of Discrimination & Protection of Minorities and the Human Rights Commission examine this information and that the Human Rights Commission make a thorough study of the situation and report with its recommendations to the Economic and Social Council . . . and to take whatever steps are necessary to impose sanctions by the nations of the world against the government of Great Britain until the rights of the Catholic citizens to personal safety and safety in the home, to equal opportunities in public and private employment, to participate in every phase of government, to freedom of speech and freedom of assembly and until the Ireland Act of 1920 be amended so as to eliminate the possibility of a recurrence of death and destruction which has marked the past 2 years in Northern Ireland."

Worsening Violence

Rioting erupted in Belfast Sept. 26, 1970 as Protestants returning from a soccer game marched through a Catholic neighborhood. Sporadic street fighting continued through Sept. 28, when police and British troops reported that the situation was "under decisive control." About 200 persons were reported injured in the violence, the first major disruption in Belfast in more than 2 months.

In a statement issued Sept. 28, Stormont's Prime Min. Chichester-

Clark called the disturbances "utter selfishness and utter folly." He declared: "It must stop now before Britain and the world grow completely sick of us and write us off as a community that is incapable of discipline and blind even to its own best interests."

British troops came under attack in a fresh outbreak of Catholic violence in Belfast Oct. 30-31. A British soldier shot and wounded a civilian during a 4-hour street battle Oct. 30. Sniping broke out but was brought under control by the use of riot gas, an Army spokesman said. The violence erupted shortly after a bomb had wrecked the office of Irish International Airlines, injuring 4 bystanders. 5 soldiers were wounded by bombs thrown in clashes in Belfast Oct. 31. An Army patrol also came under machine-gun fire in a Catholic area of the city, but no casualties were reported. In another Catholic stronghold, troops used tear gas after being pelted by bricks and bottles.

Fighting broke out in Londonderry between Catholics and Protestants Oct. 31 following a meeting addressed by the Rev. Ian Paisley, the Protestant extremist leader. Paisley said at a gathering of 800 followers of the Ulster Protestant Volunteers: "Protestantism in Northern Ireland has been betrayed. We must now be prepared to use the mailed fist."

 Britain announced the withdrawal of 1,000 more peace-keeping troops from Northern Ireland Nov. 11.

Violent rioting swept 2 Catholic areas of Belfast Jan. 11-17, 1971. The worst clashes occurred Jan. 15-16. Several stores in the city came under incendiary attacks and British troops used tear gas to quell the rioters, mostly teenagers. 17 persons were arrested on charges of riotous behavior. After a cabinet meeting called Jan. 17 to discuss the latest outbreak, a Stormont government spokesman charged that the violence had been "deliberately fomented and encouraged by hidden agitators. Army tactics have been unable to cope with them. Now, there is a need for . . . a harder, tougher line."

Prime Min. Chichester-Clark met in London Jan. 18 with British Home Secy. Reginald Maudling to seek more help in curbing the disorders. In a communiqué issued after the meeting, the 2 men agreed that Britain and Northern Ireland were determined to take all necessary steps to end the unrest.

A bomb Jan. 22 destroyed an electrical transformer in the city of Armagh, 40 miles from Belfast. Rioting between Protestants and Catholics broke out again in Belfast Jan. 23-25. British troops used riot gas and rubber bullets Jan. 23 to prevent about 300 Protestants from entering the Catholic Crumlin Road area. British Defense State Secy. Lord Carrington, after talks with Prime Min. Chichester-Clark in

Belfast Jan. 28–29, announced that security forces in Northern Ireland would be increased and their weapons modernized to combat terrorism.

At least 11 persons were killed in a new outbreak of clashes Feb. 3–9 between armed Catholic extremists and British soldiers in the Catholic districts of Belfast. Ulster officials and British army officers blamed the outbreaks on IRA Provisionals.

The February upsurge in violence began Feb. 3 as Catholics used submachine guns and threw bombs, grenades, stones and bottles at British troops during an arms search in the Clonard district of western Belfast. The soldiers, retaliating mainly with water cannon and rubber bullets, also returned fire 6 times. 7 soldiers were injured and more than 60 people arrested. (British troops had not previously entered the Clonard area.)

Maj. Gen. Anthony Farrar-Hockley, British commander of land forces in Belfast, Feb. 4 labeled the Clonard area a "harbor" of leaders of the IRA Provisionals and said that arms searches, which had been under way since Jan. 16, had involved only 32 houses "in the known Republican areas of Belfast." Farrar-Hockley blamed the violence on "attempts by the IRA Provisionals to stir up the whole of Belfast."

Acid and gasoline bomb attacks against troops in Catholic districts continued Feb. 5. British soldiers were reinforced by an extra batallion of troops that day and by an armored scout car squadron commanded by the Duke of Kent. (Bernadette Devlin, militant Catholic leader from Mid-Ulster, warned in Kingston, R.I. Feb. 8, during a speaking tour of the U.S., that the presence of the Duke of Kent would increase rebel resentment against the London government.) The violence intensified Feb. 6 when 4 civilians and one soldier were killed in a street battle. Prime Min. Chichester-Clark declared the same day that the armed battles represented "a trial of strength" between his government and the IRA and vowed that he would "not give in to intimidation."

Gun battles raged in the Ardoyne and Crumlin districts in Belfast Feb. 7, while in Londonderry, rockthrowing rioters also battled British troops. The same day bombs exploded in the towns of Newry, Killeen and Carrickmore, near the border of the Irish Republic. 4 teenagers were hit by machine-gun fire in Belfast Feb. 8 after a 5-year-old girl was run over and killed by a British armored car near the Catholic New Lodge Road area. About 200 persons attacked British vehicles in the area. A senior Army spokesman Feb. 8 deplored the use of women and children in the forefront of rioting crowds.

A booby trap apparently intended for British soldiers killed 5 civilians Feb. 9 on a rural mountain road outside Enniskillen, County

Fermanagh's capital. The victims were 2 British technicians for the British Broadcasting Corp. and 3 Irish construction workers.

In the Republic of Ireland, meanwhile, Prime Min. John Lynch condemned the violence Feb. 6 but attributed much of the responsibility to "political mistakes and tactical errors," an allusion to Irish criticism of the treatment of Catholics in Northern Ireland. The *Washington Post* reported Feb. 8 that IRA leader Rory O'Brady, in a statement issued from Dublin, had called on all Irishmen to stand together against British troops.

Repercussions in Irish Republic

Irish Prime Min. John Lynch dismissed Finance Min. Charles J. Haughey and Agriculture Min. Neil T. Blaney May 5, 1970 on charges of attempting to ship arms across the border to Catholics in Northern Ireland. Another cabinet member, Kevin Boland, minister for local government and social welfare, resigned in support of his 2 colleagues.

Announcing his action at a reconvened session of the Dáil Éireann (lower house of parliament) May 6, Lynch said that he had received information Apr. 19-20 that Haughey and Blaney had been linked with "alleged attempts to unlawfully import arms" for reported transshipment to Northern Ireland. He said that the 2 ministers had twice refused his request for them to resign and that he was forced to oust them after news of the charges had leaked out. Lynch assured the Oireachtas (parliament) that "this was the only intended importation of arms of the 2 members. These arms have not been imported and have not been landed in this country." Blaney and Haughey favored arms assistance for Ulster's Catholics in their struggle against the Protestant-dominated government, and they opposed Lynch's moderate policy for ending Irish partition. But the 2 former ministers denied any involvement in the illegal importation of arms for transshipment to Ulster.

Lynch won a parliamentary vote of confidence (72-65) May 7 on his handling of the crisis. He received another vote of confidence (73-66) May 10 on the issue of approving the nomination of 3 new ministers. They were Robert Molloy (local government), Gerard Cronin (defense) and Gerald Collins (post and telegraph). George Colley (Seoirse Ó Colla) former minister of industry, replaced Haughey as finance minister.

Kevin Boland told parliament May 8 that he had resigned because he could not serve a government "whose leader kept members under Gestapo surveillance." Boland accused Lynch of establishing a special force in the police to spy on cabinet ministers. Boland announced his resignation from the ruling Fianna Fáil party May 3, 1971. He said that he had lost faith in the possibility of changing the party's current policies, particularly its moderate policy for ending partition. Prime Min. Lynch won a 72–62 vote of confidence in parliament May 14, 1970 at the end of a 2-day debate on the gun-running incident.

Ex-Finance Min. Haughey and ex-Agriculture Min. Blaney were arrested May 28 on charges of conspiring to smuggle arms to Catholics in Northern Ireland. After being formally charged in a Dublin court, the 2 men were released on bail. The government's case against Blaney was dismissed from the docket of the Dublin District Court July 2 because of insufficient evidence.

A Dublin jury Oct. 23 acquitted Haughey and 3 other defendants of charges that they had conspired to import arms and ammunition illegally into Ireland for eventual transshipment to the Catholic minority in Northern Ireland. Defense attorneys during the 14-day trial contended that the arms had been brought into Ireland with the knowledge and approval of James Gibbons, then defense minister and currently agriculture minister. The other men acquitted were James Kelley, 41, a former intelligence captain in the Irish army, John Kelly, 34, a civil-rights organizer in Belfast, and Alfred Luykx, 53, of Dublin.

Prime Min. Lynch won another vote of confidence in parliament Nov. 4. The vote was 74–67. The confidence test stemmed from Haughey's acquittal.

A bomb explosion in Dublin Jan. 17, 1971 damaged a tower monument that formed part of the tomb of Daniel O'Connell, the patriot who won political emancipation for Irish Catholics in the 19th century. A bomb explosion Jan. 26 nearly destroyed a customs post in County Donegal's capital, Lifford, that separated the Irish Republic from the County Tyrone market town of Strabane in Northern Ireland.

Prime Min. Lynch retained control of the Fianna Fáil party during the party's annual convention in Dublin Feb. 20–21, 1971. His followers captured all the principal party posts. Lynch said at the convention that the government "may have to grasp nettles which might sting our pride" in order to achieve lasting peace throughout a united Ireland.

William Cardinal Conway, archbishop of Armagh and Catholic primate of all Ireland, held formal talks Feb. 25 with government leaders at Stormont, the seat of Northern Ireland's government. He was the first head of the Roman Catholic Church of Ireland to meet with a prime minister of Northern Ireland in 50 years.

Prime Min. Lynch discussed the problem of Northern Ireland with U.S. Pres. Richard M. Nixon in Washington Mar. 16. After the meeting he told newsmen that the ultimate solution was a reunification of North and South.

A visiting British Navy survey launch, the *Stork*, was seized Apr. 20 in the harbor of Baltimore, near Cork, towed to sea and blown up. No one was aboard the ship. The IRA claimed responsibility for the explosion. The ship had been engaged in a hydrographic survey in cooperation with the Irish government. The French newspaper *Le Monde* reported May 23 that police had arrested a number of suspects.

As part of a campaign to curb the IRA's activities, the Dáil Éireann June 9 unanimously approved a bill restricting the purchase and carrying of arms. The law specifically banned the holding of arms designed to be used beyond Ireland's frontier. (This was viewed as an attempt to halt the illicit traffic of arms to Northern Ireland.) Justice Min. Desmond O'Malley said the main purpose of the bill was to authorize energetic government action against armed clandestine groups. He said the police would halt such IRA activities as marches through the capital. The bill provided for an amnesty to arms holders who yielded their weapons before the law's enactment.

British Troops Vs. IRA

Stormont Prime Min. James Chichester-Clark announced new security measures against IRA terrorists Mar. 2, 1971. The measures included: (a) the dispatch to Northern Ireland of an extra battalion of British troops, raising the number there to about 8,000; (b) the maintenance of a permanent military presence in "riotous and subversive" IRA enclaves; (c) the arrogation of a right to "hot pursuit" into the Irish Republic of terrorists who engaged in armed violence; and (d) the cordoning of areas to prevent terrorists from fleeing.

The new measures came amid continuing violence between security forces and armed Catholic extremists in Belfast, including the murder of 3 British soldiers. British troops and Northern Irish police clashed with IRA extremists in Belfast Feb. 26–27. 2 policemen were killed and 4 others wounded in a gun battle with terrorists in the Ardoyne district Feb. 26. Another policeman was injured when a bomb exploded outside a police station on the outskirts of Belfast. Gasoline bombs exploded throughout the city. On the same day, police arrested 39 persons, most of them women, during fighting between Protestants and Catholics. Some of the women were charged with wearing IRA uniforms. (The government had banned the wearing of the IRA uniform Feb. 10.) Rioting erupted again between Catholics and Protestants Feb. 27, when about 400 Catholics attacked Protestants returning from a football game in Belfast. Police used water cannons to disperse the crowd.

A gang of Catholics fire-bombed a 2-man British military patrol in Londonderry Mar. 1. One soldier was burned to death. There was new rioting in the Falls Road area of Belfast Mar. 5 after troops began an arms search. British troops opened fire on bomb-throwing demonstrators Mar. 6; one civilian was killed and 5 British soldiers injured.

3 unarmed off-duty British soldiers were found shot to death near a bar on the outskirts of Belfast Mar. 10. Their bodies were discovered in a ditch in a country lane in Ligonel, 2 of the victims were brothers—John McCaig, 17, and Joseph, 18—from Ayrshire, Scotland; the other, Dougald McCaughey, 23, was from Glasgow. All 3, enlisted men in the Royal Highlands Fusiliers' regiment, were dressed in civilian clothes; the place where their corpses were discovered was by more than 2 miles off-limits to off-duty troops. (British Defense State Secy. Lord Carrington announced Mar. 12 that all British soldiers under 18 years of age were being withdrawn from Northern Ireland by Apr. 15.)

Among those making public expressions denouncing the murders was Stormont MP Austin Currie of the Social Democratic & Labor Party, who described the killings collectively as "a cowardly, brutal and savage crime" that, committed "in a so-called civilized country, is sickening and almost beyond belief." (The left-wing opposition Social Democratic & Labor Party had been formed Aug. 21, 1970 by 6 members of the Northern Irish Parliament. The leader of the new group, Gerald Fitt, said that SDLP's principal purpose was to work for the reunification of Ireland. The party's other aims included a minimum wage for all workers, equal pay for equal work, civil rights for all citizens, encouragement for cooperatives, and proportional representation.) Capt. Robert Mitchell, a Unionist MP, urged the authorities to proceed "to take into custody for questioning all those known to be associated in any way with the evil activities going on in the country."

Large-scale terrorist attacks that resulted in several deaths and numerous injuries occurred from April through early June 1971. Some observers—including Stormont's new Prime Min. Brian Faulkner—expressed the thought that the IRA had embarked on a new policy designed to provoke British soldiers to retaliate against civilians. Among developments in the violence:

● Bomb explosions damaged a city information booth in Belfast Apr. 2 and an electricity transformer near Dungannon.

● British troops and police found caches of illegal arms in predawn raids in Catholic areas of Belfast Apr. 3.

● British soldiers were injured in Londonderry rioting Apr. 11 after 2

Republican parades commemorated the 1916 Easter rebellion against the British in Dublin.

● Protestants, including a 13-year-old boy, were wounded by an unknown gunman in Belfast Apr. 13 when the Protestants were returning from their last big demonstration of the Easter weekend. The shooting touched off riots Apr. 14 when about 2,000 Protestants clashed with British troops after attacking a Catholic church. Belfast Catholics also stoned police patrols. British troops still were on full alert to prevent outbreaks of violence between Protestants and Catholics.

● Bombs exploded in downtown Belfast Apr. 16. At least 4 persons were injured and the garage of a magistrate damaged.

● Unknown gunmen ambushed a British Army vehicle May 15 in downtown Belfast. A civilian was killed and 2 British soldiers and 2 civilians were wounded.

● A British soldier was killed and 2 injured in an ambush of an army night patrol in Belfast May 21-22.

● A bomb explosion in a British ex-servicemen's hall in the Belfast suburb of Suffolk May 21 injured about 30 persons.

● A bomb exploded May 24 in a pub in a Protestant area of Belfast. About 18 persons were injured.

● Terrorists threw a bomb into a Belfast police station in a Roman Catholic area of Belfast May 25. One British soldier was killed and more than 20 persons injured, including policemen, soldiers and civilians.

Shortly before the May 25 bomb attack, Prime Min. Faulkner had disclosed in Parliament that British soldiers had been authorized to shoot on sight anyone "acting suspiciously." He said that the Army was "not prepared to take half-measures with terrorists." In response to Parliamentary criticism, Faulkner explained May 26 that the order applied to circumstances in which firearms or explosives might be used.

The IRA Provisionals in Belfast May 27 claimed responsibility for 3 earlier bomb explosions. The Provisional wing in Dublin disclaimed the statement.

A series of bomb explosions shook Belfast June 5-6. At least 8 persons were wounded. One of the bombs damaged a police station.

In the continuing violence between Catholics and British soldiers, 2 Catholic civilians—George Desmont Beattie, 19, and Seamus Cusack, 27—were shot in Londonderry July 8 during a riot in which demonstrators threw bombs and the troops used live ammunition in retaliation. Both died of their wounds.

Catholics asserted that Beattie and Cusack were unarmed, and they demanded a public inquiry. In debate in the British House of Commons July 12, the minister of state for defense, Lord Balneil, rejected the demand and supported the army's conclusion that the 2 men had been armed with a rifle and nail bomb and were ready to use their arms. Bernadette Devlin accused Lord Balneil of acting as "official liar" for the army command. She announced that an independent public inquiry would be held to investigate the deaths; the tribunal would include Paul O'Dwyer, a New York lawyer.

The 2 deaths, which occurred on the 5th consecutive day of rioting in Londonderry, generated more violence. Londonderry youths threw rocks at British soldiers July 9 and tossed gasoline bombs in the streets. Rioters set fire to an American-owned factory, Essex International Brakelining, of Fort Wayne, Ind. Extremists fired machine guns at British troops July 9–10.

About 11,000 soldiers and 4,000 policemen sealed off Catholic areas and prevented violence during Protestant Orange Order parades held July 12 to commemorate the victory of Protestant William of Orange over Catholic forces in the battle of the Boyne. About 100,000 Protestants participated in the parades held throughout Northern Ireland. Before the parades, which the Catholics traditionally regarded as humiliating provocation, a series of bomb attacks July 12 had destroyed stores and damaged the central post office along the main parade route in Belfast. 9 persons were injured. Other bombings took place in Belfast suburbs and outlying towns. (A Belfast court Oct. 8 sentenced a man to 15 years' imprisonment and a woman to 9 years on charges of exploding a bomb in a shopping arcade July 12.)

Away from the parade routes, a British soldier was killed by a sniper in a Catholic neighborhood of Belfast July 12. Another soldier was killed in a Belfast ambush July 13. The IRA Provisionals claimed responsibility for the 2 deaths as a retaliatory action for the 2 killings in Londonderry. (The *N.Y. Times* reported July 14 that 2 policemen, 10 soldiers and 15 civilians had been killed in Northern Ireland thus far in 1971, compared to 16 civilians, 2 policemen and no soldiers in all of 1970.)

In Londonderry, Catholics exchanged gunfire with troops and set fire to a shirt factory and 2 other buildings July 12. About 100 youths attacked armored cars and police in Londonderry July 24 after an army truck knocked down and killed a 9-year-old boy.

Lynch Proposes Reunification

Irish Republican Prime Min. John Lynch called on Britain July 11 to abandon its military and financial support of Northern Ireland and to declare its interest in reuniting Ireland. The speech, which was denounced by the Stormont government, was seen as a change of policy for Lynch, who previously had stressed peaceful coexistence rather than reunification.

Anthony Royle, British state undersecretary for foreign and Commonwealth affairs, wrote July 26 in reply to Lynch that his speech "contained . . . [some] passages . . . distinctly unhelpful at the present time." Royle added that London's views on Northern Ireland's status had repeatedly been made clear, most lately to Irish Foreign Min. Patrick Hillery July 21 by Britain's ambassador in Dublin. (Hillery Mar. 3 had had the name of his portfolio restyled; it had formerly been known as the External Affairs Ministry.)

Extremist Pressures Mount, Chichester-Clark Resigns

Ex-Home Affairs Min. William Craig asserted Aug. 10, 1970 that he and the extreme right-wing faction of the ruling Unionist Party were determined to bring down the Stormont government of Prime Min. James Chichester-Clark. The Rev. Ian Paisley had made a similar statement Apr. 17. But this goal eluded both men's political art until Chichester-Clark finally resigned Mar. 20, 1971—over what he reportedly considered to be a lack of British support for his aims.

Craig, opposed to the government's policy of concessions to Catholic grievances, charged that the régime "has committed the country to policies which have made law and order the laughing stock." He advocated greater force to crush any violence perpetrated by Catholics to achieve "political ends." Craig suggested the rearming of the Royal Ulster police force, whose guns had been taken away following their action in the 1969 riots in Londonderry and Belfast, and of reestablishment of the "B-Specials," the part-time volunteer police force of Protestants.

British Home Sec. Reginald Maudling warned the Stormont government Aug. 10 not to abandon its civil-rights and social-reform program. He said that "to go back on what has been done, or depart from the ideal of impartiality and reconciliation, would endanger the present constitutional arrangements under which Northern Ireland governs its own affairs."

Chichester-Clark won a 97–87 vote of confidence for his policies during a stormy local Unionist Party meeting Aug. 10 in Maghera, a town in eastern County Derry at the foot of the Sperrin Mountains. Right-wing party members charged, however, that the voting was irregular. Chichester-Clark's cabinet announced its unanimous support of his civil-rights program following a meeting Aug. 11. (The prime minister had asked for the vote of confidence.) Chichester-Clark received similar support from a majority of the Unionist Party's members of the Stormont Parliament Aug. 13.

The Executive Committee of the Unionist Party passed a vote of no confidence in Chichester-Clark's law-and-order policies Sept. 18; the resolution was adopted by 18–2 vote, although the committee consisted of 40 members. The resolution was intended to be private but was leaked to the press. A spokesman explained that the move was not a vote of no confidence in Chichester-Clark or in the government but merely in their law-and-order policies.

Chichester-Clark declared Oct. 26 that the majority of Northern Ireland's citizens wanted their land to remain part of Britain. Speaking at a meeting of Belfast members of the ruling Unionist Party, Chichester-Clark said: "The will of the great majority of our people to remain in association with our fellow British citizens is not to be set aside by any course of agitation of violence." He also said that his government was "determined to restore proper respect for law and lawfully constituted authority."

The Stormont Parliament Jan. 28, 1971 rejected by 29–7 vote a resolution of the right-wing splinter faction of the ruling Unionist Party to oust Chichester-Clark for failure to maintain law and order. The resolution was introduced by 7 Protestant Unionists, including the Rev. Ian Paisley and 2 former cabinet ministers—William Craig and Harry West. Citing earlier Catholic rioting, the resolution accused the government of "consistent and deplorable failure to appreciate and adequately deal with the origins of subversion in the community."

James Stewart, assistant secretary-general for the Northern Area of the Communist Party of Ireland, and Betty Sinclair, member of the party's National Executive, Feb. 15 strongly condemned "the methods of individual terror and physical coercion applied by the [IRA] Provisionals . . . , [which] only help the antidemocratic policy of the authorities, diverting attention from the real tasks and correct methods of political struggle." The party demanded the withdrawal of British troops but not before a political settlement was reached.

The murder of the 3 unarmed, off-duty British soldiers on the outskirts of Belfast Mar. 10 apparently intensified Protestant anxiety over the use of violence by Catholic terrorists demanding a union of Northern Ireland with the Irish Republic. British Home Secy. Reginald Maudling told the Westminster House of Commons Mar. 11 that the security forces in the 6 counties would not be provoked into reprisals. He promised, however, that the search for the terrorists would be intensified.

About 3,000 to 6,000 shipyard workers marched through Belfast Mar. 12 in protest against the killing of the 3 soldiers Mar. 10. In a petition to the Unionist Party, they demanded tough actions against the IRA, including internment without trial and the rearming of the police. (Both factions of the IRA—the militant Provisionals and the leftist Officials—denied responsibility for the murders, although the police remained convinced of their culpability. The London *Times* reported Mar. 11 that leaders of the IRA Provisional and Official factions had agreed to a truce Mar. 10 in the internecine warfare to which their policy rift had led. 600 British soldiers began Mar. 14 what was described as the biggest security operation in 2 years in their search for the killers.

Chichester-Clark found his moderate policies under increasing attack. He flew to London Mar. 16 for talks with Maudling, British Defense State Secy. Lord Carrington and Prime Min. Heath. He reportedly threatened to resign unless the government authorized stronger measures—including the dispatch of 4,000 additional troops—against the terrorists. Radar was installed along Northern Ireland's border with the Irish Republic to intercept arms and munitions, it was reported Mar. 16. The introduction of radar followed the discovery of a large machine-gun ammunition cache.

Chichester-Clark announced Mar. 18 that Britain would send 1,300 additional soldiers, bringing the total in Northern Ireland to more than 9,500. He also reported that Britain would not consent to the internment of Catholic guerrillas without trial and described British policy as "more physical presence on the ground in dangerous areas, more patrols, more controls of movement, more vigorous and frequent action both in Belfast and throughout the country."

Reportedly angry over what he considered lack of British support, Chichester-Clark resigned Mar. 20, 1971 as prime minister of the Stormont government. He said that he saw "no other way of bringing home to all concerned the realities of the present constitutional, political, and security situation." (British Prime Min. Heath immediately postponed a 4-day trip to West Germany and Berlin, scheduled to begin Mar. 21.)

The London *Sunday Times* Nov. 21 ascribed Chichester-Clark's downfall to an excess of faith in the decency and self-control and good judgment of the citizens of Northern Ireland. The editorial said: "Chichester-Clark was among the optimists of Ulster. When the troops moved into Derry and Belfast in the 1969 riots, he thought they would be back in barracks within 12 months. When those 12 months in fact ended with the Orange parades and the Falls curfew, he thought the first a success and the 2d justified. When the winter of 1970 seemed quiet, Chichester-Clark and his cabinet colleagues began to murmur that the trouble was over. The Army was disconcerted. 'We used to tell them: "For God's sake your troubles are ahead of you," ' one senior Army officer recalled. 'But they wouldn't listen.' The root of Chichester-Clark's optimism did him credit, however. In 1969 he, like most Ulstermen, had blamed the trouble on the IRA. But while his cabinet colleagues had remained of that fundamentalist persuasion, Chichester-Clark had in 1970 come to believe the IRA at that time was secondary. 'The trouble really is communal discontent,' he once said privately. And this he thought his reform program would assuage."

Chichester-Clark's resignation was followed by the imposition of stiffer measures against the IRA and the introduction in Aug. 1971 of internment for suspected terrorists. This policy, carried out by the British Army, was condemned by Catholics as a case of the British bowing to militant Protestant pressure. (The greater part of the violence had already shifted from large-scale communal violence to urban guerilla warfare between the IRA and the British Army.)

First 4 Months of Faulkner Government

Development Min. Brian Faulkner, 50, a Protestant moderate, was elected as the 6th prime minister of Northern Ireland Mar. 23, 1971, replacing Chichester-Clark. Faulkner, by 26-4 vote, defeated his hard-line opponent, William Craig, for leadership of the ruling Protestant Unionist Party. (Faulkner, born in 1921, had been a Stormont MP since 1949 and had served as the Unionist Party whip 1956-9. He was home affairs minister 1959-63, then minister of commerce 1963-9 and minister of development since 1969.)

Faulkner immediately pledged to restore confidence in Northern Ireland through a vigorous law-and-order campaign. He called for greater coordination between the British Army and the provincial police—the Royal Ulster Constabulary (RUC)—to combat terrorism, but he ruled out repressive measures. He also pledged "early talks with all shades of opinion" and promised that the civil rights "program for progress" would be "energetically continued." (Prime Min. John Lynch of the Irish Republic Mar. 23 lauded Faulkner for his announced intention of holding talks with all shades of opinion and said that his government would cooperate with Faulkner.)

William Craig, who had been expelled from the Unionist Party in 1970 for his militant position, immediately warned that Faulkner's administration would quickly collapse unless the prime minister adopted tougher policies against Catholic militants. Extreme right-wing Protestants urged the internment without trial of members of the IRA, a larger British Army presence in Catholic districts in Belfast, thorough searches for men and arms after terrorist incidents, the rearming of the RUC and the creation of a special armed militia under RUC control. (Catholic terrorists had been detained without trial during the IRA campaign in 1956–61. The RUC had been disarmed after the 1969 riots in Londonderry and Belfast, and the "B-Specials" had been disbanded after Catholics had complained that both units were violently anti-Catholic.)

Britain had opposed harsher security measures on the ground that they would further alienate the Catholic community. In a statement to the House of Commons Mar. 22, Prime Min. Heath had said that Britain would not sanction the rearming of the RUC or the reconstitution of the B-Specials. He also said he would support any government that cooperated in "implementing the policies which we judge right" for economic and social progress and for maintaining "law and order." He reaffirmed that Britain had "the ultimate authority and responsibility" for Northern Ireland. Observers saw a threat of direct rule from London if Northern Ireland did not pursue the 1969 civil-rights and social-reform program.

Prime Min. Faulkner revised his cabinet Mar. 25 in an effort to establish what he called "a broadly based government." His major appointments were seen as an effort to heal the breach between the feuding left and right wings of the ruling Unionist Party.

Harry West, a Protestant hardliner in the Unionist Party, was appointed agriculture minister. In an unprecedented move, a member of the opposition nonsectarian Northern Ireland Labor Party, David Bleakley, was named minister of community relations. Bleakley, a university lecturer, had been chairman of the East Belfast Peace Committee since 1969. The other new appointments were Roy Bradford, former minister of commerce, as minister of development; Nathaniel Minford as minister of state at the Ministry of Development; Robin Bailie as minister of commerce; and Capt. John Brooke as chief whip and minister of state at the Ministry of Finance.

Faulkner said that he himself would retain the post of home affairs minister and retain John Taylor as state minister for home affairs. Committing himself to concentrate on security, he announced that he would establish "a small but high-powered" branch for the coordination of security.

Faulkner said that every member of his cabinet had "fully endorsed the principles of policy which I outlined on taking office." They included a strong law-and-order policy and support for the reform program designed to eliminate discrimination against Catholics.

West, a rightist opponent of the reform policies, said he had joined the government because "the interests of Ulster would not best be served by pursuing past disagreements to the point where they could give comfort to our enemies or threaten our position within the United Kingdom." West had been a strong supporter of William Craig, who had challenged Faulkner in his bid to become prime minister.

Shortly after the appointment of the cabinet, a bomb explosion rocked the headquarters of the Unionist Party in Belfast. No injuries were reported.

Faulkner's cabinet won a vote of confidence, 27–8, from a standing committee of Unionist Party members Mar. 26. Most of the opposing votes came from the right wing, although liberal members expressed reservations over West's appointment. One Unionist MP, Anne Dickson, resigned from the party in protest against West's inclusion in the cabinet. The Stormont Parliament, by 199–71 vote, gave Faulkner a vote of confidence Apr. 1.

Faulkner Mar. 30 announced an amnesty period until Apr. 8 for people turning in illegal arms and gelignite. Faulkner reported Apr. 6 that more than 340 guns and 20,000 rounds of ammunition had been surrendered, representing only a small fraction of privately held arms in Northern Ireland.

Faulkner conferred in London Apr. 1 with Prime Min. Heath and other British ministers. A joint communiqué said the ministers agreed that "the forces available have the capability" to take all measures necessary for the restoration of peace and stability in Northern Ireland. The London *Times* reported Apr. 2 that the ministers had also agreed to a suggestion by Faulkner for the creation of a joint working party of Belfast and London officials to review prospects for Northern Ireland's economic and social development. (The number of unemployed in England, Scotland and Wales totaled 774,533, or 3.4% of the total work force. In Northern Ireland, 39,656 persons—7.7% of the work force—were unemployed.)

The Social Democratic & Labor party (SDLP), the main opposition party, announced July 16, 1971 that it would boycott the Northern Irish Parliament when it reconvened in October and would create an alternative assembly. The party's decision followed the refusal of the British government to order an independent public inquiry into the killing of 2 Catholic civilians—George Beattie and Seamus Cusack—July 8 by British troops in Londonderry. In addition to the 6 SDLP Parliamentary members, others of the 13-member opposition said they would boycott the autumn session of the Stormont Parliament.

In the face of mounting violence and the boycott threat by the opposition, Faulkner had appealed to SDLP members July 15 to back his government in its efforts to face "the enemy whose aim is to engulf us all in chaos and destruction." He offered the people of Londonderry a choice between the "social and economic benefits of an imaginative development plan" or "the fruits of riot, destruction, injury and death." In an earlier attempt to reach accomodation with the opposition, Faulkner had offered June 23 to establish 3 new Parliamentary policy committees in addition to the one existing committee. Opposition Catholic members would be entitled to at least 2 committee chairmanships. The new groups would cover social, environmental and industrial services. Opposition members reportedly welcomed Faulkner's offer.

INTERNMENT POLICY: 1971 – 2

Faulkner Begins Preventive Detention

Prime Min. Brian Faulkner invoked Northern Ireland's 1922 Special Powers Act's provisions Aug. 9, 1971 and imposed a policy of preventive detention and internment without trial of suspected IRA members throughout Northern Ireland. Faulkner took the step after consulting in London Aug. 5 with British Prime Min. Edward Heath and other British officials. Nocturnal rioting Aug. 7–8 in Belfast and the resultant loss of life and damage to property became the Stormont government's *apologia* for resorting to this recourse.

Tension had been again aroused in Belfast when a British soldier Aug. 7, 1971 shot to death a Catholic on his rounds as the driver of a delivery truck. The Army said initially that the soldier had opened fire after shots had been fired from the truck, but witnesses said that the sentry had mistaken a backfiring for the sound of a gunshot. Rioting occurred the nights of Aug. 7–8. Nail bombs, guns and stones were used in the Catholic Springfield Road, Falls Road and Ardoyne areas of Belfast Aug. 8. 3 British soldiers were wounded, one fatally.

A new wave of even more intense rioting erupted Aug. 9. The fighting was reported to be the heaviest in Northern Ireland in 50 years; the death toll reportedly rose to at least 21 Aug. 11. The commander of British Army ground forces, Maj. Gen. Robert Ford, had reported late Aug. 9 that the Army had been engaged in "a constant war of attrition against terrorists." He said that the Army and police had killed 5 men, 2 of them while they were raiding an Army post in central Belfast. One soldier, who had been shot by a sniper the night of Aug. 8 before the internment measures were invoked, died early Aug. 9. About 16 soldiers were reported wounded.

The crisis began with a series of dawn raids Aug. 9 when British army and police patrols seized more than 300 people for questioning. Later that morning, Stormont's Prime Min. Faulkner announced that he had resorted to preventive detention and the internment without trial of suspected IRA members. He said that he had taken the step "solely for the protection of life and the security of property." Faulkner, stressing that the measures were not aimed at "responsible and law-abiding" Catholic citizens, urged the moderate Catholic community to cooperate. He said that the "main target is the Irish Republican Army, which has been responsible for recent acts of terrorism, and whose victims have included Protestant and Roman Catholic alike." Faulkner continued:

Every means has been tried to make terrorism amenable to the law. Nor have such methods been without success, because a substantial number of the most prominent leaders of the IRA are now serving ordinary prison sentences. But the terrorist campaign continues at an unacceptable level, and I have had to conclude that the ordinary law cannot deal comprehensively or quickly enough with such ruthless viciousness.

I have therefore decided, after weighing all the relevant considerations, including the views of the security authorities and after consultation with her majesty's government in the United Kingdom last Thursday, to exercise where necessary the powers of detention and internment vested in me as minister of home affairs.

Accordingly, a number of men have been arrested by the security forces at various places in Northern Ireland this morning. I will be making internment orders in respect of any of these men who constitute a serious and continuing threat to public order and safety. This will be done only after a careful scrutiny of information furnished to me in respect of each such person, sufficient to convince me that the individual in question is a threat to the preservation of peace and the maintenance of order. Any such person will then have the right to have his case considered by an advisory committee, which will hear his representations and make recommendations to me.

Faulkner made it clear that the internment policy was directed against terrorists and not against the Catholic civil-rights movement. But he warned that "we will not hesitate to take strong action against any other individuals or organizations who may present such a threat in the future."

Under the internment order, which was authorized by a Special Powers Act applicable only to Northern Ireland, people could be arrested and held for 48 hours—longer if necessary—without being charged. Within 14 days, Faulkner was to review the case of every arrested person and decide whether to intern the suspect for an indefinite period. Anyone interned would have the right to appeal. At the same time (Aug. 9), Faulkner also announced a ban on religious parades in Northern Ireland for 6 months. The ban cancelled a march scheduled for Aug. 12 in Londonderry by the Protestant Apprentice Boys of Derry in commemoration of a Protestant victory over Roman Catholics in 1689.

Faulkner said that the 2 measures involved sacrifices by all segments of the population. He justified their use on the ground that Northern Ireland was "at war with the terrorist." He said the measures were designed to free the province from the "fear of the gunman, of the nightly explosion, of fire-raising [arson], of kangaroo courts, and all the appartus of terrorism." Faulkner said his decision had been made after consultation in London Aug. 5 with British Prime Min. Heath and other officials. (As a result of the meeting, the British government announced Aug. 6 a decision to send 1,800 more British troops to Northern Ireland, increasing the number there to 12,000, in anticipation of violence threatened by the IRA.)

The Catholic detainees were mainly rank-and-file members of the IRA, although news reports said that the leader of the IRA's Official wing had also been arrested. According to a London *Times* report Aug. 12, the police had arrested 70% of the suspects they sought. IRA spokesmen contended, however, that most of the key figures had escaped. Others unofficially reported arrested Aug. 9 included about 30 members of the Civil Rights Association on Northern Ireland, including its chairman, Ivan Barr, and Michael Farrell, a leader of People's Democracy, a Marxist theoretical group. Faulkner Aug. 11 signed an order detaining 230 of the approximately 300 persons arrested. They were being held on board a former British Navy submarine supply ship and in a local prison pending a final decision on internment. About 70 persons were released.

Rioting erupted in Belfast, Londonderry, Newry and Fermanagh immediately after the first dawn arrests Aug. 9, hours before Faulkner's announcement. In Belfast, Catholics set fire to buildings, threw nail and gasoline bombs and exchanged gunfire with British troops. 12 buses were hijacked. The city came to a standstill as pubs and restaurants shut down and public transportation ceased. Protestant families in predominantly Catholic neighborhoods and Catholic families in Protestant areas fled their homes. Protestants set fire to their own houses to ensure that Catholics would not occupy them. One Protestant woman was shot to death by a sniper as she fled from her home in the predominantly Catholic Ardoyne section of Belfast.

In Londonderry, where 60 persons had been detained, 4 British soldiers were shot and 6 were injured by thrown objects. Catholics attacked a police station with machine guns and gasoline bombs. Conflicting statistics of Aug. 9's death toll ranged between 7 and 12. All police leaves were canceled, and 4,000 Army reservists were called into full-time duty.

The crisis moved almost immediately beyond the borders of Northern Ireland. Irish Republican Prime Min. John Lynch Aug. 9 deplored the internment measures as "evidence of the political poverty of the policies" of Protestant Ulster's government. He called for a conference of all interested parties in order to obtain "a new form of administration for Northern Ireland." He also instructed that army camps be opened near the Northern Irish border for the dependents of people detained.

In continued fighting Aug. 10, a British soldier was killed in Londonderry and at least 4 others were wounded by snipers there and in

Belfast. Soldiers battled stone-throwing mobs in the primarily Catholic sections of Belfast with tear gas and rubber bullets. Bombs were thrown at a bank and a movie theater. Many cars were set afire and used as barricades. The British government sent 550 additional soldiers to Northern Ireland Aug. 11, raising the number of troops there to 12,500. It was the most troops in Protestant Ulster since the riots of 1969.

At least 4 men were killed by British soldiers in gun battles with terrorists in Belfast Aug. 11. Arson and sniper fire broke out there as well as in Londonderry and Armagh. The death toll rose to at least 21 persons Aug. 11, according to a London *Times* report Aug. 12. The unofficial death toll was estimated at 25. Nearly 3,500 Catholics had reportedly sought refuge in 8 army camps in Ireland. An Aug. 12 *N.Y. Times* report estimated that about 2,000 Protestants had fled their homes in Belfast's predominantly Catholic Ardoyne area. Nearly 350 homes were believed to have been burned by Protestant owners.

Ireland's Foreign Min. Patrick Hillery conferred Aug. 11 with British Home Secy. Reginald Maudling and other officials in London on the crisis. No details were disclosed, although an Aug. 12 *Washington Post* report suggested that the possibility of a tripartite summit meeting had been discussed. Prime Min. Faulkner said Aug. 11 that he would confer with anyone who wanted to improve the situation in Northern Ireland, but he insisted the constitution was "inviolate." He said he was "not prepared to discuss the constitutional position with anyone, whoever they are."

Faulkner that night defended his use of internment. He said that it had drawn "the gunmen out into the open instead of hiding behind, doing their explosions and their dirty work." Faulkner's action, however, had evoked strong criticism within Northern Ireland. The leading opposition group, the Social Democratic & Labor Party, had called for civil disobedience against internment Aug. 9 and urged people not to pay rent or taxes. The same day, Bernadette Devlin returned to Northern Ireland from London to organize resistance in her constituency. The Rev. Ian Paisley, leader of the right-wing Protestants, denounced the internment measure Aug. 9 as a piece of "political expediency" by Faulkner "to bolster up his tottering premiership." In a meeting with Faulkner the next day, Paisley urged the convocation of a special session of the Northern Irish Parliament to discuss stiffer measures against rioters.

The British Airline Pilots Association Aug. 10 declared Belfast a "hostile area" and expressed support for any pilot who refused to fly into Northern Ireland. In New York, 4 Irish Republican sympathizers were arrested Aug. 10 after an 8-hour sit-in at the British consulate. They were part of a group of 8 demonstrators.

Dublin & Belfast in Bitter Dispute

In the face of internments without trial of suspected Catholic terrorists and subsequent rioting in Northern Ireland, Irish Republican relations with Great Britain and Northern Ireland deteriorated in mid-August in an exchange of increasingly harsh statements by government leaders. As fighting ebbed after 3 days and nights of violence, a bitter political dispute exploded between the governments of Northern Ireland and the Irish Republic.

The dispute stemmed from the appeal Aug. 12, 1971 by Irish Prime Min. John Lynch for the replacement of the Stormont government by an administration—possibly a commission—in which the minority Catholics would share power with the ruling Protestants. Lynch urged all Irishmen to take united political action to topple the Stormont government, which, he charged, had "consistently repressed" the Catholics. He reiterated his opposition to terrorist tactics by militant Catholics, while making a special plea to the British people to work toward a change in Protestant Ulster's administration.

Northern Ireland's Prime Min. Faulkner Aug. 13 "rejected utterly" Lynch's statement. He said that "no further attempt by us to deal constructively with the present Dublin government is possible." Faulkner accused Lynch of "cant, hypocrisy and falsehood" and with tacit support of the IRA, which he said was based, trained and organized in the Irish Republic. He charged that Lynch had committed himself "to support by political means what the IRA seek to achieve by violent means—the overthrow of the Northern Ireland government."

Following up his request that Catholics share power with Protestants in Northern Ireland, Irish Prime Min. Lynch warned Aug. 19 that he would support the opposition policy of passive resistance unless Britain stopped attempting military solutions" in the 6 counties.

In a telegram to British Prime Min. Heath—timed to arrive when Stormont's Prime Min. Faulkner was meeting in London with Heath, Home Secy. Reginald Maudling and other British officials—Lynch wired that the violence and bitterness in Northern Ireland since the introduction of internment without trial had proved the failure of that policy and of military operations. He agreed to attend a summit meeting of "all the interested parties designed to promote the economic, social and political well-being of all the Irish peoples" if military action were replaced by a policy of finding solution by "political means." (Lynch and Heath were due to confer in London Oct. 20 at a meeting scheduled before the recent outbreaks. The British Labor spokesman on home affairs, James Callaghan, had called Aug. 15 for an earlier summit meeting of Heath, Lynch and Faulkner. He had criticized the British government for not taking new political initiatives along with internment and military operations.)

Lynch's telegram followed growing pressure within the Republic of Ireland to take stronger action toward the unification of the 2 Irelands. 7 members of the ruling Fianna Fáil party in Cork, Ireland had resigned Aug. 18. They said they would help organize the New Republican Party planned by Kevin Boland, the former cabinet minister who had quit the party in May. The defectors accused the Fianna Fáil of abandoning "all vestiges of republicanism" and said that the party's policy in later years amounted to acceptance by the government of Irish partition.

Boland, former minister for local government and social welfare, formed the Republican Unity Party in Dublin Sept. 19. He told the 1,200 founding members that the governing Fianna Fáil had failed to push its demand for a united Ireland. 2 members of the Dáil (lower house of the Irish parliament) had also quit the Fianna Fáil to join Boland's new party.

Heath replied immediately that Lynch's message was "unacceptable in its attempts to interfere in the affairs of the United Kingdom and can in no way contribute to the solution of the problems in Northern Ireland." He said that Lynch's threat to support passive resistance was "calculated" to worsen tension in Northern Ireland and to impair relations between Britain and the Irish Republic.

Lynch Aug. 20 rejected Heath's charge of unwarranted interference in Northern Ireland and linked Dublin's concern to the general unacceptability of partition. He said that "no generation of Irishmen has ever willingly acquiesced in that division; nor can this problem remain forever in its present situation."

The Stormont government Aug. 20 issued a White paper rebutting Lynch's earlier claim that Northern Ireland had "consistently repressed" its Catholic minority and had not implemented reforms stipulated in an Aug. 1969 accord. The paper claimed progress in granting full civil rights to Catholics and cited as reforms: the disarming of the police force and disbandment of the "B-Specials," a paramilitary volunteer band of Protestants; the impartial allocation of housing; and antidiscriminatory measures in voting and employment.

Lynch met in Dublin Aug. 23 at his own invitation with 13 opposition members of the Stormont Parliament who had 5½ weeks before decided to boycott coming sessions. In a joint statement issued after the talks, the group agreed that their immediate objective was to obtain equality of treatment for everyone in Northern Ireland. They added that "the great majority of the Irish people" wanted to achieve the unification of Ireland and said that all the discussion's participants had agreed that this goal should be pursued through "nonviolent political means." It was also announced that regular consultations would be held between the Irish Republican government and the Northern Irish opposition politicians.

Prime Min. Faulkner responded Aug. 24 that "the state of Northern Ireland is not going to be brought down." He said that "neither the United Kingdom nor the Northern Ireland government will be shaken in their resolve to maintain Northern Ireland as an integral part of the United Kingdom by any campaign—be it outright terrorists or political blackmail."

Heath & Lynch Disagree

British Prime Min. Heath and Irish Prime Min. Lynch conferred Sept. 6-7 on the crisis in Northern Ireland but failed to resolve their differences. The 2 leaders were deadlocked over Northern Ireland's policy of internment, the campaign to smash the IRA, constitutional changes for Ulster and Lynch's demand that he participate in direct negotiations involving Northern Ireland.

Lynch said at a news conference after the meetings, held outside London, that he had insisted at the talks that he had a right to be involved in constitutional matters involving Northern Ireland because "I am the elected head of the government of Ireland and I represent the mass opinion of the Irish people." Heath had rejected this view and asserted that "as long as there was a Northern Ireland government, he would not have the Republic [of Ireland] interfering," Lynch said.

Lynch had proposed at the meetings an immediate conference of the Irish Republican, British and Northern Irish governments as well as representatives of Northern Ireland's opposition, which was largely Catholic. Heath had rejected the proposal and instead announced that British officials would meet with representatives of the Stormont government, the province's political opposition and members of the Catholic and Protestant communities in Northern Ireland. At the same time, Heath proposed a 3-way conference of himself, Lynch and Stormont Prime Min. Brian Faulkner. Lynch said in Dublin Sept. 8 that he would be interested in meeting with Heath and Faulkner because "every effort needs to be made to obtain progress through political means."

The Catholic opposition in Northern Ireland, the Social Democratic & Labor Party, Sept. 8 rejected the proposed meeting with Ulster Protestant and British representatives. They said that the only basis for such a parley was a halt in internment and the suspension of the Protestant-controlled government of Northern Ireland. Bernadette Devlin, acknowledged by younger Catholics as their leader in the civil rights drive, said that if British Home Secy. Reginald Maudling, who was to represent London in the conference, "expects the civil rights campaign to be discouraged before talks take place, the talks will not be held." She said that "the civil rights campaign will continue until internees have been released."

The Northern Ireland Labor Party and the Ulster Trades Union Council, which represented Catholic and Protestant workers, accepted the invitation to attend the talks.

Tripartite Talks 'Inconclusive'

Prime Min. Edward Heath of Great Britain, Brian Faulkner of Northern Ireland, and John M. Lynch of Ireland ended 2 days of intensive talks Sept. 28 with an appeal for "political reconciliation" in Northern Ireland and a condemnation of "any form of violence as an instrument of political pressure." They failed, however, to agree on new measures to halt the escalating violence in the 6 counties or to reach a joint position regarding the internment without trial of suspected IRA terrorists. The 3 political leaders vowed "to seek to bring violence and internment and all other emergency measures to an end without delay." The 3 prime ministers also agreed to hold another meeting, but did not set a date. The meeting—the first between the prime ministers of the 3 nations since the partition of Ireland—was held at Chequers, the country residence of the British prime minister.

The talks were denounced as "inconclusive" by Cathal Goulding, Dublin leader of the leftist IRA Officials. He said, on a Dublin TV show Sept. 29, that his men would continue to use guns and bombs "to defend nationalist areas in Northern Ireland." The leader of the IRA's militant Provisionals also warned that the campaign of violence would be "continued and intensified."

Immediately after the talks, Lynch asserted publicly that the first essential step toward ending the violence was to abolish internment. He said that this was necessary in order to persuade the leading Catholic opposition party in the Stormont Parliament, the Social Democratic & Labor Party (SDLP), to end its boycott of talks on political reform in Northern Ireland. He promised to inform the SDLP about the tripartite meeting, but he said he could not "dictate" a course of action to the party.

Faulkner, at a separate news conference after the talks, defended internment without trial, which, he asserted, had "prevented additional murder." He said he "would not be prepared to weaken on that and put back on the streets those ready to take lives." Faulkner also said that while he foresaw a wider governmental rôle for the Catholic minority, he would not give cabinet positions to Catholics determined to sever Northern Ireland's ties with Britain and to bring about union with the Irish Republic. (The SDLP held unification as its ultimate goal.)

Border Incidents & Irish-British Tension

A British soldier was shot to death Aug. 29, 1971 and another wounded when their Army patrol was ambushed by gunmen near the Northern Irish town of Crossmaglen in Southwestern County Armagh, 10 miles west-northwest of the County Louth port of Dundalk across the border with the Irish Republic. The attack occurred after 2 armored patrol cars had inadvertently crossed the border into the Irish Republic. The men fled back to Northern Ireland after hostile passersby burned one of the cars. The casualties occurred after the soldiers had returned to Northern Ireland. A British Army spokesman charged that the shots were fired from within the Irish Republic.

The incident exacerbated already tense relations between the Irish Republic, Great Britain and Northern Ireland. Irish Prime Min. Lynch Aug. 31 issued a statement denying that the shots were fired from the Irish Republic. He criticized the British government for failing to "control movements of their troops" along the border between Northern Ireland and the Irish Republic and said that British troops had made at least 30 "incursions" into Ireland within the past 2 years. He warned that "infringement could be prejudicial to the peace."

British Home Office Undersecy. Lord Windlesham announced Sept. 23 that the Army would strengthen mobile patrols and air reconnaissance at the border between the 6 counties and the Irish Republic in an effort to halt the influx of guerrillas into Protestant Ulster. His announcement was made in the House of Lords on the final day of a special 2-day debate on the Northern Irish crisis.

Britain Oct. 7 announced its decision to send 3 more Army battalions—1,750 men—to Northern Ireland to combat continuing terrorism. The additional men would raise to nearly 14,000 the number of British troops stationed there. The announcement followed 8 hours of talks in London between Northern Irish Prime Min. Faulkner and British Prime Min. Edward Heath. The statement said that the troops would be used "to strengthen control of the border [with the

Irish Republic] and to follow up more rapidly the action against terrorists."

After the meeting, Heath announced that Geoffrey Johnson Smith, undersecretary of state for the Army, had received special responsibility for the Ulster Defense Regiment, a group equivalent to a national militia. The terms of the assignment indicated that the British government would, when necessary, assume tighter control over the situation in Northern Ireland.

In an interview televised by the BBC Oct. 11, Heath said that he was "determined to get on top of the gunmen" in the 6 counties. He vowed that Britain would remain in Northern Ireland as long as most of the people there wanted it to.

Unidentified British Army sources confirmed Oct. 12 that troops had been authorized to shoot across the border into the Irish Republic at armed men if their lives were endangered. In the past, troops were prohibited from opening fire if their shots were likely to cross the border. British troops Oct. 13 began blowing up more than 50 secondary roads between Ulster and the Irish Republic in an effort to halt the flow of arms and guerrillas across the border. About 20 official crossing points would remain open.

Irish Prime Min. John Lynch announced Oct. 13 that he had protested to Britain about the blowing up of the roads. He said the action was "a retrograde step" that would "aggravate a deteriorating situation."

Lynch, in the opening speech of a 2-day debate in the Dáil Oct. 20, denounced what he said were repeated violations by British troops of the Irish Republic's border. He warned he would appeal to the UN to halt "a threat to international peace" if the incursions did not cease.

Armed Irish Republican soldiers Oct. 28 forced British soldiers to abandon explosives they had placed under a bridge near Newton Butler, in County Fermanagh, at the border between Northern Ireland and the Republic. The Irish soldiers said that the bridge was located within the Republic. The British had intended to blow up the bridge as part of their campaign to destroy secondary frontier roads and to reduce the flow of guerrillas and arms from the republic. The *Washington Post* Oct. 29 said of the incident:

A 30-man Irish army patrol led by Lt. Bernard Goulding took combat positions against the British troops as they were planting gelignite charges in the span, near Munnely in County Monaghan. The British have been cutting bridges and roads along the border, trying to reduce the flow of arms and men into the strife-ridden north.

Goulding pointed a submachine gun at his British counterpart and demanded he hand over the explosives. The tense confrontation lasted 90 minutes before maps were produced indicating that the bridge was located just inside the Republic. The British soldiers withdrew.

In Dublin, the Irish cabinet reportedly approved a plan to seek up to $7.2 million to provide the Republic's army with new firepower and to finance a recruiting drive.

Sources said a prime purpose of the plan . . . is to fortify the border between the Republic and Northern Ireland.

Irish Prime Min. Lynch urged Britain later Oct. 28 to end the "futile and dangerous" border-sealing operation. He said it was "time for the British government to show genuine concern and statesmanship" in the crisis.

In an incident Oct. 30, IRA terrorists blew up 8 British customs posts along the Irish border.

Terrorist activities extended to London and further complicated the relations between Britain and Ireland. A bomb explosion severely damaged the top floors of the Post Office Tower in London Oct. 31. 6 hours after the blast, a man with an Irish accent telephoned the British Press Association, a news agency, and said a London branch of the IRA was responsible for the bombing. He warned that Parliament would be the next target. Both the Official and Provisional branches of the IRA in Dublin issued statements denying responsibility for the explosion. Another bomb explosion caused minor damage to an army drill hall a quarter of a mile from Parliament Nov. 1. British police refused to speculate about who was responsible for the bombings. The Angry Brigade, a group of young revolutionaries who had claimed credit for previous explosions, also claimed responsibility for these blasts.

Terrorism Escalates

The introduction of the internment policy Aug. 9, 1971 failed to reduce terrorist activities in Northern Ireland and even seemed to spur the IRA to greater efforts to end the British occupation. Northern Irish Catholics rioted for 3 days after the internment policy was imposed and the rioting then waned; the terrorism, however, continued and increased. According to Lewis Chester in the London *Sunday Times* Nov. 7: "Since . . . [the internment policy's] adoption, every important index of violence—number of civilians killed, number of explosions—has risen with great speed. The escalatory point is best established by a comparison of the figure of the first 7 months of this year with those for August, September and October." Chester gave these statistics for casualties in Northern Ireland during 1971:

	Jan.	Feb.	March	April	May	June	July	Aug.	Sept.	Oct.
Number of British soldiers killed	0	3	3	0	2	0	2	6	6	11
Number of British soldiers injured	5	28	5	5	6	3	15	36	34	34
Number of RUC and UDR killed	0	2	0	0	0	0	0	1	2	4
Number of civilians killed	3	6	2	0	2	0	2	28	11	17
Number of explosions	12	28	33	37	47	50	91	103	173	107
Poundage of explosive used	150	380	231	265	365	519	1,408	1,349	2,292	2,381

Referring to the above statistics Sen. Edward Kennedy (D., Mass.) declared Nov. 16: ". . . These figures strongly suggest that the policy of internment may actually be counterproductive even on its own terms, since internment may well be fueling the violence instead of reducing it. Surely, in light of figures like these, there can be no justification for a continuation of this cruel and repressive policy."

There was an intense escalation of terrorism after Aug. 12 when the rioting of Northern Irish Catholics against British troops waned.

British soldiers shot and killed a man in the Bogside district of Londonderry early Aug. 13. The Army said the man had fired on soldiers. Other British troops Aug. 13 fought a gun battle with IRA suspects near Newry, close to the border with the Irish Republic. Early Aug. 14, terrorists fired machine guns from County Donegal across the border at a police station in the frontier town of Belleek in County Fermanagh.

The British troops reportedly moved toward the border with Ireland Aug. 14 to halt terrorist infiltration and the flow of arms into Northern Ireland. A British soldier was killed by a sniper Aug. 14 in Belfast's Catholic district of Ardoyne. Later the same day, bombs exploded in downtown Belfast. 9 persons were injured in explosions at the customs and excise office on the docks.

British soldiers in Londonderry shot to death 2 armed civilians in 2 separate incidents Aug. 18. One man was killed in a gun battle between soldiers and snipers and another, a deaf mute, was killed after he failed to hear an Army order to drop a pistol he had allegedly waved after an address at a passive resistance rally by Bernadette Devlin. 2 opposition members of the Stormont Parliament—John Hume, a Catholic, and Ivan Cooper, a Protestant who supported Catholic civil rights—were arrested Aug. 18 after they and 300 supporters tried to block soldiers from entering the Catholic Bogside district of Londonderry. They were released on bail. Hume and Cooper were convicted and fined Sept. 8 on charges connected with their participation in the attempt to prevent British troops from dismantling barricades.

Scattered terrorist incidents occurred Aug. 21-25. Bombs wrecked a Ministry of Health & Social Services building and a car showroom in

Belfast Aug. 21. Terrorists Aug. 22 blew up the gates of Belfast's heavily guarded Crumlin Jail, where nearly half of the 230 suspected terrorists were interned. 2 prisoners and 2 prison officers were injured. A British sentry was shot to death Aug. 23 by a sniper in Belfast's Ardoyne area, and a civilian shot 2 weeks earlier died in a hospital.

A bomb exploded in the suburban offices of the Electricity Board of Northern Ireland in Belfast Aug. 25, killing one person and injuring 35. The IRA Official wing denied responsibility and called the explosion a "cowardly attack on a nonmilitary target."

Daily and nightly bomb explosions added to the violence and fear among the civilian population. A wave of noontime bomb blasts in the center of Belfast Sept. 2 caused injuries to 39 persons and wrecked part of the ruling all-Protestant Unionist Party headquarters.

Terrorists firing at British soldiers Sept. 3 in the Catholic Falls Road section of Belfast killed a 17-month-old girl. Earlier the same day, a private in the Irish Ulster Defense Regiment was fatally shot on sentry duty in Kinawley, County Fermanagh, near the border. A British soldier was killed Sept. 4 and 2 other soldiers injured when their scout car hit a mine in the County Fermanagh town of Bessbrook near the border with the Irish Republic. 2 young sisters, aged 15 and 12, were injured Sept. 5 when a bomb exploded at a supermarket next to their home in Belfast.

A 14-year-old girl was killed in Londonderry Sept. 6 when she was caught in a gun battle between British soldiers and snipers. A British armored car struck and killed a 3-year-old boy in a Londonderry traffic accident Sept. 9. The incident, combined with riots after the funeral of the 14-year-old girl, incited crowds to throw stones and gasoline bombs at troops in Londonderry's Bogside district.

Catholics and Protestants exchanged gunfire in the Catholic Ardoyne district of Belfast Sept. 11. One civilian was wounded.

Street riots erupted in Londonderry Sept. 12 after the funeral of the 3-year-old boy run over by the British Army truck. Troops fired rubber bullets and nausea gas in an effort to crush the fighting. The same day, riots broke out in Belfast after a civil disobedience rally staged by Catholics.

A soldier was shot to death and 2 others were wounded in Belfast Sept. 17 while they were dismantling a gelignite bomb. Later in the day, terrorists killed a policeman in Strabane, near the border with the Irish Republic. A British soldier was critically wounded Sept. 20 at an observation post in Londonderry by what the Army said was a dum-dum bullet, outlawed by the Geneva Convention on rules of warfare,

(Dumdum bullets split on impact, causing multiple wounds.) The IRA claimed responsibility for the shooting, but denied any use of a dumdum bullet.

A bomb explosion killed 2 persons and wounded 25 in a crowded bar in the Protestant Shankill Road district of Belfast Sept. 29. The bomb exploded while the bar was filled with soccer fans after a game.

Protestants fought with Catholics in stone-throwing incidents in Belfast Sept. 30, a day after an explosion in a bar frequented by Protestants killed 2 persons. The 2 IRA factions Sept. 30 denied responsibility for the blast.

The terrorism continued into October. A British soldier was shot to death and a civilian sniper was shot and captured in incidents in Belfast Oct. 1. Terrorists shot to death Patrick Daly, 57, a Stormont Agriculture Ministry inspector, when he was caught in a gunfire exchange between British troops and IRA snipers in the Catholic Falls Road area of Belfast Oct. 3. A bomb explosion in a shop in the Catholic Springfield Road area of Belfast killed one British soldier and wounded 9 other soldiers and civilians Oct. 4. Terrorists blew up a pumping station at a Belfast reservoir Oct. 8, causing extensive flooding and cutting water off from Catholic homes. A bomb explosion in a bar frequented mainly by Belfast Catholics killed a woman and injured 14 people Oct. 9. The London *Times* Oct. 11 reported growing speculation in Northern Ireland that the blast might be the work of a clandestine Protestant terrorist force.

4 men were arrested in the Irish Republic Oct. 14 after a gun battle between British soldiers and IRA guerrillas near the border in County Armagh, Northern Ireland. The suspected terrorists had crossed into the Irish Republic after they had ambushed a British demolition squad destroying roads between Northern Ireland and the Irish Republic. The men were the first IRA guerrillas to be detained in Ireland since the outbreak of violence in Ulster in 1969.

2 Northern Irish plainclothesmen, members of the Royal Ulster Constabulary, were killed by machine-gun fire in downtown Belfast Oct. 15. A group called the Irish Republican Movement Oct. 16 claimed responsibility for the killing of the policemen. They said one of the policemen had been a member of a "police murder group" that had killed a man in Londonderry in 1969.

A British soldier was shot to death by a sniper during a clash between troops and rioters in Londonderry Oct. 16, and terrorists shot and killed a British soldier in the Catholic Ballymurphy area of Belfast Oct. 17.

In a fresh upsurge in the continuing violence, British soldiers

Oct. 23 shot and killed 2 sisters, aged 30 and 19, who had been riding in a car in a Catholic district of Belfast. The sisters were reportedly members of the Clonard Women's Action Committee, a vigilante group that warned Catholic residents of Army raids. The Army contended that shots had first been fired from the car, an assertion denied by the driver and witnesses. Army officials explained that no weapons had been recovered from the car because hostile onlookers had prevented soldiers from reaching the vehicle immediately after the shooting. In a statement to the House of Commons on Oct. 25, Lord Robert A. L. Balniel, British minister of state for defense, said: "I have received the following report. At about 4:30 a.m. on Saturday, Oct. 23, soldiers of the 3d Battalion, the Royal Green Jackets, were engaged in search operations in Cape Street in the Lower Falls area of Belfast. A Ford saloon car was driven at speed along Cape Street. As it reached the junction of Cape Street and Ross Street, the rear window was broken from inside and 2 shots were fired from inside the car towards soldiers in Cape Street. 3 soldiers returned a total of 9 rounds at the car, which swerved across Ross Street into the junction with Omar Street. By the time that the soldiers could regroup to follow up, a crowd had gathered about the car, which had crashed into a wall. When the soldiers had dispersed the crowd, they found 2 women shot dead in the back seat. These have been identified as Mrs. Mary Ellen Meehan and Miss Dorothy Maguire."

British soldiers Oct. 23 had shot to death 3 apparently unarmed men attempting a robbery in Newry.

Clashes between Catholics and soldiers erupted after the 2 incidents. Soldiers used nausea gas to curb an angry mob in Newry. A man was shot to death in Belfast and a woman wounded Oct. 24 after police spotted them, along with another man, planting a bomb outside a nightclub. The bomb exploded, but no one was injured. In fresh protests against Army shootings, mobs in Newry Oct. 24 looted, set fire to stores and wrecked mail trucks. Rioters also attacked police and Army posts in Londonderry. In Belfast, 3 soldiers were shot and injured.

British troops attempting to blow up a frontier road leading to the Irish Republic Oct. 26 engaged in a gun battle with snipers firing from across the border.

A Protestant laborer was found bound, gagged and shot to death in Belfast Oct. 26, reportedly the victim of an IRA "revenge" killing. 2 soldiers were killed when a bomb was thrown at an Army observation post in Londonderry Oct. 27—in reprisal for the shooting of the 2 sisters Oct. 23 in Belfast, an IRA Provisional spokesman said in Dublin.

A police sergeant was shot to death Oct. 27 and a constable seriously wounded in an ambush on the outskirts of Belfast. (Earlier Oct. 27, an Army officer warned that soldiers would shoot to kill any child or adult man or woman firing guns at them.)

7 policemen and 2 civilians were injured Oct. 28 in a series of terrorist attacks on homes of policemen in Belfast. A policeman was killed and 2 injured when terrorists bombed a Belfast police station Oct. 29. 2 plainclothesmen were machine-gunned to death Nov. 1 at a shopping center in Belfast. 2 bomb explosions near a police station in suburban Belfast killed a man and a woman and injured 35 persons Nov. 2.

A housewife was shot to death by British soldiers in Londonderry Nov. 6 during a house-to-house search for terrorists. The woman was apparently caught in an exchange of shots with terrorists.

More than 20 bomb explosions in Belfast Nov. 8 struck a suburban shopping center, hosiery factory, restaurant, hairdressing salon, cafe, a bus and Army patrols. A British soldier was shot to death by snipers while on observation-post duty in Londonderry Nov. 9.

British Army units discovered arms caches throughout Ulster in a series of raids Nov. 4–9. 52 persons were detained for questioning in Belfast Nov. 4 during house-to-house raids that also netted sizable quantities of arms, ammunitions and explosives. The Army reported Nov. 6 the discovery of a bomb factory in Carrickmore in County Tyrone. (According to figures released Nov. 9, arms searches in 1971 had netted 62,121 rounds of ammunition and 369 weapons, of which 124 were rifles and 10 were machine guns.)

Enraged Londonderry women Nov. 10 tied Martha Doherty, 19, to a lamp post, shaved her head, and covered her with tar for dating a British soldier. She subsequently married the soldier. 2 other girls were seized by women in Londonderry and publicly humiliated Nov. 8 and Nov. 10 for dating British soldiers.

A soldier and 2 civilians were killed and a wave of bomb explosions shook Ulster Nov. 27. The soldier was shot by a sniper in the Catholic Falls Road area of Belfast. The 2 civilians were killed at a customs post near Newry by gunfire that a British army spokesman said came from the Irish Republic side of the border.

In another of several terrorist incidents in November, a Dutch sailor was machine-gunned to death in a dentist's waiting room in Belfast Nov. 12. He was believed to be the first non-Irish, non-British victim of terrorist violence. His death was thought to be a case of mistaken identity.

2 civilians manning a British customs post near the border town of

Newry were killed Nov. 27 by gunfire allegedly coming from the Irish Republic side of the border. 4 other frontier posts were attacked by terrorists during the day. Gunmen also shot and killed a British soldier in the Catholic Falls Road area of Belfast.

15 Catholic civilians, including 2 children, were killed Dec. 4 when a bomb destroyed (Thomas) McGurk's Bar, a Belfast saloon. McGurk was injured. This was the highest toll for a single terrorist incident in the more than 2 years of Northern Ireland's civil unrest. Police hypothesized that the bar might have been used as a transfer point when the bomb exploded accidentally. Both the Official and Provisional IRA factions disclaimed responsibility. Catholics were said to be convinced the incident was the work of an extremist Protestant terrorist group.

IRA terrorists Dec. 7-10 shot to death 3 members of the Ulster Defense Regiment in what was seen as a campaign to demoralize the volunteer force. 2 of the victims were Catholic, one was Protestant. Pvt. Sean Russel, one of the Catholic victims, was killed Dec. 9 in front of his 5 children in his Belfast home. The other killings took place in the villages of Clady and Curlough in County Tyrone. A bomb explosion in a crowded furniture store in the Protestant Shankill Road area Dec. 11 killed 2 men and 2 babies in carriages and injured at least 19 other persons. William Cardinal Conway Dec. 12 denounced the murderers of Sean Russell and the killers of the Belfast furniture shop victims from the pulpit of St. Patrick's Cathedral in Armagh. Conway said: "The person who could shoot a man dead in his own sitting-room in front of his wife and children was a monster, and the person who planted a bomb among innocent people was a foul murderer. The same could be said of other horrible killings which have taken place during the past 2 weeks. Nothing can cloud a cold clear condemnation of these deeds. To condone them in the slightest degree, even in thought, would be to become murder-soiled oneself."

Conway and 5 Catholic bishops in Northern Ireland had joined Sept. 12 in issuing the following statement:

In the present dangerous situation in Northern Ireland, it is important that people should see facts clearly. On a future occasion we may find it necessary to speak at some length on certain aspects of the present situation about which Catholics feel a very real sense of grievance.

In this short statement, however, we wish to focus attention on one fact in particular. This is that in Northern Ireland at the present time there is a small group of people who are trying to secure a united Ireland by the use of force. One has only to state this fact in all its stark simplicity to see the absurdity of the idea. Who in his sane senses wants to bomb one million Protestants into a united Ireland?

At times the people behind this campaign will talk of "defense." But anyone who looks at the facts knows that it is not just defense. They themselves have admitted openly that they are engaged in offensive operations. Moreover, their bombs have killed, maimed and terrorized innocent people, including women and girls. Their campaign is bringing shame and disgrace on noble and just causes. It is straining people's nerves to the breaking-point. It is destroying people's livelihood. It is intensifying sectarian bitterness. It is pushing the union of minds and hearts between men and women of all Ireland further and further away.

All this because a handful of men, without any mandate from the people, have decided that this is the way to achieve a united Ireland. This is the way to postpone a really united Ireland until long after all Irishmen and women now living are dead.

We are well aware that this campaign of violence is not the sole cause of the present terrible situation. We know as well as anyone the very real depression which the minority feels at the thought of having to live forever under a government of the same political party as has ruled here for 50 years, the deep indignation which the recent internment swoops caused, the humiliation of innocent men, the allegations of brutality and worse, many of which we are convinced are well founded.

Many Protestants in Northern Ireland, good Christian people, will not like our mentioning these things. We ask them to realize that these facts are part of the total situation. What we want to emphasize is that we are painfully aware of these facts and nevertheless we condemn the violence.

We also condemn the vicious evil of intimidation, from whatever source and on whatever side. This is a deadly poison which eats away at the very roots of personal freedom in society.

We appeal also to Catholics to realize the genuine fears and deep frustrations of the Protestant community at the present time. Understanding each other's fears and feelings can smooth the path to peace.

The problems of this divided community will never be solved until a radical reform of the institutions of democracy here is introduced. Mathematical "majority rule" simply does not work in a community of this kind.

Sen. John Barnhill, 63, a right-wing member of the ruling Unionist Party, was shot to death and his house was bombed by IRA terrorists Dec. 12. Barnhill's wife charged that the gunmen shot her husband as he opened the front door, then dragged his body into the living room, where they placed a bomb under his body. The IRA Officials Dec. 13 claimed responsibility for the killing and the bomb explosion but said they had intended only to destroy the house. The statement, issued in Dublin, said Barnhill had been shot after he attacked 2 IRA members who had asked him and his wife to evacuate the house because they planned to bomb it. The Officials said the bombing was in "reprisal for the destruction of working-class homes throughout the province" by the British Army.

Denouncing Barnhill's killing as Northern Ireland's first political assassination since 1922, Prime Min. Brian Faulkner accused the Irish Republic Dec. 13 of offering a "safe haven" to the men responsible for the deed. He said that unless the Irish Republic arrested the killers and cracked down on the terrorists who, he said, moved freely across the border between Northern Ireland and the Republic, Dublin would "bear an awful guilt for the neglect of their unmistakable duty." Barnhill's home was located at Strabane, about 200 yards from the border.

British Foreign Secy. Sir Alec Douglas-Home informed the British Parliament Dec. 13 he would make "renewed and urgent" representations to the Republic for stronger action to curb the gunmen crossing the border. He said Dublin "must accept some responsibility of control."

Shortly afterward, Irish Republic Prime Min. John Lynch condemned Barnhill's killing but denied that his government had sheltered the terrorists. He also reiterated a suggestion he had made in September that the British and Irish Republican governments jointly request the UN Security Council to provide a "UN observer group to operate on both sides in the border area" to insure stability.

The homes of 5 prominent Belfast residents in the exclusive Malone area came under bomb and gunfire attacks Dec. 14, but 3 of the attacks were frustrated by women at least 50 years old who drove off young gunmen apparently out to kill their husbands. One of the women, 68, suffered a grazed scalp from a gunshot while successfully defending her husband. A territorial Army sergeant was wounded on his own doorstep elsewhere in Belfast by self-styled book salesmen.

Implicitly acknowledging the difficulties in curbing the escalating terrorist violence, British Home Secy. Reginald Maudling said at a news conference in Belfast Dec. 15 that the British Army had the power to reduce the level of violence "to something which is acceptable." He condemned the "new and more vicious forms" of violence that had been used in the preceding month. The right-wing militant Protestant leader Rev. Ian Paisley replied in the Stormont Parliament that no level of violence was acceptable to the Northern Irish. Maudling had made his statement after a 2-day fact-finding visit.

A bomb set by IRA operatives Dec. 30 destroyed the County Down country home of Maj. Ivan Neill, speaker of the Stormont Parliament. No one was hurt in the blast.

Continuing violence in Northern Ireland had taken 193 lives in 1971. Since the violence began in Aug. 1969, 202 persons had been killed.

Dutch Seize Czechoslovak Arms

Dutch police seized a 3½-ton cargo of Czechoslovak-made arms and ammunition on a Belgian charter plane from Prague Oct. 16 at Amsterdam's Schiphol Airport. The haul, 116 crates of submachine guns, automatic rifles, bazookas, rocket launchers, rocket grenades, hand grenades, and other ammunition, had been consigned to "Wendamount Ltd. of City Road," London—a nonexistent company, Scotland Yard detectives discovered after having been asked by Dutch police to investigate. The Amsterdam authorities' suspicions reportedly had been aroused by an irregularity in the cargo manifest. The arms were thought to be destined for the Irish Republican Army in Northern Ireland.

The Dutch police arrested the Belgian pilot (but later released him) and an American, Ernest Koenig, 43, whom they held on charges of violating Holland's firearms code. Amsterdam authorities issued warrants for the arrest of David O'Connell, 33, and Moira McGuire, 23, who reportedly had registered at an Amsterdam hotel as "teacher" and "student," respectively. O'Connell, whose Gaelic name was Daithi O'Conaill, had been released after serving 3 years of an 8-year prison sentence imposed on him as a young IRA operative in 1960 in Northern Ireland for possession of arms and explosives. He reached the Republic of Ireland later in Oct. 1971, as did Miss McGuire.

The official Czechoslovak press agency CTK Oct. 18 described as "without foundation" reports that Czechoslovakia had sent or sold the arms.

Irish Republic customs officials Oct. 19 seized 6 suitcases of weapons thought to be destined for Ulster's IRA from luggage taken off the liner *Queen Elizabeth 2* in Cobh, the port of Cork.

Protestant Militants Challenge Faulkner

Stormont Parliament members of the ruling Protestant Ulster Unionist Party Aug. 17, 1971 unanimously pledged their support of Prime Min. Faulkner's policies to end the scourge of terrorism. But a group of hardline right-wing Protestants and former members of the Unionist Party accused Faulkner the same day of irresolute action in ending Catholic violence, and they announced the formation of a temporary alliance dedicated to preserving Northern Ireland as a British province. The group—which included the Rev. Ian Paisley and former Stormont Home Affairs Min. William Craig—suggested the possibility of discussions between the governments of Northern Ireland, Britain and the Irish Republic.

Dissatisfied with government action against the terrorists, more than 2,000 members of the disbanded "B-Specials," the Protestant paramilitary force, announced plans Sept. 3 to prepare Protestant forces "to defend this country in its time of need under the lawfully constituted government." The group urged that the B-Specials or "a like auxiliary police force be raised under the direct control of the Northern Ireland government."

Home Affairs Deputy Min. John Taylor Sept. 13 called for stronger measures against the IRA. Speaking at a Unionist Party meeting he said that a "3d armed force" should be established outside British control unless recruitment for the Ulster Defense Regiment—the new provincial militia—improved within the next few weeks. In an attempt to blunt the mounting pressure for a Protestant volunteer police force, Prime Min. Faulkner Sept. 2 had urged Northern Irish to join the Royal Ulster Constabulary Reserve and the Ulster Defense Regiment.

Desmond Boal and John McQuade, members of the Stormont Parliament, resigned from the Ulster Unionist Party Sept. 13 and 14, respectively, in protest against Faulkner's decision to attend the scheduled tripartite talks in London with the prime ministers of Great Britain and the Irish Republic. They opposed the decision on the ground that it retreated from the traditional Unionist attitude that the Irish Republic should not be involved in the internal affairs of Northern Ireland.

The Rev. Paisley conferred in London Sept. 30 with British Home Secy. Maudling. Paisley, who had requested the meeting, demanded that Protestant vigilante groups that had sprung up to guard Belfast roads should be mobilized into what he called an "unarmed civil defense corps." He called for the destruction of all unapproved roads between Northern Ireland and the Irish Republic and the abandonment by the British Army of its policy of containment for more aggressive antiterrorist action.

2 more Ulster Unionist Party members, James Craige and Councillor William Spence, the chairman of the Belfast transport department, resigned from the party Sept. 30 in protest against what they called the government's inadequate antiterrorist policy. Craige and Spence expressed an interest in joining a new right-wing group, the Ulster Loyalist party, according to an Oct. 1 London *Times* report.

A meeting of the Ulster Unionist Party council Oct. 8 reflected rising opposition of the party's right wing to Faulkner's policies. He still received the backing of the party's majority, however. This support was given after Faulkner had met in London Oct. 7 with British Prime Min. Edward Heath, Foreign Secy. Sir Alec Douglas-Home, Home Secy. Maudling, Defense Secy. Lord Carrington and Lord President of the Council William Whitelaw. At this meeting he had received pledges of more British troops. In a speech to the Stormont Parliament Oct. 5 before leaving for London, Faulkner had said: "Ulster alone cannot win this war. Nothing would end it more rapidly than a demonstration from Westminster by all parties of an inflexible determination not to yield to terror in a part of the United Kingdom. In our hour of need we, who have been proud to be British and who have made our own sacrifices for Britain, look to our fellow citizens not to give way to war weariness in Ulster. It is vital that people throughout the United Kingdom should appreciate to the full not only the extent of our problem but its urgency." "We will keep this country a part of the United Kingdom against the efforts of gunmen who try to shoot us into an Irish Republic or political lunatics who speak the absurd language of UDI [Unilateral Declaration of Independence, an allusion to militants urging Stormont to emulate Rhodesia's secession in Nov. 1965 when Britain demanded that Africans receive a share in Rhodesia's government]."

Defending his policies, Faulkner declared in a speech to the Stormont Parliament Oct. 21 that the country was confronted with a choice between civilized society and murderous thuggery. He said that the issues at stake were highlighted by continuing IRA atrocities and by the "sinister implications" of the discovery of arms shipments in Amsterdam and Cork. Concluding that both Protestants and Catholics would have to compromise, he declared: "Protestants must not look on every Catholic demand for 'a bigger say in things' as a veiled attempt to undermine the state from within. . . . I am . . . convinced that there is a very great number of Catholics who would like this community, and the politics of this community, to be concerned with bread and butter issues—with the raising of living standards, the creation of better job opportunities for themselves and their children, better houses, better services and so on—and who want to participate in, or be identified with those who participate in, the full life of the Northern Ireland community. We would be making a great mistake if we did not welcome and foster such a spirit."

The government Nov. 3 yielded to police demands and authorized the arming of 1,000 members of the Royal Ulster Constabulary Reserve force. The police had threatened to strike unless they were armed. Announcing the move, Faulkner said the police could not be denied "the minimum weapons necessary for their personal protection." The unarmed RUC reserve force had been formed on the recommendation of Lord Hunt's British government commission in 1969. The police strike threat followed mounting terrorist attacks on policemen in previous weeks. The Northern Ireland Police Authority announced Nov. 12 that the Royal Ulster Constabulary, Ulster's regular police force, would receive machine guns when needed to protect police stations that had been disarmed on the basis of another recommendation by the Hunt commission in 1969 but were often permitted to carry revolvers in trouble spots.

British Prime Min. Edward Heath paid a surprise 10-hour visit to Northern Ireland Dec. 23; this was his first trip to Ulster since he took office. He visited military bases in Londonderry, Armagh and Belfast.

IRA Factions Call Truce, Split Again

British Army officers and IRA leaders traded claims and counter-claims quite early about the impact of internment and the resulting violence. Brig. Marston Tickell, chief of staff of the British armed forces in Northern Ireland, claimed Aug. 13, 1971 that British troops had virtually defeated "the hard core" of the IRA. He asserted that 20 to 30 IRA men had been killed in Belfast and Londonderry. IRA leaders immediately disputed the claim. At an impromptu news conference in Belfast later that day, Joe Cahill, chief of staff of the IRA Provisionals, said that only 30 members—none of them leaders—had been arrested and that only 2 IRA men had been killed in the battles. He said the British action "was only a pinprick" to the IRA.

Cahill announced that the 2 rival factions of the IRA—the Officials and Provisionals—had declared a truce between themselves and would regroup their forces. But the 2 factions apparently split again Aug. 14 in a dispute over tactics. A militant IRA spokesman, John Kelly, former chairman of the Belfast Citizens Defense Committee, warned that unless British troops ceased their "repressive measures" in support of the Stormont government, the Provisionals would launch a bombing campaign in major British cities against government installations and big business companies. Kelly had been acquitted in Dublin in Oct. 1970 of smuggling arms into Ireland for eventual transshipment to the 6 counties.

The Officials said later Aug. 14 that they would not support reprisals in Britain. They called for an end to confrontation with British troops and urged a campaign of civil disobedience instead. In response to the Officials' call, Roman Catholics staged a general strike Aug. 16 in protest against internment. In Londonderry, Catholic leaders said that the work stoppage was about 2/3 effective and that most material services—including bus service and postal deliveries—had been halted.

The Provisionals Aug. 16 announced plans for the formation of an underground government that would work to topple the existing Stormont régime. The parliament would have 40 members, the cabinet 6. The Provisionals Sept. 5 issued a 5-point plan "to end the agony of our people." It included demands for the withdrawal of British troops, the release of political prisoners, and the abolition of the Stormont Parliament.

Séan MacStiofain, IRA Provisional chief of staff, said Oct. 24 at a Dublin annual conference of his group's political arm, the Provisional Sinn Fein, that the IRA campaign had "changed from a defensive to a retaliatory and offensive campaign in all parts of the occupied area of the North." Vowing revenge for army shootings Oct. 23 and 24 in Belfast, he said the final phase would "be more intensive than anything so far."

Ruairi O'Bradaigh (Rory O'Brady), elected president of the Provisional Sinn Fein, defined the group's program: to bring down the Stormont government by making the province ungovernable; to conduct an intensive campaign to force British withdrawal; and to consider a temporary neutral peace-keeping force after success was obtained in the first 2 areas. The Sinn Fein, was then to lead both northern and southern Irish in building a democratic Socialist republic.

Moderate Catholics Oppose Internment

Within Northern Ireland, a campaign of passive civil disobedience was launched by Catholic opposition Parliament members and the non-violent Official wing of the outlawed IRA. 9 of the 13 opposition members in the Northern Irish Parliament had agreed Aug. 14, 1971 on a campaign of civil disobedience, beginning Aug. 15 and lasting until all detainees were released.

The civil disobedience campaign, which included a rent strike and a general refusal to pay income and real estate taxes, gained momentum with the resignation Aug. 19 of more than 30 leading Londonderry Roman Catholics from public office in protest against what they termed the British Army's "reign of repression" against Catholics. They criticized the policy of internment without trial and the arrest of 2 members of the Stormont Parliament for leading a sit-down protest against the removal of Catholic barricades in Londonderry's Bogside district.

More than 100 opposition local councillors decided in County Tyrone Aug. 21 to withdraw from their elected seats and to urge all other non-Unionist councillors—about 300—to support civil disobedience. They also urged the establishment of a "rival" Ulster government.

The opposition Social Democratic & Labor Party (SDLP) Sept. 7 rejected an invitation made earlier that day in London by British Home

Secy. Reginald Maudling to attend discussions in London on ways of giving Northern Ireland's Catholic minority more of a rôle in Ulster's public affairs. Maudling had made it clear that all participants in the talks would have to "agree [in advance] that there can be no support for or tolerance of violence and that civil disobedience should be discouraged." The SDLP said:

Mr. Maudling's statement and the offer in it are unacceptable. Both reveal a dangerous lack of real knowledge of the situation in which we find ourselves and do not offer a basis of solution to the grave and deteriorating situation which obtains in Northern Ireland.... Our position remains unaltered. The first step on the road to peace, justice and stability is the rejection of their present policies by the Westminster government. The removal of internment will convince us that they have turned their back on present policies. Without this first step talks will serve no useful purpose. It is our earnest wish to reach a political settlement of the present serious crisis in Northern Ireland, but we would be less than honest if we misled people into thinking that talks based on the present offer represented a realistic basis for a solution.

Talks can take place on the basis of the following conditions, which we have already made public: (1) release of all detainees held without trial; (2) suspension of the present system of government in Northern Ireland which has failed so miserably and with such tragic consequences to provide a basis of peace, justice and stability; (3) appointment for a limited period of time of a commission or council of state to administer Northern Ireland; (4) quadripartite talks to discuss in detail a more permanent solution.

We condemn the continued failure of the British government to disarm all sections of this community of their legal and illegal arms. It must be obvious to them that the remarkable growth in licensed weapons is designed to strengthen the power of threat by right-wing Unionists whose intolerant behaviour lies at the root of Northern Ireland's problems. In the meantime, we call on our supporters to remain fully committed to our campaign of civil disobedience and passive resistance.... We pledge ourselves to continue to give firm and determined leadership out of a deep conviction that violence should be rejected as a means. We are confident that ... a firm adherence to our policies will lead to a situation in which Catholic, Protestant and Dissenter can live together in peace and justice.

Maudling conferred in London Sept. 13 with officials of the Northern Ireland Committee of the Irish Congress of Trade Unions. Committee Chairman Brendan Harkin said later that he and his colleagues had asked Maudling for a "massive investment scheme" of £20 million by the British government to "provide the basis for state enterprise in all spheres of [economic] activity" in Northern Ireland.

The Northern Ireland Labor Party sent to London a delegation led by Vivian Simpson, its only member in the Stormont Parliament. The group met with Maudling Sept. 15 in the first of his proposed talks with Northern Ireland's opposition politicians. Simpson's group proposed as an alternative to internment the setting up of a mixed British-Northern Irish legal security commission under a Commonwealth judge as chairman. It called for the immediate summoning of a conference of all Northern Irish democratic political and social interest groups that "forswear violence" by both Maudling and ex-Home Secy. James Callaghan of the British Labor Party's shadow cabinet and invitations to an all-party sampling of British Parliament members as observers. Simpson's group also proposed: (a) the "conclusion of a realistic treaty between the United Kingdom and the Republic of Ireland which will prevent gunmen of whatever faction [from] hiding behind a legal smokescreen"; (b) the bolstering of both the Royal Ulster Constabulary and the Ulster Defense Regiment—the provincial guard; and (c) the immediate establishment of a community government fairly representing all the people of the 6 counties.

Maudling received a delegation from the Northern Irish Alliance Party, led by Oliver Napier, at the British Home Office Sept. 17. Napier said afterwards that he had told Maudling that internment would have to be halted before any "package solution" could be reached. He also said that he had emphatically urged the widest possible agenda for any Northern Irish political conference.

In an attempt to stem the mounting violence that swept the 6 counties after the introduction of internment without trial of suspected IRA members. Maudling Sept. 22 proposed major political concessions to the Catholic minority that would give them "an active, permanent and guaranteed place in the public affairs of Northern Ireland." Maudling's speech highlighted the first day of a special 2-day session of the House of Commons convened at the request of the opposition Labor Party to discuss the crisis.

Maudling said that the government was prepared to discuss constitutional changes designed to give Catholics a representative share of the power now held solely by the Protestants. His proposals included the use of proportional representation in future elections and enlargement of the Stormont Parliament. Maudling urged the main opposition group in the Stormont Parliament, the Social Democratic & Labor Party, to talk with him about his proposals.

On the eve of the debate Sept. 21, Northern Irish Prime Min. Brian Faulkner had also shown a more conciliatory attitude toward the Catholics. He indicated that his government was prepared to study ideas for constitutional changes, such as proportional representation.

British Labor MP Gerard Fitt, who was also an SDLP member in Stormont, said during the debate that Northern Ireland's Catholic minority had no faith in the impartiality of Protestant Ulster's courts and law-and-order forces and noted that 219 men were currently interned in the only "concentration camp" in western Europe. The Rev. Ian Paisley, a Protestant Unionist on the Conservative side of the

House of Commons, denounced the disarming of the Royal Ulster Constabulary, the disbanding of the "B-Specials" and the freedom of IRA members to march in Northern Irish streets in the mourning for comrades shot by legal security forces. Bernadette Devlin said that the civil-disobedience campaign, already costing Stormont £70,000 weekly in withheld payments, would last until internment ended.

Jeremy Thorpe, leader of the House's 6 Liberal Party members and of the party itself, welcomed the scheduling of talks among Irish Prime Min. John Lynch, British Prime Min. Heath and Prime Min. Faulkner and condemned the use of violence by "any quarter." He observed: "It is the most extraordinary situation that British troops were commit- ted to Northern Ireland to protect the Catholic community from Protestant Ulster gunmen and yet when those who are a threat to the peace are rounded up there is not a single Protestant amongst the internees." Of suggestions that any or all Irish citizens receive the privileges of dual nationality as a future right, Thorpe declared: "The position of the U[nited] K[ingdom's] citizen in the Republic of Ireland and that of the citizen of the Republic in the UK is very special. The British Nationality Act recognized the act of secession but for all practical purposes enshrined most of the continuing rights as though it had never happened. . . . By the British Nationality Act, Irish citizens were not UK citizens but they were expressly defined as not being aliens. Because we have a common travel area, the Commonwealth Immigrants Acts are not enforced, although in law technically they apply. I should like to see the possibility being considered of dual nationality for those who would opt for it, so that men and women honorably could owe allegiance to both countries. I know that there are difficulties in international law. . . . But if we cannot have dual alle- giance. . . , we must try to see if we can accord privileges of a mutual and reciprocal nature as between citizens of the Republic and those of the UK."

Labor Party Leader Harold Wilson critized the government during the Commons debate Sept. 22 for its failure to offer any political initiatives during the 5 weeks of violence following the introduction of internment. (Wilson Sept. 8 had proposed a 12-point plan that would have sharply increased Westminster's authority over the Northern Ireland government and would have given Catholics a wider government rôle. The proposals included one for the appointment of a British cabinet minister responsible for Northern Irish affairs, another for the formation of an all-Ireland council representing the Belfast and Dublin Parliaments, and a 3d for the introduction of a proportional represen- tation system of voting.)

Labor Party leaders decided not to press for a vote of censure at the end of the debate in order not to harm the forthcoming Lynch–Heath–Faulkner tripartite talks. Left-wing Labor members Sept. 23, however, forced a protest vote against government policy on a technical motion of adjournment. The vote was defeated 203–74.

Community Relations Min. David Bleakley resigned his post Sept. 26 in protest against the government's policy of internment without trial. Bleakley, a member of the opposition Northern Ireland Labor Party, would have been obliged to resign Oct. 1 because he did not hold a Parliament seat and was consequently limited to a 6-month cabinet term. Bleakley had been the only non-Unionist figure to hold a cabinet post in Northern Ireland. In his letter of resignation, Bleakley criticized one-party rule, internment and what he considered inadequate political initiatives. He proposed the introduction of proportional representation, an expansion of the Senate, the creation of a Ministry of Reconstruction and a commission to prepare a plan for parliamentary reform.

In an effort to win support from the Catholic community, the Stormont régime Oct. 26 presented a document outlining preliminary reform proposals to widen Catholic participation in the government. The document suggested the possibilities of proportional representation in future elections, the enlargement of the Northern Irish House of Commons by 20 or 30 seats from the current 52, and a proportionate increase in the Senate (from 26 to about 40 seats). The document rejected as "fundamentally unrealistic" a system that would allot Cabinet posts in proportion to a party's Parliamentary strength. It said the formula "would simply not be workable in Northern Ireland conditions given the deep divisions of opinion which exist on quite fundamental issues." It reaffirmed that Northern Ireland must remain an integral part of the United Kingdom.

More than 50 persons, among them opposition Catholic legislators who had quit the Northern Irish Parliament in protest against the government's policy toward Catholics, attended the first meeting of their newly created Assembly of the Northern Irish People at Dungiven Oct. 26. John Hume, a member of the leading opposition Social Democratic & Labor Party (SDLP), was elected Assembly president, and Gerard Lennon, Opposition leader in the Stormont Senate, was chosen Assembly chairman (or speaker). Hume called for an end to the administration of Prime Min. Faulkner and its replacement by a system that would recognize the right of Catholics to have a proportionate share of government posts. (The SDLP had refused to discuss reforms with Ulster and British officials while internment was in force.) After adopting a motion of formal withdrawal from the Stormont government, the Assembly affirmed its determination to work non-violently for equality of treatment for all people in the province, regardless of their religious or political affiliations, until the reunification of the 2 Irelands could be achieved.

Prime Min. Faulkner Oct. 26 appointed William McIvor, a Protestant Unionist member of Parliament, as minister of community relations to replace David Bleakley, who had resigned in protest against Stormont's internment policy. Albert Anderson, a retired naval commander and MP for Londonderry, was appointed to a new post as senior Parliamentary secretary to the Ministry of Home Affairs with special responsibility for recruitment to the Royal Ulster Constabulary Reserve and the Ulster Defense Regiment.

The Stormont Parliament earlier in October had passed legislation empowering the government to deduct citizens' debts from all forms of social security payments (family allowances, supplementary benefits and old-age pensions, for example) and even, when necessary, to levy a distress on personal wages. Stormont Development Min. Roy Bradford said in a British Broadcasting Corp. interview Oct. 17 that the Catholics' civil disobedience campaign had so far cost the provincial economy £500,000 ($1.2 million) and that about 26,000 of the 140,000 people in public housing were withholding all rent and tax payments until all persons detained or interned as IRA suspects had been released.

Dr. Gerard B. Newe, 64, a Catholic layman with no previous political experience, was appointed Oct. 27 as minister of state in the prime minister's office. He was the first Catholic ever named to a Stormont cabinet. Newe had been secretary of the Belfast Council of Social Welfare, a welfare agency for both Protestants and Catholics. Shortly after his appointment, Newe said that he would work "to create as soon as possible the circumstances" in which internment without trial of suspected IRA members would be discontinued. He continued: "Naturally I am conscious of the symbolism of an action by which, for the first time, a member of the half-million strong Catholic community comes into a Northern Ireland government. All who know me need no assurance that it is not a step I have taken lightly, or without satisfying myself that it is intended to be very much more than a token or a symbol...."

"I have no mandate from anybody," Newe said, "and I would not claim to speak for the Catholic community. If I have a specific course of policy to announce it is the improvement of the quality of life for all in Northern Ireland. To this objective ... I am guided by the social teachings of my church, rather than by the arguments of political or social theorists...." He took the position that Northern Ireland's constitutional status could be changed only by democratic methods and only with majority consent. "This proposition seems to me to be based both on morality and on common sense," he continued. "It also seems to me indisputable that, at this point of time, a majority wish to retain the constitutional link with Great Britain." Newe said he believed citizens had the right "by all legitimate peaceful and democratic means" to advocate and work for Ireland's ultimate unification.

Newe asserted that "if I had been a member of the cabinet when internment was under discussion, I would undoubtedly have been opposed to it. Now that it is an accomplished fact, I think the important thing is to create as soon as possible the circumstances in which it can rapidly be ended, and in the meantime to ensure that what is inevitably a distasteful business is conducted with fairness and humanity."

Announcing Newe's appointment, Faulkner said: "I am asking Dr. Newe to consider how best to establish and maintain contact with the various elements of the Catholic population. In so doing, I am recognizing the importance of letting it be clearly seen that the point of view of the religious minority in Northern Ireland is adequately taken into acount by the government."

Wilson's Plan to End Crisis

British Prime Min. Heath Aug. 23, 1971 rejected a formal request by Labor Party leader Harold Wilson for a recall of Parliament from its summer recess to debate the crisis in Northern Ireland. The rejection was considered unusual since an opposition request for a debate on a critical issue was generally granted.

Wilson Sept. 8 proposed a 12-point program as a "constructive attempt to restore the balance in Northern Ireland." He said:

(1) The appointment of a Parliamentary commission comprising equal numbers of members of the Westminster and Stormont Parliaments should be made as soon as possible, with some of Stormont's representatives being selected from an enlarged Senate designed to include members "capable of speaking for a wider range of interests and views than those at present represented in the elected chamber."

(2) The commission should have all the powers of a Westminster select committee (such as the new Select Committee on Expenditure), including the powers to examine all relevant books and accounts and to subpoena persons and papers.

(3) The commission should be directed to examine all proposed Stormont legislation, including ministerial orders and Orders-in-Council, bearing on any aspects of human rights and the provisions of the Downing Street Declaration of Aug. 1969—a 7-point joint statement of Protestant Ulster-British responsibilities, rights and purposes by then Stormont Prime Min. James Chichester-Clark and

Wilson. Stormont legislation not approved by the Commission with an appropriate majority (such as 2/3) should not come into effect unless approved by a specific resolution of the Westminster Parliament.

(4) The commission should be authorized to make reports to the 2 Parliaments proposing new legislation in the field covered in the transfer of authority to the commission. Such a report, if approved by both Parliaments, would be up to Stormont to enact. If it were approved by Westminster alone, however, or refused or ignored by the Stormont Parliament, it would be up to the Westminster Parliament to act on it under Section 75 of the Government of Ireland Act of 1920.

(5) The commission should report annually to the 2 Parliaments on the detailed operation of Northern Ireland's 1922 Special Powers Act and on actions taken under its authority.

(6) The Special Powers Act should require the approval of the Westminster Parliament from year to year to continue and should lapse without it.

(7) The commission should be required by statute to prepare and submit to both Parliaments an annual report on Stormont's finances, taxation and expenditure, with particular attention to accounting for the disposal of subventions, grants and other direct and indirect aids for industrial development and expansion.

(8) All subventions and other financial aid for Northern Ireland should no longer be included in the Consolidated Fund and should be subject to annual estimates and votes by the Westminster Parliament.

(9) Even before the appointment of the commission, a minister of Cabinet rank for Northern Irish affairs should be appointed as a member of the British government. He would have no executive functions but serve mainly to maintain liaison with the Stormont government. The minister would be stationed in Northern Ireland but would report to the British cabinet and Parliament.

(10) New legislation should stipulate that future elections for the Stormont Parliament would be based on proportional representation.

(11) An All-Ireland Council, representing the 2 Irish Parliaments, should be established by statute as a consultative body whose members would be chosen in proportion to the elected strengths of the several parties represented in both Parliaments. The Council would debate all matters of common interest to Ireland, North and South.

(12) Immediate legislation should be introduced in the Stormont Parliament or else at Westminster to ban the private possesion of and unlicensed traffic in firearms. Such a measure should also provide for the revocation of all but a few firearms licenses, with these specific exceptions spelled out by Parliament and subject to an annual report by the Parliamentary commission.

Britons Disillusioned with Occupation

Opinion samplings of 1,910 people throughout Britain in mid-Sept. 1971 indicated widespread disagreement with official policy on the Northern Irish crisis. According to the London *Daily Mail* Sept. 24: "The majority of people in Britain want the Army brought home from Northern Ireland now."

The newspaper reported a poll conducted Sept. 14–20 among nearly 2,000 voters in 100 constituencies throughout Britain. According to the *Daily Mail*:

The poll's big surprise is the strength of feeling on the use of British troops. This was the question:

"Some people think the British troops should be brought back home now. Others think they should stay in Northern Ireland. What is your opinion?"

Answer: Brought back home 59%, stay in Northern Ireland 35%, don't know 6%.

The figures, revealed as Parliament's 2-day emergency debate on Ulster ended last night, will be a shock for ministers. With the opposition front bench, they are committed totally to the necessity of troops in Ulster until violence is quelled.

Tory voters are more inclined to favor the use of troops. But a narrow majority of these—49% compared with 45% in favor of the Army staying—wants the troops brought home.

Labor supporters are far more certain—67% say the men must be brought out now. Only 28% say they should stay. . . .

One irony in the polls: The majority that now wants the Army brought home is roughly the same size as that which favored the troops being sent to keep peace in Ulster 2 years ago.

The independent London weekly *New Statesman* Oct. 22 published an article entitled "Ulster—Our Vietnam?" The piece began:

"Unless the Labor opposition wakes up and does its duty, this government will soon turn Ulster into our Vietnam. We shall be unable to extricate ourselves from an unwinnable civil war which corrupts our political morals and destroys our Army as a fighting force. The real tragedy of Vietnam was that the Americans did not will it: they slithered into it. Indeed they hardly knew they were at war until it was too late to withdraw without dishonor and without breach of faith. Much the same is happening to us now in Northern Ireland. Already the shooting of a couple of soldiers a week is no longer rated front-page news: it has become part of the normal process of upholding law and order in Northern Ireland. Internment without trial, which shocked us a few weeks ago, is now accepted as part of that same process. To judge by their previous facility for blind acquiescence, the government will soon be defending the methods of our investigators in the camps as inevitable in the circumstances. The most deadly disease of British and American democracy is the way we acclimatise ourselves to the evils done in out-of-the way places on our behalf."

Direct Rule from London Opposed

Amid growing speculation that Britain might impose direct rule on Northern Ireland to curb the mounting violence, Prime Min. Faulkner warned Oct. 28, 1971 that "direct rule would lead to a terrible battle, civil war." He said the takeover would be interpreted as a "move in the direction of Dublin and a weakening of our constitutional position." According to the *N.Y. Times* of Nov. 10: "At the highest level of the Protestant-dominated provincial government there is growing anxiety that the semi-independent Parliament at Stormont Castle will be suspended and some form of direct rule from London will take its place. With that the precarious dominance of the million Ulster Protestants over the half-million Catholics will topple."

About 20,000 Protestants marched peacefully in downtown Belfast Nov. 11 in protest against a visit by 2 former British Labor cabinet members, ex-Home Secy. James Callaghan and ex-Technology Min. Anthony Wedgwood Benn. The men held talks with representatives of the 3 branches of the Labor Party in Northern Ireland and the Irish Republic. The march had been organized by militant Protestant groups, who feared that Britain—and particularly the Labor Party—would soon advocate unacceptable political changes.

Wilson Proposes New Peace Plan

British Labor Party leader Harold Wilson proposed in the House of Commons Nov. 25, 1971 a radical new peace plan for Northern Ireland that was designed to lead to the creation of a united Ireland after a 15-year transitional period. At the same time he rejected left-wing Labor pressure to end the bipartisan policy on the government's program to crush the IRA. Backing the Conservative government's security policy, Wilson said there would have to be a "military solution" to crush the IRA terrorist campaign before a political solution could be implemented. He insisted "the men of violence must be destroyed or compelled to retire."

Wilson opened his political proposals with a call for interparty talks in Britain and Northern Ireland that would pave the way for the creation of a constitutional commission representing the major parties of Britain, Northern Ireland and the Irish Republic. The commission would be directed to examine the possibility of creating a united Ireland, whose draft constitution would be ratified by the 3 parliaments and would go into effect 15 years from the date of agreement, "provided violence as a political weapon has come to an end."

Wilson also proposed: membership for the new united Ireland in the British Commonwealth of Nations: the maintenance of a British military force in Northern Ireland during the 15-year transitional period and possibly for 5 to 10 years after unification; an end to internment without trial as soon as the security situation improved; a guarantee of minority rights in both Northern and Southern Ireland; the representation of minority views in Protestant Ulster's government during the 15-year transitional period; and the alignment of social service provisions for the new Ireland, involving health, education and social security, with British policies.

Wilson offered his plan after fact-finding visits to Northern Ireland Nov. 15–18 and to the Irish Republic Nov. 18–19. In Northern Ireland, Wilson had conferred with Stormont's Prime Min. Brian Faulkner and with other responsible government and opposition party leaders. In Dublin he had conferred with Prime Min. John Lynch and other political leaders.

Lynch Nov. 25 welcomed Wilson's proposals as "a serious contribution to finding a way forward by political action." He did not comment on the other suggestion, including the proposed Irish membership in the Commonwealth. Northern Ireland's Prime Min. Faulkner rejected the Wilson plan Nov. 26 and reiterated the determination of the province's Protestant majority to remain an integral part of the United Kingdom. However, he welcomed any "constructive and useful cooperation" between the 6 counties and the Republic.

In a debate in the House of Commons Nov. 29, British Prime Min. Edward Heath described the proposals as "constructive" and accepted the call for talks between the Labor and Conservative parties on the situation. He said the talks would not be committed to specific policies in advance. During the same debate, Home Secy. Reginald Maudling indicated that the unification issue could be included on the agenda. He termed the hope for a united Ireland "legitimate" and predicted that Britain would welcome a united Ireland if the North and South agreed to it.

Growing opposition within the Labor Party to Wilson's bipartisan policy on Ulster surfaced in the Commons debate with a motion regretting the failure of the government's current policies and calling for an end to internment without trial. The motion also criticized the "extraction of information from detainees by methods which must never by permitted in a civilized society," a reference to torture charges. The motion was defeated, 293 to 259.

Irish Republic Prime Min. Lynch said at a Parliamentary press gallery luncheon in London Dec. 6, 1971 that the constitution of a united Ireland was negotiable. His comment, indicating a willingness to rewrite the Republic's constitution to accommodate the Protestants of Northern Ireland, was a follow-up to Wilson's Nov. 25 proposals on eventual Irish unification. Lynch said that Wilson's speech was "a turning point not only in British domestic politics but also in Anglo-Irish relations." Lynch urged the British government to "declare its interest in encouraging the unity of Ireland" and to exert pressure on Ulster's Protestatns to move toward that goal. He said that a genuine union would be based on "agreement among all the people of Ireland."

Internment Policy's Impact

Prime Min. Faulkner announced Sept. 15 that he had signed internment orders for 219 of the approximately 240 persons detained in Northern Ireland since Aug. 9 as suspected IRA terrorists. He said the cases of 20 other detainees were still being studied. The internment orders formally signified that the detainees could be held in prison without trial for an indefinite period.

337 persons had originally been rounded up in the predawn raids that had sparked the continuing wave of violence. Perhaps 12 internees had been released from prison Sept. 14; the others had been freed earlier. Among those released Sept. 14 were Michael Farrell, a prominent left-wing leader, and Kevin McCorry, organizer of the Northern Ireland Civil Rights Association.

The London *Times* reported Oct. 11 that Prime Min. Faulkner had signed detention orders for an additional 20 persons, raising the number of people detained to about 240.

15 IRA suspects were arrested in police raids throughout the province Oct. 12 in the 2d big raid within a week. A suspected IRA leader, James Sullivan, had been arrested Oct. 9 after a 2-month police search.

Rioting prisoners at the Long Kesh internment camp, 10 miles from Belfast, held 4 guards hostage Oct. 25 and then released them unharmed. The internees were believed to be protesting living conditions in the camp.

Red Cross Inspects Internment Camps

British Prime Min. Edward Heath had announced Sept. 23, 1971, during the Westminster House of Commons' debate on the internment crisis, that the International Red Cross would inspect the internment facilities in Northern Ireland at the end of September and that an all-party British Parliamentary delegation also would be allowed to visit them.

2 officials of the Swiss Red Cross visited the Crumlin Road prison in Belfast Oct. 5 and the Long Kesh camp (10 miles outside Belfast)

Oct. 6. The 2 officials acted in behalf of the International Committee of the Red Cross (ICRC). The ICRC Nov. 29 published a report of their findings on the conditions in both internment centers.

At the Long Kesh camp, where most of the IRA suspects were interned, the 2 Red Cross officials found "overcrowding": 180 internees were lodged in a facility with a capacity for 110 persons, the camp commandant admitted. Each detained suspect was limited to one 30-minute visit each week from 3 adults and 2 children under 12—5 persons at most. Many of those detained complained to the 2 Red Cross officials of brutal predetention treatment by soldiers but said that conditions at the camp were "fair." Their biggest complaints, aside from the accommodations, concerned the complete lack of recreational facilities and the inadequate access of Catholic internees to religious services: ". . . A priest held mass in the camp every Sunday, but . . . only part of the internees were authorized to attend for security reasons."

The 2 Swiss recommended that "2 or more priests should hold a service each Sunday for all the internees" at Long Kesh. They asserted as their belief that "the reduction of the conditions of overcrowding and the provision of recreational facilities would greatly contribute to a reduction of the extreme tension" that they found in the camp.

At the Crumlin Road prison, the 2 ICRC delegates found 115 IRA suspects doubled up 2 to a cell, apart from 749 other prisoners, in a 130-year-old building intended to house 475 persons. ". . . The prison could be more readily considered overcrowded from a psychological viewpoint," the 2 Swiss asserted. ". . . In the opinion of the convicted prisoners, who work 8 hours a day, the small cells were inhabitable since they spent little time in them. On the other hand, for the internees and detainees without work, the confines of the small cells were hardly tolerable. Privacy was nonexistent."

The 2 ICRC observers concluded that these factors would "lead invariably to mental and psychosomatic disorders" and recommended "the development of recreational facilities" and "speeding up the circulation of books among the various wings and the setting up of a workshop for wood, leather and other crafts under a skilled craftsman who could give courses."

Stormont's Home Affairs Ministry Nov. 29 issued an accompanying statement of its own to the effect that it had reduced the overcrowding by $\frac{1}{3}$ and had provided recreational and educational facilities at Long Kesh.

ICRC representatives returned Dec. 14–16 for another look at the camps and the first look at the floating internment camp HMS *Maidstone*, a converted submarine tender then housing 15 detained IRA suspects, moored in Belfast Lough. In their report, published Apr. 25, 1972 by the British government, the ICRC representatives commented favorably on the authorities' "considerable efforts" to improve conditions at the Long Kesh camp since early Oct. 1971—although they still found overcrowding—but deplored the "grave deterioration," due to anxiety, in the suspects' morale and in the camp's atmosphere. They recommended a further reduction by $\frac{1}{3}$ in the number of men held in each compound. (They had found 426 men interned at Long Kesh in mid-Dec. 1971 and 119 internees at the Crumlin Road prison.)

The number of suspects detained or interned steadily increased to the end of 1971. The London *Times* Nov. 7, 1971 had published figures released by the British government on the number of suspects arrested and detained in Northern Ireland since the introduction of internment in August. Of 882 people arrested under the Special Powers Act, 476 had been released. Of the 406 persons being held, 278 were interned, 112 were detained for questioning and held after a detention order had been served, and 16 were being held for questioning for up to 48 hours without being charged before a further decision on detainment was reached. Those detained were generally held 28 days before a final decision to release or intern them. The *Times* commented: "The figures indicate that the security forces have been casting the net pretty wide in their effort to bring in the gunmen and the bombers of the IRA, and that arrests are still going on at a high rate. But the quick release of 54% does point to a rather poorer flow of intelligence than the Army has been claiming."

According to the *N.Y. Times* of Nov. 10: "Internment has been turned into an even more emotional issue by charges that prisoners have been tortured. Yesterday the widely respected London-based organization, Amnesty International, reported internees' allegations of torture and brutality. In the Catholic community leaders have asserted that internment is an anti-Catholic measure and that Protestant gunmen have been ignored. This was denied by Mr. Faulkner, who said: 'I can't tell you, in fact, whether there are any Protestants who have been interned but I would accept, certainly, that at least 90% of those who have been interned are Catholics. This is because the IRA has such a grip in the Catholic community. But I say this—that the vast majority of the Catholic community, probably 90% of them, are totally opposed to the thugs and murderers in the IRA.' "

3 IRA detainees escaped from the Crumlin Road prison of Belfast Dec. 3. Unidentified IRA sources said the 3 fled to the Irish Republic. 2 of the men—Martin Meehan and Anthony (Dutch) Doherty—were reportedly considered among the most important IRA leaders arrested

since the introduction of internment without trial. The incident followed the escape Nov. 16 of 9 other IRA suspects from Crumlin Road prison. 6 of those fugitives reached Dublin; 2 were recaptured in Northern Ireland.

Compton Group Charges Mistreatment of Suspects

A controversial report by a 3-man British commission, presented Nov. 16, 1971, concluded that suspected Catholic terrorists detained without trial in Northern Ireland had been subjected to "physical illtreatment" but not to "cruelty or brutality." The commission was headed by Sir Edmund Compton, Northern Ireland's ombudsman, named Aug. 31 by British Home Secy. Reginald Maudling to lead an official investigation into the adequacy of grounds for interning persons arrested after the Stormont government had invoked its internment powers.

The investigation, originally announced by the British Defense Ministry Aug. 21, had been ordered at the request of Lt. Gen. Sir Harry Tuzo, commander of British troops in Northern Ireland. Tuzo had asked for an "independent inquiry" after he had met with Catholics from Londonderry. The Catholics had urged a formal look into reports of brutality by British troops and Northern Irish police toward interned suspects during the first 48 hours of detention. Brig. Marston Tickell, Tuzo's chief of staff, said that only 2 complaints had officially been made against the Army and 6 against the Royal Ulster Constabulary.

(William Cardinal Conway, archbishop of Armagh and Catholic primate of Ireland, had called Aug. 14 for an inquiry into alleged brutality toward detainees and had added his voice to other Catholic criticism of internment without trial.)

According to the London Sunday Times of Oct. 17, "there is now a weight of circumstantial evidence which cannot be brushed aside that the interrogation methods being used in Ulster 'ought'—to quote a Stormont opposition MP—'to be unacceptable in a civilized country.'. . ." The Times account also said: "The facts are these. The compound at Palace Barracks [in Belfast] houses an interrogation center set up by a unit of MI 12—the section of Military Intelligence dealing with Ulster. The center is using top-secret 'disorientation' techniques of interrogation to break down suspected IRA men. . . . The 'disorientation' technique of interrogation is among the most secret areas of the British armed services' training techniques. Using Russian brainwash techniques, it was refined for British service use by an RAF [Royal Air Force] wing-commander who committed suicide later. It is taught to select military personnel at the Joint Services

Interrogation Center, whose location is an official secret." The *Sunday Times* said it had statements from 11 detainees that described the "torture" techniques.

British Prime Min. Edward Heath himself Oct. 18 ordered an official inquiry into alleged torture of detained terrorist suspects in Northern Ireland. He arranged for the probe after he had met with Labor Party Leader Harold Wilson and former Labor Home Secy. James Callaghan. The Labor leaders had requested the meeting following the *Sunday Times* Oct. 17 report. It was announced shortly thereafter that the already existing Compton commission would examine the allegations. In addition to Compton, the members of the commission were Dr. Ronald Gibson, ex-chairman of the British Medical Association Council, and Edgar Fay, a judge.

Renewed charges that suspected terrorists interned without trial in Northern Ireland had been subjected to "savage beatings" and torture were published Nov. 8 by Amnesty International, the London-based organization concerned with political prisoners. Amnesty called for an international commission of inquiry to investigate the charges. Acknowledging that its report was based on *prima facie* (self-evident) evidence, the organization said that the men had been beaten, given electric shocks, injected with hallucinatory drugs and subjected to "physical abuse of genital organs." The report was sharply criticized Nov. 10 by Anthony Marreco, a British lawyer who had been treasurer of Amnesty International until his resignation shortly before the report was published. He charged the group had "merely accepted unconfirmed affidavits" from released detainees without making an independent investigation.

In the course of their 8-week investigation, the 3 members of the Compton commission and supporting legal and administrative secretaries examined 40 individual complaints and 5 groups of allegations. Evidence was taken from 11 doctors, 11 prison personnel, 26 police officers and 96 Army personnel. The resulting 73-page report said that detainees had been hooded, subjected to "continuous and monotonous noise," fed only bread and water, deprived of sleep and forced to stand against a wall for hours. The commission described these interrogation methods as ill-treatment, not brutality. (It defined brutality as "inhuman or savage form of cruelty" whereas "cruelty implies a disposition to inflict suffering, coupled with indifference to, or pleasure in, the victim's pain.") The commission rejected the more serious charges of brainwashing, 3d-degree methods, savage beatings and torture. It reported that the interrogation methods had been applied by the Royal Ulster Constabulary in the presence of British Army "advisers."

Home Secy. Reginald Maudling who presented the report to the

House of Commons, announced that the government would set up a 3-man panel under Lord Parker, a former chief justice, to re-examine the army's interrogation methods in Northern Ireland. He denied that the methods were cruel or brutal.

In an emergency debate in the House of Commons Nov. 17, Maudling again defended the interrogation methods as necessary to combat terrorism. He said: "inevitably there have been cries of 'whitewash' from some quarters. One expected that. . . . I do not believe that any credence will be given to that by the House of Commons. Those of us who know Sir Edmund Compton and have read his report know that this was no whitewashing operation; it was a genuine operation designed to ascertain and make clear the facts. . . ."

Referring to the methods used to interrogate IRA suspects, Maudling explained: "First, they are designed to ensure the security of both those who are interrogating and those being interrogated. This is a very important point. In a situation where murder is rife, the identification of individual members of the security forces, and the identification, either in interrogation or possibly even in newspapers, of people who, under interrogation, have given information, may lead to their murder. . . . The 2d purpose of these methods is to create a feeling of fatigue, a sense of isolation, which is part of the process of interrogation to obtain the information which the security forces need for the battle they are fighting. . . . In this case there is a wide range of degree between, at the one extreme, asking suspects whether they will give particular information and, at the other, torturing them. Torture is not acceptable, but merely asking people if they would be good enough to help in the investigation is equally not acceptable."

The report drew sharp criticism from Catholics. The Northern Ireland Civil Rights Association Nov. 16 called it a "whitewash" of the internment procedure. (The IRA Nov. 17 vowed to take "ruthless action" against British intelligence men whom it accused of torturing suspects.) William Cardinal Conway, archbishop of Armagh, and a number of bishops Nov. 21 condemned the "interrogation in depth" of suspected terrorists as "immoral and inhuman." The statement, issued in Armagh, said there was "disturbing medical evidence of the physical beating of arrested persons even in recent weeks."

The Irish government announced Nov. 30 that it would ask the European Commission on Human Rights to investigate the charges of brutality toward detainees.

Pursuing an outspoken stand on the Ulster crisis, U.S. Sen. Edward M. Kennedy (D., Mass.) Dec. 8 denounced as "sheer hypocrisy" the conclusion of the Compton commission that IRA suspects had been subjected to ill treatment but not to torture. His statement was published in a letter to the London *Times*.

In a report published in the U.S. *Congressional Record* Feb. 16, 1972, the British Society for Social Responsibility in Science criticized the Compton report. The society cited psychological studies that indicated that the interrogation procedure used on internees was more harmful than the Compton report admitted. The society concluded: "We believe that a consideration of the effects of the procedure will show that the value-judgment implied in the report's attempt to distinguish between ill-treatment and brutality is not viable. The history of certain aspects of this procedure is widely known. The techniques resemble those used by the KGB in Russia for interrogation purposes.... Clearly for the detainees, the psychological pressures must have been enormous. Sudden arrest in the middle of the night, being physically beaten and dreading what the future might hold can be expected to interact traumatically with the sensory deprivation situation. This could be expected also to increase greatly the pliability of the detainees under interrogation, as sensory deprivation increases the suggestibility and lowers intellectual competence...."

Graham Greene, the British novelist and essayist, in an article in the *N.Y. Times* of Dec. 2, 1971, described the Compton report as "worthy of Orwell's *1984*." He wrote: "Mr. Maudling in his blithe jolly style reminiscent of that used by defenders of corporal punishment when they remember their school days, suggests that no one has suffered permanent injury from this form of torture, by standing long hours pressed against a wall, hooded in darkness, isolated and deprived of hearing as well as sight by permanent noise, prevented in the intervals of the ordeal from sleep—these were the methods we condemned in the Slansky trial in Czechoslovakia and in the case of Cardinal Mindszenty in Hungary. Slansky is dead; he cannot be asked by Mr. Maudling how permanent was the injury he suffered, but one would like to know the opinion of the cardinal on methods which when applied by Communists or Fascists we call 'torture' and when applied by the British become down-graded to 'ill treatment.'.... The effect of these methods extends far beyond the borders of Ulster. How can any Englishman now protest against torture in Vietnam, in Greece, in Brazil, in the psychiatric wards of the U.S.S.R. without being told, 'You have a double standard: one for others and another for your own country.' And after all the British tortures and Catholic outrages, what comes next?"

Reporting on her visit Dec. 31 to Long Kesh, Dr. Rona Fields, a psychologist at California State College in Los Angeles, described conditions among the internees as fostering "maximal psychological uncertainty." According to the report, as placed in the U.S. *Congressional Record* Feb. 16, 1972, Dr. Fields wrote: "Every person in these camps has been subjected to extreme physical and psychological torture prior to arrival. None have any assurance of release nor of subjection to further torture. They suffer physical pain, an aftermath of hallucinations, disorientation and extreme anxiety symptoms. . . . Psychological torture (ranging from the very crude to the very sophisticated) and physical torture have been applied to persons as young as 12 and has resulted in severe consequences. These effects also indicate that there is a high probability of permanent damage for those so treated. . . . The process of visiting an internee has become familiar experience for the women and children of Northern Ireland. Each detainee is allowed ½ hour visit per week. This is allotted to the 'next of kin.' Since the majority of families of detainees are without private automobiles and the camp, located on a swamp, is some miles distant from Belfast (about 40 minutes drive), there are enormous complications involved in visiting. . . . The half hour permitted for 'family togetherness' transpires in an airless cell-like cubicle, the door to which has a large window. The wardens assigned to that cubicle peer frequently through the window. . . . Cognizant of the overcrowded and damaging conditions of the camps, the governor of Long Kesh has been pressuring inmates to appeal to the Advisory Board for release. . . ."

Dr. Fields, in her report, related 2 other serious charges against political and military authorities:

There is little continuity between the conduct of the British regiments who were originally sent in to 'keep the peace' and the behaviors of the military as to Dec. 1971. This discontinuity can be laid to the fact that prior to the invocation of the Special Powers Act, special Scots regiments were installed in Northern Ireland. These particular regiments have traditions and identity from their historic deployment in actions to 'subdue Irish rebels.' The combination of this tradition and the training of the officers in anti-insurgents' campaigns in Indonesia, Palestine, Aden and Cyprus provides a task-orientation consistent with the tactics of the Stormont régime. The troops are kept closely quartered and are allowed out only on patrol. They have very limited contact with their homes and families and are very restricted as to contact with civilians. They exemplify British military discipline. The Scots Guards, for instance, have notably maintained their posture and presence despite heckling harassment by tourists while on sentry duty at Buckingham Palace and elsewhere. This discipline is maintained through allowing certain mechanisms for 'tension release.'

Initially the routines of physical brutality were conducted with the utmost attention to the legalisms (*i.e.*, the military conducted 'interrogations' at the direction and under the supervision of the RUC Special Branch). By December of 1971, such 'niceties' were no longer required. There were attested incidents of persons being 'lifted,' taken to RUC stations, dismissed by the RUC and carried away by their military captors to regimental barracks for 'a couple of hours of beating about.' British military doctors are, significantly, the only persons knowledgeable about the extent of injuries and deaths directly attributable to mistreatment. Like all other British military personnel, they are subject to the 'Official Secrets Act,' according to which they cannot publicly reveal anything concerning their duties. When civilian physicians have been asked to treat the victims they have been compelled to sign release forms disclaiming the extent of injury and necessary follow-up treatment. In some instances, even without such release forms, civilian physicians who do not want to be bothered by the military have modified accounts of effects or overlooked significant symptoms. This keeps the 'records straight.'

Dr. Fields put at "more than 1,800" the number of "men and boys (some as young as 12) who have been detained . . . in the months since Aug. 9, 1971. . . ." She cited no source for these figures.

Edward Kennedy Proposes British Withdrawal

The Massachusetts State Senate approved by voice vote Aug. 12, 1971 a resolution urging Britain to withdraw its troops from Northern Ireland and to allow the province to join the Republic of Ireland.

U.S. Sens. Edward M. Kennedy (D., Mass.) and Abraham Ribicoff (D., Conn.) introduced in the U.S. Senate Oct. 20 a resolution urging Pres. Richard M. Nixon to seek an end to the violence in Northern Ireland and the withdrawal of all British troops there. An identical resolution was introduced in the U.S. House of Representatives the same day by Rep. Hugh Carey (D., N.Y.). In addition to calling for a withdrawal of British troops from Ulster, the Kennedy-Ribicoff resolution demanded the termination of Stormont's internment policy, full respect for the civil rights of all persons in Northern Ireland, the implementation of reforms promised by Britain since 1968 in the spheres of law enforcement, housing, employment and voting rights, the dissolution of the Stormont Parliament and the convening of a meeting of all interested parties to plan for the unification of Ireland.

Speaking in favor of the resolution in the Senate, Kennedy warned that Northern Ireland was becoming Britain's Vietnam. He charged that "the government of Ulster rules by bayonet and bloodshed." Kennedy added: "if only the cruel and constant irritation of the British military presence is withdrawn, Ireland can be whole again." Pending reunification, Kennedy called for direct British rule over Northern Ireland. According to Kennedy: "The conscience of America cannot keep silent when men and women of Ireland are dying. Britain has lost its way, and the innocent people of Northern Ireland are the ones who now must suffer. The time has come for Americans of every faith and political persuasion to speak out. . . . The explosive situation in Northern Ireland transcends the traditional feelings of those who believe America ought not to intervene in the affairs of another nation. That principle is utterly without application here. There are ties between America and Ireland that simply cannot be ignored.... In another sense as well, the tragedy of Ulster is the tragedy of America in Indochina. For Ulster is becoming Britain's Vietnam. Indeed, it is fair to say that Britain stands toward peace in Northern Ireland today where America stood in Southeast Asia in the early 1960s."

Kennedy concluded: "We believe that the sum of these proposals offers the only real hope for the freedom of the people of Northern Ireland and an end to the reign of violence and terror that threatens to consume that land. No one doubts that Ireland stands today on the brink of a massive civil war. The specter we face is nothing less than the senseless destruction of Ireland herself. No American who loves Ireland or who remembers her proud and noble history can stand silent in the face of the tragedy and horror now unfolding in Ulster."

Speaking in favor of the resolution, Sen. Ribicoff declared: "This resolution is being introduced because the current tragedy in Ulster involves a denial of the basic principles of human decency and social justice. Concern for those oppressed and persecuted because of their religion or skin color has been an historic tradition of our country, and I would hope we never become so jaded that we ignore such problems. Discrimination against Catholics in Northern Ireland is just as abhorrent as the discrimination practiced against black people in our own country, Bengalis in East Pakistan or Jews in the Soviet Union. It is morally wrong and can only bring shame on its perpetrators and spawn desperate reactions by those oppressed.... British neglect and misrule in Northern Ireland have left a legacy of fear and hate that the deployment of thousands of more British troops will never erase. Belated and half-hearted attempts at reforms are too late. The distrust and bitterness felt by the Catholic minority toward a tyrannical majority runs too deep. Britain, in whose hands the ultimate fate of Northern Ireland lies, must finally face up to the festering conflict it has so long sought to ignore. The only long-term solution consistent with the principles of self-determination and liberty is the unification of Ireland."

Dissociating the Nixon Administration from the resolution, Charles W. Bray 3d U.S. State Department spokesman, noted Oct. 20 that the U.S. embassy in London had said that Kennedy's action "in no way reflects American policy."

Northern Irish Prime Min. Brian Faulkner Oct. 21 sharply criticized Kennedy's statement and reiterated the desire of "the overwhelming majority of the Ulster people to remain part of the United

Kingdom." He deplored Kennedy's failure to mention the campaign being waged by IRA terrorists.

About 60 members of the British Parliament Oct. 21 signed a motion deploring Kennedy's "unfortunate outburst."

Asked to comment on Kennedy's remarks, the Earl of Cromer (George Baring), British ambassador in Washington, said Oct. 20: "The Northern Ireland problem is not a colonial problem. The prime minister of the Republic of Ireland, Mr. Lynch, himself has said, 'There is no real invader here. . . This whole unhappy situation is an Irish quarrel.' British withdrawal would not make the Northern Ireland problem disappear. Successive British governments have indicated that if a majority of the inhabitants of Northern Ireland said that they wished to join the Irish Republic, Britain would not stand in their way. The crucial point is that the inhabitants of Northern Ireland have for the past 50 years continuously voted by overwhelming majorities to remain part of Britain. There are over a million people in Northern Ireland, out of a total population of a million and a half, who are determined to remain British. Cardinal Conway, primate of all Ireland, and the Catholic bishops, in a statement last September, asked—and I quote—'Who in his sane senses wants to bomb a million Protestants into a united Ireland?' "

Editorial opinion in the U.S. was largely hostile to the Kennedy-Ribicoff resolution. The *Christian Science Monitor* Oct. 23 described it as a "totally unwarranted intrusion into British internal affairs." The *Memphis Press-Scimitar* (Tenn.) Oct. 25 referred to the resolution as "uninformed advice from abroad." The *Richmond Times-Dispatch* (Va.) Oct. 25 denounced Kennedy for stirring "a hornet's nest in the United Kingdom," and the *Omaha World Herald* Oct. 26 declared that "we expected a little better from Kennedy." The *Philadelphia Inquirer* Oct. 27 described the resolution as "gratuitous" and "muddle-headed," while the *Philadelphia Bulletin* suggested Oct. 27 that a "great disservice" had been done to the people of Ulster. Several of the editorials alleged that the resolution had been introduced to further Kennedy's domestic political ambitions. The *Portland Press Herald* declared Nov. 1 that Kennedy's speech would have been suitable "if delivered before a St. Patrick's Day meeting of the Ancient Order of Hibernians in South Boston," and the *Arizona Republic* Oct. 28 termed the speech "irresponsible and uninformed."

In Congress, Rep. William J. Scherle (R., Ia.) said Nov. 15: "It is not the responsibility and it is a dubious right of any individual American, particularly a political spokesman, to make emotional and shortsighted demands on a foreign government's internal policy."

Sen. Fred Harris (D., Okla.) Nov. 16 proposed UN intervention in Northern Ireland. He said: "Ireland, then, faces a painful dilemma. On the one hand, the presence of some peacekeeping force in Northern Ireland seems essential. On the other hand, using British troops for any peacekeeping rôle seems likely to lead to continued and increased violence. So what is to be done? I believe the [U.S.] Congress must urge the creation by the UN Security Council of a United Nations peacekeeping force for Northern Ireland. This force should be constituted as soon as possible so that the British can announce and hasten their final and irrevocable withdrawal. The UN peacekeeping force should be charged with protecting the civil rights of all the people of Northern Ireland and with ending all forces of discrimination: political, social, economic or religious."

Rep. Mario Biaggi (D., N.Y.), concerned by reports of large numbers of Ulster Catholics fleeing into the Irish Republic, introduced a bill Nov. 18 to provide for "25,000 emergency refugee visas for those trying to escape the war in Northern Ireland."

At its national convention in Miami, Fla., the American Federation of Labor & Congress of Industrial Organizations (AFL-CIO) Nov. 22 adopted a resolution on the crisis. The resolution condemned "insidious practices [of the British and Stormont governments] which have caused so much bloodshed," called for the withdrawal of British troops and their replacement by a UN peacekeeping force, an end to the "Hitlerian policy of internment the dissolution of the Stormont régime and the establishment of a "free and independent United Ireland." The resolution urged the U.S. Congress and the President "to make our people's wishes known to the government of Great Britain" in order to achieve these ends.

Interrogation Abuses Curbed

British Prime Min. Edward Heath Mar. 2, 1972 barred the use of harsh interrogation methods against detained terrorist suspects in Northern Ireland. He told the House of Commons that "interrogation in depth" would continue in the fight against terrorism but that "severe techniques will not be used." Heath promised that the government would seek prior Parliamentary approval if it felt the need to resume the methods. (The tactics barred included putting hoods over detainee's heads and subjecting suspects to continuous noise, sleep deprivation and bread-and-water diets.) Heath said that 14 prisoners had been subjected to the harsh questioning tactics since the introduction of internment without trial in Aug. 1971.

Heath's decision followed the publication Mar. 2 of the results of an official inquiry into army interrogation methods in Ulster. The 3-man committee, headed by Lord Parker, a former lord chief justice, had split 2-1 in favor of authorizing harsh questioning methods "in cases where it is considered vitally necessary to obtain information." The dissenting opinion—by Lord Gardiner, a former lord chancellor—opposed the techniques as morally unjustifiable. Lord Parker and John Archibald Boyd-Carpenter, a Conservative, wrote the majority opinion.

The government decision was derided in Dublin by a spokesman for Sinn Fein, the political arm of the IRA Officials, as a "sop to left-wing liberal opinion in Britain." The Sinn Fein, however, welcomed the "reassurance that this kind of thing will not happen again in Ireland."

LONDONDERRY MASSACRE & ITS CONSEQUENCES: 1972

13 Catholic demonstrators in Londonderry were killed Jan. 30, 1972 by British paratroopers after other troops had curtailed a forbidden protest march. The deaths brought the turmoil to a new and more dangerous point in Northern Ireland. Catholics, enraged by the killings, promised to take revenge, and demonstrations against British rule in Ulster took place throughout the world.

Agitation Against Internment

The "Londonderry Massacre" was preceded by a month of continued gunfighting and several demonstrations by Catholics for an end to Stormont's internment policy. In the year's first major incident Jan. 2, 2,000 Catholic protesters staged anti-internment parades in Belfast in defiance of the official prohibition on marches since mid-Aug. 1971.

In an effort to curb the continuing terrorist violence in Northern Ireland, the British Army Jan. 5 authorized its soldiers in Ulster to use machine guns, as well as rifles and pistols, on city streets, according to revised orders reported by the press Jan. 5. The commander on the spot could order machine-gun fire against identified targets rather than only the "single, aimed shots" previously authorized. Soldiers were also authorized to open fire without warning at moving cars and to shoot without warning armed persons. The use of machine guns had previously been authorized for the defense of police stations.

A controversial inquiry into the Northern Irish crisis by the British Broadcasting Corp., a publicly financed broadcasting system, was televised Jan. 5 despite strong British government opposition. The program, which officials considered tendentious, consisted of a distinguished 3-man panel listening to proposals for a solution to the crisis from various representatives of Northern Irish opinion.

The government opened its 2d internment camp Jan. 16 with 50 prisoners transferred from the prison ship *Maidstone* in Belfast harbor. The new center was Camp Magilligan near Londonderry. 7 suspected IRA terrorists escaped Jan. 17 from the *Maidstone.* Previous escapes had occurred from the Crumlin Road prison. Both prisons were used as transit centers prior to formal internment. (99 more IRA suspects had been captured in security raids Jan. 1–15, according to a British Army announcement.)

Stormont Prime Min. Brian Faulkner Jan. 18 ordered a one-year extension of the 6-month ban on all parades. (The original ban had been imposed in Aug. 1971 with the introduction of internment with-

153

out trial of suspected terrorists.) The measure was taken, Faulkner said, to avoid exposing security forces to "unnecessary risks." The ban, affecting both Protestant and Catholic marches, was sharply criticized by both sides. The Rev. Ian Paisley charged in the Stormont Parliament Jan. 18 that "the government has capitulated to the policy of terror. Today, the IRA has won."

The ban was defied by Catholics Jan. 22-23 when they staged anti-internment demonstrations in Armagh, at the Magilligan internment camp and in other areas in the province. British troops clashed with the demonstrators during the protest at the Magilligan camp. Witnesses charged the soldiers with brutality in their handling of the crowd. The continuing violence in Northern Ireland included bomb and mine explosions throughout the province as well as gunfire. It resulted in the murder Jan. 1-27 of at least 9 persons, including 2 British soldiers, one member of the Ulster Defense Regiment (UDR) and 3 members of the Royal Ulster Constabulary Reserve force.

But the worst single day of violence in Northern Ireland in 50 years took place Jan. 30, 1972 when British paratroopers shot to death 13 civilians participating in a banned protest march in Londonderry. 15 demonstrators and one soldier were wounded in the incident. The slayings were denounced as a massacre by witnesses and defended by British Army and government sources as justifiable defense in the face of violent provocation. (The clash brought to 25 the number of persons who had died in Northern Ireland's civil unrest in 1972, the *N.Y. Times* reported Jan. 31). An immediate controversy arose over the events that led to the shootings.

At least 3,000 to 5,000 persons reportedly had participated in the Londonderry march, staged in defiance of the government's ban on all demonstrations. The marchers had gathered in protest against the internment without trial of suspected IRA terrorists. When the demonstrators found themselves blocked by Army barricades, they proceeded to a meeting point in the Bogside, a Catholic area, where Bernadette Devlin was scheduled to address a rally. The demonstrators began to pelt the soldiers with stones, bottles and debris. The soldiers responded with gradually escalating violence, first spraying the demonstrators with purple dye and then firing rubber bullets and—according to some early reports—riot control gas canisters. (British authorities later charged that a demonstrator had thrown the first canister.) As the tension increased the paratroopers were sent over the barricades to scatter the mob.

An Army statement said later that more than 200 paratroopers were ordered forward and that they had opened fire only after they came under nail bomb attack and sniper fire. The Army said that more than 200 rounds were fired indiscriminately at the soldiers during the 30-minute battle that followed and that soldiers had returned fire "only at identified targets." The British paratroop commander, Lt. Col. Derek Wilford, said later that the troops had first been fired at by 2 snipers, both of whom were killed by the soldiers. He acknowledged that no weapons were found on the 2 bodies. The Army commander in charge of the operation, Maj. Gen. Robert Ford, also insisted that the soldiers had fired only at snipers and grenade throwers. British Army spokesmen reported that, of the 13 men killed in the shooting that began after the bulk of the 3,000 marchers had been peacefully dispersed, 4 were on the security force's wanted list. One man had 4 nail bombs in his pocket. All the victims were between the ages of 16 and 40.

The *Washington Post* of Jan. 31 quoted an IRA leader as saying: "At no time did any of our units open fire on the British Army prior to the Army's opening fire." The IRA unequivocally denied that its men had initiated the gunfire exchange.

Northern Irish Prime Min. Faulkner had issued a statement Jan. 30 blaming the incident on the IRA and the organizers of the march.

Witnesses, including several leading Northern Irish politicians and some priests, countered with charges that the paratroopers had been the first to open fire and had fired directly into the crowd. Miss Devlin denounced the killings as "mass murder" by the Army. Lord Brockway, a Labor peer who was present to address the rally, said that the march, though illegal, had seemed to be "a perfectly peaceful procession" and that there would have been no violence if it had been allowed to proceed.

Both the militant Provisional and the leftist Official wings of the IRA Jan. 31 vowed reprisals against the British. The Londonderry Provisional leader said: "We will avenge every death in Derry today." In Belfast that day, a 100-pound bomb exploded in a department store arcade, critically injuring a policeman. Northern Irish Catholics responded to an IRA call Jan. 31 and began a general strike that was to last until the Londonderry victims were buried. Hundreds of shops, offices and factories were closed in Londonderry and in other cities. Sitdown protests and demonstrations took place throughout the province.

A British soldier was shot to death in Belfast Feb. 1 and a man was shot to death in rioting in Belfast's Catholic districts after funeral services for 12 of the 13 Londonderry victims Feb. 2. The same day a bomb explosion in a Belfast suburban pub killed one person.

Reaction in Britain

While defending the paratroops' action in Londonderry before a tense session of the House of Commons Jan. 31, British Home Secy. Reginald Maudling announced that an impartial judicial inquiry into the clash would be held. Shortly after his announcement, Maudling was physically attacked on the House floor by Bernadette Devlin, who had been refused permission to give an eyewitness account of the Londonderry events. She called the home secretary a "murdering hypocrite," then pulled his hair and punched him.

British Prime Min. Edward Heath Feb. 1 named Britain's lord chief justice, Baron John Passmore Widgery, to conduct an independent inquiry into the Londonderry incident. Heath declared of Lord Widgery Feb. 6: "No one can doubt the impartiality of the Lord Chief Justice or his ability to carry through the heavy task entrusted to him. Should any individuals or groups concerned take a considered decision not to give evidence to the tribunal they must not be surprised at the natural conclusion which opinion here and abroad will draw."

An emergency debate in the British House of Commons Feb. 1 was marked by the Labor Party's sharpest attack to date on the Conservative government's handling of the Ulster crisis. The government, by 304-266 vote, defeated a Labor Party motion expressing disappointment at the government's "procrastination" in organizing all-party talks on the Ulster crisis. Labor Party leader Harold Wilson, who had first proposed such talks in 1971, said that he would not accept confidential talks restricted to the Labor Party and the government. Wilson accused Maudling of "dragging his feet" on talks that would include all parties to the dispute. Wilson also demanded the transfer of all responsibility for security from the Northern Irish government to the British government.

Maudling replied that the government had been striving to arrange all-party talks for months but that Northern Irish Catholic groups had refused to cooperate. He again defended the Army, insisting that troops had been brought in only when law and order were threatened and had used only the degree of force necessary to respond to attacks by persons using bullets and bombs. He also insisted that the organizers of the illegal march bore "a heavy responsibility" for the consequences.

Lord Balniel, minister of state for defense, asserted: "If we analyze the recent activities of bombers and gunners, we do not see a picture of growing strength but rather one of growing desperation. The continuing build-up of information has enabled the security forces to form a clearer picture of the organizations, tactics and whereabouts of the

IRA. . . . Civil-rights marches suit the IRA's tactics and purposes well—not just because of their propaganda value but also because they give it a chance to create further trouble. . . . Intelligence information had given the security forces good reason to believe that the IRA would exploit the opportunities afforded by the march and subsequent rioting to mount attacks on the security forces."

Speaking in the Feb. 1 Commons debate, Bernadette Devlin warned that the Londonderry events might "doom the last vestige of British rule" in Northern Ireland. Another Catholic politician from Ulster, Gerard Fitt, said that the killings had "dramatically changed the whole political outlook" in Ireland; he called for the withdrawal of all British troops from Ulster.

15 Oxford University students were arrested Feb. 1 after they refused to end an occupation of the Army recruiting office in Oxford, England, staged in protest against the Londonderry shootings.

About 4,000 demonstrators clashed with London police Feb. 5 after trying to deliver 13 coffins representing the Londonderry victims to No. 10 Downing Street, the residence of the British prime minister. More than 90 policemen and civilians were injured as the demonstrators threw rocks and bottles at the police. Other protests were held in Birmingham, Manchester, Leeds, Glasgow and elsewhere in Great Britain.

Addressing the Young Conservative Conference at Harrogate, Yorkshire Feb. 6, Prime Min. Heath emphasized British responsibility for the future of Northern Ireland. He pointed out ". . . first, . . . that the status of Northern Ireland as part of the United Kingdom cannot be changed except by consent . . . [and] 2d . . . that the minority in Northern Ireland must be assured of a real and meaningful part in the taking of the decisions which shape their future. . . ." "The 2d responsibility on the government must be to maintain by the means at our disposal the greatest possible security for the people of Northern Ireland, to whichever community they belong," Heath said. Many observers inferred from this that the British government was planning to take over the administration of Northern Ireland from the Stormont régime.

Relations Between Dublin & London Worsen

The Irish government recalled its ambassador to Britain, Dr. Donal O'Sullivan, Jan. 31, 1972. It declared itself "fully satisfied that there was an unprovoked attack by British troops on unarmed civilians in Derry." The government protested the Londonderry shootings and issued a statement demanding the withdrawal of British troops from Londonderry and Catholic areas in other cities, an end to "harassment" of Catholics and internment without trial and a conference to settle the crisis.

British European Airways Feb. 1 cancelled flights to the Irish Republic after airport workers in Dublin, Shannon and Cork refused to service British planes. Irish dock workers also refused to unload British ships in Irish ports.

The Irish government Jan. 28 had arrested 7 IRA Provisionals in the County Louth seaport of Dundalk and had charged them with illegal possession of arms. The arrests, which the British government had hoped would signal a tougher policy toward the IRA, followed a 2-hour gun battle Jan. 27 between the IRA Provisionals and the British Army at Dungooley, on the border between Northern Ireland and the Republic. A British Army patrol reportedly had been fired on by IRA terrorists from the Republic side of the border. Among those arrested was Anthony (Dutch) Doherty, who had escaped from the Crumlin Road prison in Belfast in 1971. Martin Meehan, another escapee from the prison, was being sought by police in connection with the incident. (A leading IRA suspect, Francis McGuigan, escaped from the Long Kesh internment camp southwest of Belfast Feb. 7. This was the first escape from that internment camp.)

In a violent protest against the Londonderry killings, members of a crowd of about 25,000 persons besieged and burned down the British embassy in Dublin Feb. 2. The embassy had been evacuated earlier that morning after 2 days of firebombing. The attack followed a march through downtown Dublin organized as part of the Irish Republic's official day of mourning on the burial of the Londonderry victims. The crowd overwhelmed the police patrolling the march and prevented firemen from getting to the blaze.

The destruction of the embassy was the most dramatic of several events indicating a sharp deterioration in relations between the Republic and Britain over the Northern Irish crisis.

Irish Republic Foreign Min. Patrick Hillery Feb. 2 urged the U. S. and other governments to put pressure on Britain to abandon its "lunatic policies" in Ulster. He charged that the "brutal onslaught on a defenseless civil rights demonstration" in Londonderry constituted a "new policy directed against the entire minority population of Northern Ireland." Hillery made his comments at a press conference in New York after delivering a message on the crisis to UN Undersecy. Gen C. V. Narasimhan. Hillery reiterated charges that British troops had made incursions across the border and had fired into Irish Republic territory.

In an interview on NBC's "Today" TV program in New York Feb. 2, Hillery outlined Ireland's policy and voiced Dublin's frustration over Britain's apparent intransigence: "We can only hope that the United Nations . . . , and other governments too, may impress upon the British that their policies in the North of Ireland are lunatic, they're aggressive, they're warlike politics . . . on a peaceful nation. They're going to cause war in our country. . . . We have followed peaceful policies, but it is not possible to control all our people, and the IRA you mentioned will have some support from the rest of our country. . . . The withdrawal of the British troops now from the ghetto areas where they're not wanted, where they spend their time harassing the populace, breaking down their doors, searching their houses, driving their children from their studies. Letting people out of internment. They were interned to prevent violence, and violence has escalated. These things must stop for Ireland at once, then we could get down to talking about the type of Ireland in which the North—the Protestants—there are a million Protestants in the North—and the rest of Ireland could live together."

British Foreign Secy. Sir Alec Douglas-Home in Britain's House of Commons Feb. 3 warned Ireland that continuation of its critical attitude on the Ulster crisis, as exemplified by Hillery's comments, could do "lasting damage" to British-Irish relations. He condemned the burning of the embassy as an "outrage."

Irish Republic Prime Min. Lynch, in a speech at an emergency session of the Irish parliament Feb. 3, also condemned the embassy burning and described those responsible for it as "a small minority who under the cloak of patriotism seek to overthrow the institutions of this state." He warned that the government would take strong action against the extremist groups and promised that the government would pay full compensation to Britain for the building. He reiterated his call for the immediate withdrawal of British troops from Catholic areas of Northern Ireland.

Silent marches of sympathy for the Londonderry victims' families and meetings in protest against the British military presence in Northern Ireland took place in Dublin, Cork, Limerick and other towns in the Irish Republic Feb. 6

Foreign Reaction

A small group of demonstrators protesting the Londonderry killings cut down the British flag flying in front of the British Consulate in New York Jan. 31 and tried to set it afire. Police arrested 2 of the demonstrators for disorderly conduct and starting an open fire in the street. The protest was organized by the National Association for Irish Freedom. The British news service Reuters reported the same day that a man claiming to represent "the Irish Minutemen" had phoned a warning that "all British industry in New York is going to be a target."

Condemning British policies in Northern Ireland, U. S. Sen. Abraham Ribicoff (D., Conn.) declared Jan. 31: "The tragic killings yesterday in Londonderry of 13 persons and the wounding of another 16 is another dark blot on Great Britain's sorry record in Northern Ireland. This bloody incident makes it even more obvious that the current British policies in Northern Ireland have failed and that their continuation can only prolong the agony of Ulster. I hope that any official inquiry into this tragedy will go beyond the terrible events of Jan. [30] and go to the root causes of the mounting violence in Northern Ireland."

Calling for the withdrawal of the British Army from Protestant Ulster, Ribicoff asserted: ". . . The presence of these troops in increasing numbers is a crucial element. Had British paratroopers and armored cars, according to the *Washington Post*, not stormed into the Catholic Bogside ghetto in pursuit of demonstrators at a banned protest march, this slaughter would not have taken place. From the first newspaper reports of the killings, including an eyewitness account by a Manchester *Guardian* correspondent, it appears that British troops deliberately fired into the crowd and at people fleeing the scene. The British Army commander's allegations that his men came under a sustained attack by snipers and grenade throwers are refuted by the very fact that only a single British trooper was reportedly wounded. What is perfectly clear, however, is that more of the same repressive policies, such as internment without trial and brutal interrogation, and more British troops are not solutions for the festering of problems of Northern Ireland. It has been said that the British genius for policies seems to disappear when it comes to Ireland. This was tragically evident yesterday."

Several other U. S. Senators, including Edward M. Kennedy (D., Mass.) and James L. Buckley (Conservative, N.Y.) called Feb. 2 for the U.S. to urge Britain to withdraw its troops from Northern Ireland.

Irish Foreign Min. Patrick Hillery met in Washington with Secy. William P. Rogers Feb. 3 to discuss the Ulster situation. Rogers told newsmen after their talks that "it would be both inappropriate and counterproductive for the United States to attempt to intervene in any way in the area." He said that the U.S. would consider playing "a useful rôle" in the dispute only at the request of the Irish Republic and Britain, but he expressed "serious reservations about whether there is a useful rôle we could play." He stressed that the crisis must be resolved by "the people in the area."

More than 100 Irish-Americans picketed the British consulate in New York Feb. 4. The Rev. Robert I. Gannon, former president of Fordham University, assailed British policy in Ulster as "stupid and bungling." He made his attack in a sermon delivered Feb. 6 at New York's St. Patrick's Cathedral during a mass for peace and justice in Ulster.

Thousands of Irish-Australians staged peaceful protest demonstrations in downtown Sydney and Melbourne Feb. 6.

UN Secy. Gen. Kurt Waldheim said at a news conference at UN headquarters in New York Feb. 7 that he had offered to help settle the Ulster crisis in response to a request from the Irish Republic. He said that his intervention would be conditional on British consent because the issue was an internal matter. Britain declined the offer Feb. 8, stating that "the matter does not lend itself to intervention from outside."

Canadian External Affairs Min. Mitchell Sharp Feb. 8 rejected a request by Irish Foreign Min. Hillery that Ottawa press Britain to change its Northern Irish policy. He said that Canada would only communicate the Irish Republic's representations to Britain. Sharp made his comment to newsmen after meeting with Hillery in Ottawa. Hillery had gone to Canada after a brief visit to the U.S. He left Ottawa Feb. 8 on a similar mission to France.

Yuri Yasnev, a Soviet correspondent, gave this Soviet view in the Feb. 2 issue of *Pravda*, the official organ of the Soviet Communist Party:

The world has been shocked by the horrible shooting of a peaceful demonstration in Londonderry. 13 people were killed, 18 seriously wounded—such is the result of the tragedy which broke last Sunday in this ancient Irish town.

Thousands of people who took part in the demonstration at the call of the Civil Rights Association advanced legitimate demands: to free their relatives and friends put into concentration camps and prisons without trial and investigation. They demanded work and houses. Bullets were the answer.

The volleys of British paratroopers against peaceful marchers in whose ranks were women and children have completely revealed the essence of the hypocritical policy of British colonialists in Ulster. How many times Heath and Maudling asserted in Parliament that British troops in Northern Ireland were discharging extremely humane mission—to maintain 'law and order.' This is a lie from beginning to end.

The author of these lines happened to visit Northern Ireland twice: in 1969, a month after the British troops entered the country, and quite recently, this January. It was not difficult to notice what an escalation of 'law and order' took place during this period.

Giving sanctions to intern 'suspicious persons' in accordance with the notorious 'law of emergency powers,' the Heath government tried to justify these measures, saying they would allegedly reduce the number of losses among the civilian population. Facts reveal another picture. From Aug. 9, 1971, when the interning began, to the end of the year, 142 civilians were killed in Northern Ireland, that is 7 times as many as within the corresponding period in 1970. The people of long-suffering Ulster pay by tears and blood for London's unasked 'humane mission.' Northern Ireland today is a land of ruined economy, of the completely bankrupt unionist régime, isolated from the broad sections of people, and of unbridled terror of British invaders.

The heinous crime of British imperialists in Londonderry cannot leave anybody impartial to the further destiny of Northern Ireland. The Soviet people, who are always on the side of the fighters for freedom and independence, together with the progressive public of the whole world, share the grief and anger of the Irish people and demand an end to the horrible crimes of British colonialists in Ulster.

Ulster Catholics Protest

15,000 to 30,000 Catholics defied a government ban on demonstrations in Northern Ireland and staged a silent march in Newry Feb. 6 in protest against British policy and the "Londonderry Massacre." The demonstration was held despite urgent appeals by British Prime Min. Edward Heath and Northern Irish Prime Min. Brian Faulkner for its cancellation.

The feared violence never materialized in the Newry march. The protesters stayed away from barricades set up by British troops and Northern Irish police in the center of Newry, where a post-march rally had been scheduled to be held. The march was diverted to another part of Newry, where Catholic politicians and the organizers of the march addressed the crowd, claiming victory for defying the ban on parades and demanding the end of internment without trial, the removal of British troops and the abolition of the current Protestant-dominated Ulster government.

The parade, organized by the Northern Ireland Civil Rights Association, was joined by Catholics from the Irish Republic as well as from Northern Ireland. Also present as an observer was U.S. Congressman Mario Biaggi (D., N.Y.).

A "day of disruption"—civil disobedience—in protest against the internment policy was organized by the Northern Ireland Civil Rights Association Feb. 9, the 6-month anniversary of the introduction of internment. Demonstrators blocked streets, closed post offices in Newry and a Catholic district of Belfast, staged small rallies and shut down some stores in the province's Catholic areas. They failed, however, in their objective of seriously disrupting government administration and phone service.

Stormont's Prime Min. Faulkner had warned Feb. 8 of "a long and bloody struggle" if Roman Catholics continued to press for a united

Ireland. In a speech to the Stormont Parliament, Faulkner said that "the whole method of the Republican state—the structure of its constitution and of its laws"—were "repugnant" to the Northern Irish. He urged Irish Republic Prime Min. Lynch to set aside the issue of unification and "lend his influence to the cause of a realistic settlement."

Maurice Hayes, chairman of Northern Ireland's Community Relations Commission, resigned Feb. 9 because, he said, the government's security policies made his efforts to seek reconciliation between Protestants and Catholics "impossible." The resignations of a number of Catholics from public office in Northern Ireland were reported by the *N.Y. Times* Feb. 5. Among those listed were 3 senior public prosecutors, the vice chairman of the Hospital Authority and 2 members of the Police Authority. The opposition Social Democratic Labor Party, whose members had begun a boycott of Parliament in 1971, had urged Feb. 2 that all Catholics resign from public office in Northern Ireland. The party said that it would abandon its efforts to seek political reform in Northern Ireland in order to concentrate on achieving a united Ireland.

3,000 to 4,000 Catholics marched peacefully through the border town of Enniskillen Feb. 13 in protest against the Londonderry killings and to demand the end of internment without trial and the abolition of the Stormont government. The march, organized by the Northern Resistance Movement, a militant civil rights group, was held in defiance of a government ban on demonstrations.

Widgery Report Clears British Army

The official British inquiry into the killing of 13 civilians by British soldiers in Londonderry in January issued a report Apr. 19, 1972 that absolved the Army of primary responsibility for the deaths. The inquiry report was based on hearings held in Coleraine, Northern Ireland, and London Feb. 21–Mar. 20. Testimony was taken from Army and civilian witnesses by Lord Widgery, who had served as an officer in the Royal Artillery throughout World War II.

Details of the conduct of the investigation into the Londonderry events had been given by Widgery Feb. 14 at a preliminary hearing held in Coleraine, County Derry, 27 miles east-northeast of the municipality of Londonderry. He said: "This is a judicial inquiry, and the tribunal has the independence of a judge, and the proceedings will be conducted on the instructions of the tribunal alone. This is also essentially a fact-finding exercise, by which I mean that the purpose of the inquiry is to reconstruct with as much detail as is necessary the precise events which led to the shooting of a number of people in the streets of

Londonderry on the afternoon of Sunday, Jan. 30 last. The tribunal is not concerned with making moral judgments. Its concern is to try and form an objective view of the precise events and the sequence in which they occurred so that those who are prepared to form judgments will have a firm basis on which to reach their conclusions. The primary concern of the tribunal, therefore, is to listen to witnesses who were present on the occasion and who can assist in reconstructing the events from evidence of what they saw with their own eyes or heard with their own ears. It is well-known that a number of versions of these events have been stipulated and I want to hear evidence from those who support each and every one of those different versions."

In his report Apr. 19, Widgery rejected Catholic claims that the Army had acted without provocation. Widgery, Britain's lord chief justice, concluded that an Irish Republican Army sniper had been responsible for the first shot fifed. The sniper was said to have fired on paratroopers from the Rossville Flats housing development in Londonderry's Bogside, a Roman Catholic district. Widgery based this conclusion on the testimony of TV newsmen present during the incident and on his own deductive reasoning. Noting that soldiers had initially limited themselves to making arrests, Widgery found "no reason to suppose that the soldiers would have opened fire if they had not been fired upon first." He asserted that if the soldiers had engaged in gross wrongdoing, "they were parties in a lying conspiracy which must have come to light in the rigorous cross-examination to which they were subjected" in the course of the inquiry.

Widgery placed a major share of responsibility for the incident on the organizers of the march, because "there would have been no deaths" if the organizers had not "created a highly dangerous situation in which a clash . . . was almost inevitable."

The Army's share of responsibility, Widgery said, stemmed from its decision to arrest "hooligans" participating in an illegal civil rights march, rather than simply to contain the marchers. Without the arrest operation, he said, "the day might have passed without serious incident." Widgery concluded that Brig. Pat McLellan, the paratrooper's brigade commander, who had issued the arrest orders, had underestimated the dangers to civilians. Despite his finding that the firing by some troops had "bordered on the reckless" when men were killed apparently "without justification" in Glenfada Park, Widgery denied there had been any general breakdown in Army discipline.

While generally backing the Army, Widgery nevertheless found no proof of the Army's claim that soldiers had fired only at identified gunmen and bombers. He noted that no weapons were found by the

Army and that none of the photos of the march showed a civilian holding an object that could be identified as a firearm or bomb. He also noted the absence of injuries among the soldiers from firearms or bombs.

Despite the fact that none of the civilians killed or wounded were proved to have been shot while handling a firearm or bomb, Widgery said there was "strong suspicion that some . . . had been firing weapons or handling bombs" during the afternoon. He based this conclusion on paraffin tests on the hands of the victims. 7 of those killed bore traces of lead particles indicating they had possibly handled firearms or had been close to someone who did. One of the 7 victims so suspected was discovered to have had 4 nail bombs in his pockets, although 2 previous medical examinations had failed to turn up any such evidence. Widgery said that the bulky objects should have been noticed during the medical examinations but, he declared, "the alternative explanation of a 'plant' is mere speculation."

Excerpts from the report and Lord Widgery's conclusions:

* * *

Security Background: Events in Londonderry During the Previous 6 Months

10. The Bogside and the Creggan [districts], the Republican views of whose people are well known, were the scene of large scale rioting in 1969 and have suffered sporadic rioting by hooligans ever since. In the early summer of 1971 a good deal of progress had been made towards restoring normal life. The Royal Ulster Constabulary was patrolling almost everywhere in the area on foot, the Army was little in evidence, the hooligan element had been isolated and the IRA was quiescent. At the beginning of July, however, gunmen appeared and an IRA campaign began. Widespread violence ensued with the inevitable military counteraction. Nevertheless at the end of August it was decided, after consultation with a group of prominent local citizens, to reduce the level of military activity in the hope that moderate opinion would prevail and the IRA gunmen be isolated from the community.

11. From the end of August to the end of October an uneasy equilibrium was maintained. In a conscious effort to avoid provocation the Army made itself less obvious. Though parts of the Bogside and Creggan were patrolled, no military initiative was taken except in response to aggression or for specific search or arrest operations. The improvement hoped for did not, however, take place. The residents of the Bogside and Creggan threw up or repaired over 50 barricades, including the one in Rossville Street which figured prominently in the proceedings of the inquiry; frequent sniping and bombing attacks were made on the security forces; and the IRA tightened its grip on the district. . . .

12. At the end of October, 8 Infantry Brigade, within whose area of command the City of Londonderry lay, was given instructions progressively to regain the initiative from the terrorists and reimpose the rule of law on the Creggan and Bogside. Hooligan activity was to be vigorously countered and arrest operations were to be mounted. As a result, a series of operations was carried out in the Bogside and Creggan at battalion strength with the object of clearing barricades,

making arrests and searching premises about which intelligence reports had been received. These operations hardened the attitude of the community against the Army, so that the troops were operating in an entirely hostile environment and as time went on were opposed by all elements of the community when they entered the Bogside and Creggan. The Army's static positions and observation posts were fired on and a large number of youths, many of them unemployed, gathered daily at the points of entry into the areas which were guarded by troops in order to attack them with stones and other missiles. Many nail and petrol bombs were thrown during these attacks. Gunmen made full use of the cover offered to them by the gangs of youths, which made it more and more difficult to engage the youths at close quarters and make arrests. The Creggan became almost a fortress. Whenever troops appeared near there at night search-lights were switched on and car horns blazed. The terrorists were still firmly in control.

13. Early in 1972 the security authorities were concerned that the violence was now spreading northwards from William Street, which was the line on the northern fringe of the Bogside on which the troops had for some considerable time taken their stand. Bombing and arson attacks on shops, offices and commercial premises were taking place with increasing frequency in Great James Street and Waterloo Place. The local traders feared that the whole of this shopping area would be extinguished within the next few months. A few figures will show the serious threat not only to the commercial areas of the City but also to the lives of the security forces. From 1 Aug. 1971 to 9 Feb. 1972 in Londonderry 2,656 shots were fired at the security forces, 456 nail and gelignite bombs were thrown and there were 225 explosions, mostly against business premises. In reply the security forces fired back 840 live rounds. In the last 2 weeks of January the IRA was particulary active. In 80 separate incidents in Londonderry 319 shots were fired at the security forces and 84 nail bombs were thrown at them; 2 men of the security forces were killed and 2 wounded. The Londonderry Development Commission has estimated that between 1 Aug. 1971 and about the middle of Feb. 1972 damage amounting to more than £6 million was inflicted in Londonderry. Since then there has been further heavy damage.

14. At the beginning of 1972 Army foot patrols were not able to operate south of William Street by day because of sniper fire, although the Army continued to patrol in the Bogside at night and to enter by day if there was a specific reason for so doing. There were no foot patrols by day during January. The hooligan gangs in Londonderry constituted a special threat to security. Their tactics were to engineer daily breaches of law and order in the face of the security forces, particularly in the William Street area, during which the lives of the soldiers were at risk from attendant snipers and nail bombers. The hooligans could be contained but not dispersed without serious risk to the troops.

15. This was the background against which it was learned that, despite the fact that parades and processions had been prohibited throughout Northern Ireland by law since 9 Aug. 1971, there was to be a protest march in Londonderry on Sunday 30 January, organized by the Northern Ireland Civil Rights Association (NICRA). It was the opinion of the Army commanders that if the march took place, whatever the intentions of NICRA might be, the hooligans backed up by the gunmen would take control. In the light of this view the security forces made their plans to block the march.

The Army Plan to Contain the March

16. The proposed march placed the security forces in a dilemma. An attempt to stop by force a crowd of 5,000 or more, perhaps as many as 20 or

25,000 might result in heavy casualties or even in the overrunning of the troops by sheer weight of numbers. To allow such a well publicized march to take place without opposition however would bring the law into disrepute and make control of future marches impossible.

17. Chief Superintendent Lagan, the head of the Royal Ulster Constabulary in Londonderry, thought that the dangers of interfering with the march were too great and that no action should be taken against it save to photograph the leaders with a view to their being prosecuted later. His opinion was reported to the Chief Constable of Northern Ireland and to the commander 8 Infantry Brigade (Brig. MacLellan) who passed it to [Maj.] Gen. [Robert] Ford, the commander Land Forces Northern Ireland. The final decision, which was taken by higher authority after Gen. Ford and the chief constable had been consulted, was to allow the march to begin but to contain it within the general area of the Bogside and the Creggan Estate so as to prevent rioting in the City center and damage to commercial premises and shops. On 25 January Gen. Ford put the commander 8 Infantry Brigade in charge of the operation and ordered him to prepare a detailed plan. The plan is 8 Infantry Brigade Operation Order No. 2/72 dated 27 January.

18. The brigade commander's plan required the erection of barriers sealing off each of the streets through which the marchers might cross the containment line. Though there were 26 barriers in all, the inquiry was concerned with only 3: No. 12 in Little James Street; No. 13 in Sackville Street; No. 14 in William Street.

The barriers, which were to consist of wooden knife rests reinforced with barbed wire and concrete slabs, were to be put in place early in the afternoon of 30 January. At some of them, notably at barrier 14, an armored personnel carrier was placed on either side of the street close behind and almost parallel with the barrier to reinforce it and to give the troops some cover from stone throwing. Each barrier was to be manned by the Army in platoon strength with representative RUC officers in support. . . . The troops at the barriers were to be provided by units normally under command of 8 Infantry Brigade. The following troops and equipment were to be brought in as reinforcements and reserves: 1st Battalion Parachute Regiment (hereafter referred to as 1 Para); 1st Battalion Kings Own Border Regiment; 2 companies of the 3d Battalion Royal Regiment of Fusiliers; 2 water cannon.

19. The Operation Order provided that the march should be dealt with in as low a key as possible for as long as possible and indeed that if it took place entirely within the Bogside and Creggan it should go unchallenged. No action was to be taken against the marchers unless they tried to breach the barriers or used violence against the security forces. CS gas* was not to be used except as a last resort if troops were about to be overrun and the rioters could no longer be held off with water cannon and riot guns. (These guns, which fire rubber bullets, are also known as baton guns; and the rubber bullets as baton rounds.)

20. Under the heading of "Hooliganism" the operation order provided: "An arrest force is to be held centrally behind the check points and launched in a scoop-up operation to arrest as many hooligans and rioters as possible." This

---

*Conditioned Stimulus gas. The sort generally used for crowd control in the British Isles is orthochloro-benzylidene malononitrile, a substance producing a pricking sensation in the eyes and nose, a streaming from the eyes and nose, retching, vomiting, chest pains and constricted breathing—depending on the volume applied to a given area.

links up with the specific task allotted to 1 Para which was in the following terms:

"1. Maintain a brigade arrest force to conduct a scoop-up operation of as many hooligans and rioters as possible.

"(a) This operation will only be launched either in whole or in part on the orders of the brigade commander.

"(b) .... [Censored from original report]

"(c) .... [Censored from original report]

"(d) It is expected that the arrest operation will be conducted on foot.

"2. A secondary role of the force will be to act as the 2d brigade mobile reserve."

21. The operation order, which was classified "Secret," thus clearly allotted to 1 Para the task of an arrest operation against hooligans. Under cross-examination, however, the senior Army officers, and particularly Gen. Ford, were severely attacked on the grounds that they did not genuinely intend to use 1 Para in this way. It was suggested that 1 Para had been specially brought to Londonderry because they were known to be the roughest and toughest unit in Northern Ireland and it was intended to use them in one of 2 ways: either to flush out any IRA gunmen in the Bogside and destroy them by superior training and fire power: or to send a punitive force into the Bogside to give the residents a rough handling and discourage them from making or supporting further attacks on the troops.

22. There is not a shred of evidence to support these suggestions and they have been denied by all the officers concerned. I am satisfied that the Brigade Operation Order accurately expressed the brigade commander's intention for the employment of 1 Para and that suggestions to the contrary are unfounded. 1 Para was chosen for the arrest rôle because it was the only experienced uncommitted battalion in Northern Ireland. Other experienced units were stationed in Londonderry as part of the normal content of 8 Infantry Brigade, but being committed to barrier and other duties they were not available for use as an arrest force. The arrest operation was vigorously carried out. At the end of the afternoon 54 people had been arrested by 1 Para, about 30 of them by Support Company.

*   *   *

The March as It Happened

24. The marchers assembled on the Creggan Estate on a fine sunny afternoon and in carnival mood. At first amounting to some hundreds only they toured the estate collecting additional numbers as they went and eventually the total may have been something between 3,000 and 5,000 people. At their head was a lorry carrying a Civil Rights Association banner and travelling upon the lorry were some of the leaders of the march. . . . The marchers did not move in any kind of military formation but walked as a crowd through the streets, occupying the entire width of the road, both carriageway and pavements. The marchers, who included many women and some children, were orderly and in the main good humored. . . . When in due course they appeared at the west end of William Street it was obvious that their direct route to the Guildhall Square lay along William Street itself and that the march would come face to face with the Army at barrier 14 in that street. At this stage it became noticeable that a large number of youths, of what was described throughout the inquiry as the hooligan type, had placed themselves at the head of the march; indeed some of

them were in front of the lorry itself. . . . Some relatively minor exchanges took place between these youths and the soldiers manning the barriers which the march passed on its way to William Street, but nothing of real consequence occurred until the marchers reached the barriers in Little James Street and William Street. When the leaders of the march reached the junction of William Street and Rossville Street the lorry turned to its right to go along Rossville Street and the stewards made strenuous efforts to persuade the marchers to follow the lorry. . . .

25. However, this change of direction was not acceptable to a great many of the marchers. The stewards' attempts to divert the march were greeted with jeers and cat-calls. In the event although large numbers of nonviolent marchers were persuaded to turn to their right into Rossville Street a substantial number, not all of them youths, continued into the *cul-de-sac* created by the William Street barrier. The television films made by the BBC and Independent Television News show graphically how this crowd approached to within touching distance of the barrier itself. . . . The pressure of the crowd from behind was heavy and a densely packed mass formed at the barrier, which was 'manned by men of the Royal Green Jackets. The television films taken from behind the troops at the barrier show that the conduct of these soldiers was impeccable, despite the ugly situation which developed. The films show at least one middle-aged man making some attempt to move the barrier aside. Had other members of the crowd followed his example, the results might have been disastrous. A steward managed to divert this particular man from his intention. There is a very illuminating view in the television films of the packed crowd standing at the barrier spitting and shouting obscenities at the troops behind it. . . . After a time the movement of the crowd at the rear reduced the pressure on those at the front in William Street and the crowd at the barrier began to thin out somewhat. The hooligans at once took advantage of the opportunity to start stone-throwing on a very violent scale. Not only stones, but objects such as fire grates and metal rods used as lances were thrown violently at the troops in a most dangerous way. . . . Some witnesses have sought to play down this part of the incident and to suggest that it was nothing more than a little light stoning of the kind which occurs on most afternoons in this district and is accepted as customary. All I can say is that if this in any way represents normality the degree of violence to which the troops are normally subjected is very much greater than I suspect most people in Britain have appreciated. The troops responded with controlled volleys of rubber bullets but this was in some degree countered by the hooligans bringing forward an improvised shield of corrugated iron behind which they could shelter from the bullets. . . . Accordingly a water cannon which had been held in reserve was brought up behind the barrier and proceeded to drench the hooligan crowd with water colored with a purple dye. Unfortunately, from the soldiers' point of view, a canister of CS gas thrown by a member of the crowd happened to explode underneath the water cannon incommoding the crew who were not wearing their gas masks. The water cannon was therefore withdrawn for a few minutes and rubber bullets were fired again with little more effect than on the previous occasion. When the gas had cleared from the water cannon it was brought forward a 2d time and used upon the crowd to some effect. At about 1555 hours [3:55 p.m.] the troops appeared to be reaching a position in which they might disperse the rioters and relieve the pressure upon themselves. . . . It was at this point that the decision to go ahead with the arrest operation, for which 1 Para was earmarked, was made.

The Launching of the Arrest Operation

26. Since the tactics of the arrest operation were to be determined by the location and strength of the rioters at the time when it was launched, the brigade order left them to be decided by Lt. Col. Wilford commanding officer of 1 Para. He had 3 companies available for the arrest operation: A Company, C Company and Support Company, the latter being reinforced by a composite platoon from Administrative Company. (A 4th Company had been detached and put under command of 22 Light Air Defense Regiment for duties elsewhere in Londonderry.) In the event these 3 companies moved forward at the same time. A Company operated in the region of the Little Diamond and played no significant part in the events with which the inquiry was concerned. C Company went forward on foot through barrier 14 and along Chamberlain Street, while Support Company drove in vehicles through barrier 12 into Rossville Street to encircle rioters on the waste ground or pursued by C Company along Chamberlain Street. The only company of 1 Para to open fire that afternoon—other than with riot guns—was Support Company.

27. Before the wisdom of the order launching the arrest operation is considered it is necessary to decide who gave it. According to the commander 8 Brigade and his brigade major (Lt. Col. Steele) the operation was authorised by the brigadier personally, as indeed was envisaged in the brigade order. The order for 1 Para to go in and make arrests was passed by the brigade major to the commanding officer 1 Para on a secure wireless link, *i.e.*, one which was not open to eavesdropping. . . . The commanding officer 1 Para confirmed that he received the order and all 3 officers agreed that the order was in terms which left the commanding officer free to employ all 3 companies.

28. During the inquiry however it was contended that the brigadier did not authorize the arrest operation and that it was carried out by Lt. Col. Wilford in defiance of orders or without orders and on his own initiative. The suspicion that Lt. Col. Wilford acted without authority derives from the absence of any relevant order in the verbatim record of wireless traffic on the ordinary brigade net. This omission was due to the use of the secure wireless link for this one vital order. . . .

Should the Arrest Operation Have Been Launched At All?

31. By 1600 hours [4 p.m.] the pressure on barrier 14 had relaxed. There were still 100 to 200 hooligans in the William Street area but most of the non-violent marchers had either turned for home or were making their way down Rossville Street to attend a meeting at Free Derry Corner where about 500 were already assembled. . . . On the waste ground between the Rossville Flats and William Street there was a mixed crowd of perhaps 200 which included some rioters together with marchers, local residents, newspapermen and sightseers who were moving aimlessly about or chatting in groups. . . . This was the situation when commander 8 Brigade ordered 1 Para to move forward and make arrests.

32. In the light of events the wisdom of carrying out the arrest operation is debatable. The Army had achieved its main purpose of containing the march and although some rioters were still active in William Street they could have been dispersed without difficulty. . . .

*   *   *

The First High Velocity Rounds

35. Shortly before 4 o'clock, and before the Paras had moved across William Street, 2 incidents occurred there involving the firing of high velocity rounds. . . .

The officers of 1 Para had previously been engaged in the morning on reconnaissance of various routes that could be used if the battalion were called upon to move forward and make arrests in the area of Rossville Street and William Street. Obviously the battalion could move the barriers and go through them; but at one time it was thought that they might wish to enter William Street somewhat to the west of Little James Street in order to outflank the vacant land at "Aggro Corner" (the corner of William Street and Rossville Street). The company commander of the Support Company found a route over a wall by the side of the Presbyterian Church which he considered might be useful for this purpose, but which was obstructed by wire. Accordingly he sent a wire-cutting party to make this route usable if required. Whilst some soldiers from the Mortar Platoon were cutting the wire a single high velocity round was fired from somewhere near the Rossville Flats and struck a rainwater pipe on the side of the Presbyterian Church just above their heads. A large number of witnesses gave evidence about this incident, which clearly occurred, and which proves that at that stage there was at least one sniper, equipped with a high velocity weapon, established somewhere in the vicinity of the Rossville Flats and prepared to open fire on the soldiers.

36. The company commander of Support Company had sent a number of men forward to cover the wire-cutting party. Some of these men established themselves on the 2 lower floors of a 3-story derelict building on William Street, just to the west of some open land near the Presbyterian Church. They had not been there very long before their presence was noticed by some of the youths who were throwing stones in Little James Street. . . , a substantial party of whom shifted their attention to the soldiers in the derelict building. A hail of missiles was thrown at these soldiers. After a time Soldier A fired 2 rounds and Soldier B fired 3 rounds. There is no doubt that this shooting wounded Mr. John Johnson and Mr. Damien Donaghy. Evidence from civilians in the neighbourhood, including Mr. Johnson himself, is to the effect that although stones were being thrown no firearms or bombs were being used against the soldiers in the derelict building. Having seen and heard Mr. Johnson I have no doubt that he was telling the truth as he saw it. He was obviously an innocent passer-by going about his own business in Londonderry that afternoon and was almost certainly shot by accident. . . .

37. What then is the explanation of this incident from the Army side? Soldier A, a corporal; described the incident as follows. He was on the middle floor of the building. From the window he saw some young men, who were hanging around after the main body of the march had passed, start throwing stones and bottles at the soldiers on the ground floor, some of whom replied with rubber bullets. He then saw 2 smoking objects, about the size of a bean can, go sailing past the window; and heard 2 explosions, louder than the explosion of the rubber bullet guns. As the 2 smoking objects went past the window he shouted 'Nail bombs' as a warning to the men on the ground floor. His platoon sergeant called back an order that he was to shoot any nail bombers. He then saw, about 50 yards away on the other side of the road, a man look round the corner and dart back again. The man reappeared carrying an object in his right hand and made the actions of striking a fuse match against the wall with his left hand. When he brought his 2 hands together Soldier A assumed that he was about to light a nail bomb, took aim and fired at him. His first shot missed, so Soldier A fired again immediately and this time saw the man fall. Other people at once came out from the side of the building and dragged the man away.

38. Soldier B's description of the incident was in similar terms. He was on

the ground floor of the building with his platoon sergeant and 3 other soldiers of the platoon. A group of about 50 youths was throwing stones at them, undeterred by shots from the 2 baton guns which the soldiers had with them. Some of the stones came through the window space. He heard the explosion of 2 nail bombs on the waste ground to the left of the building, but did not see them in flight because he was putting on his gas mask at the time. He noticed one man come out from the waste ground across William Street carrying in his right hand a black cylindrical object which looked like a nail bomb. With his left hand he struck the wall with a match. Thinking that the man was about to light the nail bomb, and that there was no time to wait for orders from his platoon sergeant, Soldier B took aim and fired. As the first shot had no effect, he fired 2 more shots, whereupon the man fell back and was dragged away by 2 of his comrades. . . .

39. I find it impossible to reach any conclusion as to whether explosive substances were thrown at these soldiers or not. Mere negative evidence that nail bombs were not seen or heard is of relatively little importance in a situation in which there was already a great deal of noise. . . . Having seen Soldiers A and B vigorously cross-examined I accept that they thought, rightly or wrongly, that the missiles being thrown towards them included a nail bomb or bombs; and that they thought, rightly or wrongly, that one of the members of the crowd was engaged in suspicious action similar to that of striking a match and lighting a nail bomb. The soldiers fired in the belief that they were entitled to do so by their orders. . . .

Support Company in Action

40. An ammunition check on return to barracks showed that Support Company of 1 Para had, in the course of 30 January, expended 108 rounds of 7.62-mm. ammunition. This is the ammunition which is used in the SLR rifle, with which all ranks in the company were armed, except 3 who had submachine guns. Some of the men carried, in addition to their SLR, a baton gun or baton. The only other weapon with which the company was equipped that day was the Browning machine gun on a Ferret scout car. No Browning or submachine gun ammunition had been used. 5 rounds of 7.62-mm. ammunition had been fired by Soldiers A and B as already described in paragraph 36 above and one had been ejected unfired by a soldier in clearing a stoppage in his rifle. The remaining 102 rounds were fired by soldiers of Support Company in a period of under 30 minutes between 1610 and 1640 hours [4:10 and 4:40 p.m.]. About 20 more rounds were fired by the Army in Londonderry that afternoon, but not by 1 Para and not in the area with which the tribunal was primarily concerned.

41. Support Company advanced through barrier 12 and down Rossville Street in a convoy of 10 vehicles. A photograph taken very shortly afterwards shows the Guildhall clock standing at 10 minutes past 4. . . . In the lead was the the Mortar Platoon commanded by Lt. N, comprising 18 all ranks and travelling in 2 armored personnel carriers (APCs, colloquially known to the Army as "Pigs"). Next came the command APC of the company commander (Maj. 236) with a Ferret scout car in attendance. Following Company Headquarters came 2 empty APCs belonging to the Machine Gun Platoon. The men of this platoon had been detached earlier and did not rejoin the company in time to take part in the arrests. The 2 empty APCs were followed by 2 soft-skinned 4-ton lorries carrying the 36 all ranks of the Composite Platoon, commanded by Capt. SA8. The rear was brought up by 2 further APCs carrying the Anti-Tank Platoon, which consisted of Lt. 119 in command and 17 other ranks.

42. According to Maj. 236 his orders were simply to go through barrier 12 and arrest as many rioters as possible. As the rioters retreated down Rossville Street he went after them.

43. The leading APC (Lt. N) turned left off Rossville Street and halted on the waste ground near to where Eden Place used to be. The 2d APC (Sgt. O) went somewhat further and halted in the courtyard of the Rossville Flats near the north end of the western (or No. 1) Block. The platoon immediately dismounted. Soldier P and one or 2 others from Sgt. O's vehicle moved towards Rossville Street but the remainder of the platoon started to make arrests near to their vehicles.

44. Meanwhile the remainder of Support Company vehicles had halted in Rossville Street. The company commander (Maj. 236) says that his command vehicle came under fire so he moved it with his scout car in attendance to the north end of No 1 Block of the Flats to obtain cover. The soft-skinned vehicles of the Composite Platoon halted under cover of buildings at the south-east corner of the junction of William Street and Rossville Street, where the troops dismounted. The Anti-Tank Platoon's vehicles halted behind the 4-ton lorries and the men of that platoon dismounted and moved to Kells Walk. Some of these men were to appear later in Glenfada Park. The Composite Platoon commander deployed half of his men to the east in support of the Mortar Platoon, the other half to the west of the Anti-Tank Platoon.

45. Thereafter Support Company operated in 3 areas which require separate examination: the courtyard of the Rossville Flats; Rossville Street from Kells Walk to the improvised barricade; and lastly the area of Glenfada Park and Abbey Park.

(a) The activities of Mortar Platoon in the courtyard of the Rossville Flats

46. As soon as the vehicles appeared in William Street the crowd on the waste ground began to run away to the south and was augmented by many other people driven out of Chamberlain Street by C Company. . . . Some of the crowd ran along Rossville Street on the west side of Block 1 of the Flats, whilst the remainder ran into the courtyard on the north side of the Flats themselves. The crowd ran not because they thought the soldiers would open fire upon them but because they feared arrest. Though there was complete confidence that the soldiers would not fire unless fired upon, experienced citizens like Father [Edward K.] Daly recognized that an arrest operation was in progress and wished to avoid the rubber bullets and rough handling which this might involve. . . .

47. The APCs of Mortar Platoon penetrated more deeply than was expected by the crowd, which caused some panic. The only means of escape from the courtyard was the alleyway between Blocks 1 and 2 and that between Blocks 2 and 3, both of which rapidly became very congested. As soon as the vehicles halted the soldiers of Mortar Platoon began to make arrests. . . . But within a minute or 2 firing broke out and within about the next 10 minutes the soldiers of Mortar Platoon had fired 42 rounds of 7.62 mm ammunition and one casualty (John Duddy) lay dead in the courtyard.

48. This action in the courtyard is of special importance for 2 reasons. The first shots—other than those in William Street referred to in paragraphs 35 to 38—were fired here. Their sound must have caused other soldiers to believe that Support Company was under attack and made them more ready than they would have been to identify gunmen amongst the crowd. Secondly, the shooting by the Mortar Platoon in the courtyard was one of the incidents invoked by those who have accused the Army of firing indiscriminately on the backs of a fleeing crowd.

49. I have heard a great deal of evidence from civilians, including pressmen,

who were in the crowd in the courtyard, almost all to the effect that the troops did not come under attack but opened fire without provocation. The Army case is that as soon as they began to make arrests they themselves came under fire and their own shooting consisted of aimed shots at gunmen and bomb throwers who were attacking them. This issue, sometimes referred to as "Who fired first?", is probably the most important single issue which I have been required to determine.

50. A representative sample of the civilian evidence is as follows:

   (i) *Father Daly* was in the area out of concern for some elderly parishioners who lived there. Having seen the Army carry out arrest operations before on the waste ground he did not think that the vehicles would travel beyond Eden Place. He did not run away until he saw that they were coming further and he was accordingly at the back of the running crowd. He overtook John Duddy as he ran. He heard a shot and looking over his shoulder saw Duddy fall. He saw no weapon in Duddy's hands. Father Daly ran on and after a few yards he heard a "fusillade of gunfire," a "huge number" of shots which he recognised as live bullets; so he dived to the ground. He was convinced that all the shots came from behind and thought that the rest of the crowd also believed this to be the case. Apart from one civilian with a pistol he saw no weapon in other than Army hands. . . .

   (ii) *Mr. Simon Winchester*, a *Guardian* reporter, was walking across the open ground to the north of Rossville Flats when he met a crowd of people moving away from the William Street area towards Free Derry Corner. He decided to go with the crowd. A very short time later a number of armored vehicles swept in along Rossville Street and the crowd started running. Some ran along Rossville Street towards Free Derry Corner, others towards the exits between the 3 blocks of the Rossville Flats. Mr. Winchester heard a number of shots, probably less than 10, coming from behind him. He dropped to the ground, as did everyone else. In the ensuing panic and confusion he saw an injured man, bleeding profusely from the leg. Mr. Winchester did not see or hear any nail bombs or petrol bombs, nor see any weapons other than those carried by the Army. He did not hear firing other than that which he attributed to Army rifles until after he had made his way through to the south side of the Rossville Flats. He came away from the Bogside that day with the impression that he had seen soldiers fire needlessly into a huge crowd.

   (iii) *Mrs. Mary Bonnor*, who lives in the central block of the Rossville Flats, said that from her flat she saw a crowd running towards the Rossville Flats from William Street followed by 2 armored vehicles. Some soldiers jumped out. One of them knelt down and pointed his gun; another, firing from the waist, shot a boy in the back. Mrs. Bonnor said that she heard no shots until the soldiers shot the boy (John Duddy). That was the first shot she heard.

   (iv) *Mr. Derrick Tucker*, who is English by birth and has served in the Royal Navy and the Royal Air Force, also lives in the central block of the Rossville Flats. From his flat he saw people start to run and shout as the armored vehicles drove up Rossville Street. Soldiers at once jumped out and adopted firing positions beside their vehicle. One of them started firing towards the landings of the flats in Rossville Street. Mr. Tucker saw the shooting of John Duddy and of Michael Bridge, who was injured in the leg. He estimated that the interval between the soldiers getting out of their vehicles and starting to fire was between 30 seconds and 2 minutes. During that time he heard no explosions nor any firing directed at the soldiers. The only firing he heard was of gas canisters and rubber bullets at the junction of William Street and Rossville Street. He said that he felt sickened and degraded by the action of the British Army against unarmed civilians.

(v) *Mr. Joseph Doherty*, who lives in the Creggan, ran away when he saw the Army vehicles moving up Rossville Street. As he did so he saw some soldiers coming out of the end of Chamberlain Street. One of these soldiers fired a round into the ground in front of the crowd, so Mr. Doherty ran towards the alleyway between the blocks of flats. Looking back he saw the same soldier in the same position fire an aimed shot at someone he could not see. The shot into the ground was the first shot of the day of which he was aware. He did not see shooting at any stage, or hear nail bombs at any time.

(vi) *Mr. Francis Dunne*, a Londonderry schoolteacher, said that he was drifting across the open ground in front of the Rossville Flats towards Free Derry Corner. He was just short of Eden Place when the crowd on the open ground, which was very large, probably some hundreds, began to run. He ran too, as far as the north end of Block 1 of the Rossville Flats. From there he saw the armored vehicles driving in. He made for the alleyway between Blocks 1 and 2 and found it jammed with people. Up to that stage he was not aware of any shots. He saw 3 soldiers along the back of the houses in Chamberlain Street and heard firing start. He saw the soldier at the front fire. Those 3 soldiers were not being molested, though some youths were throwing stones towards the end of Block 1. The front soldier fired at and hit a tall fair-haired young man. Mr. Dunne saw that the alleyway through the flats was no longer jammed and went through it. His impression was that shots were comming through the alleyway towards him (*i.e.*, from the direction of the soldiers) and he realized that live bullets were being fired. He was certain that there was no firing at the soldiers from the Rossville Flats as he ran across the courtyard towards the flats. Neither were there any nail bombs. He was convinced that as the soldiers came in and immediately afterwards there could not have been fire on them from the Rossville Flats without him knowing about it.

51. Evidence from the Army side about the shooting in the courtyard came from Maj. 236, Lt. N, Sgt. O and each of the soldiers who had fired in that area. Although the entire action took place in an area barely 100 yards square the general confusion appears to have been such that, like the civilian witnesses, soldiers spoke only to their immediate and personal experiences.

(i) *Maj. 236* halted his command vehicle in Rossville Street ... and said that as he and his driver dismounted a burst of about 15 rounds of low velocity fire came towards them from the direction of Rossville Flats. They immediately moved the vehicle to a position at the north end of Block 1 in order to obtain cover from the shooting. There was, he said, continuous firing for the next 10 minutes. He saw 7 or 8 members of the Mortar Platoon firing aimed shots towards the Flats but he could not see what they were firing at. He said that these soldiers were under fire.

(ii) *Lt. N* on leaving his vehicle was faced by a man throwing stones whom he tried to arrest but failed as the strap of his helmet broke. He then moved towards Chamberlain Street where he was faced by a hostile crowd and fired a total of 3 shots above their heads in order to disperse them. . . . He then fired one further round at a man whom he thought was throwing a nail bomb in the direction of Sgt. O's vehicle. By this time the relevant firing in the courtyard was over and he had seen nothing of it.

(iii) *Sgt. O*, with 10 years' experience in the Parachute Regiment, had returned from a training course in Cyprus that very morning. When his vehicle halted he said that he and his men began to make arrests but were met with fire from the Rossville Flats. He thought that the fire came from 4 or 5 sources and possibly included some high velocity weapons. He saw the strike of bullets 4 or 5 meters from one of the members of his platoon. He and his men returned to his APC to secure their prisoners and then spread out in firing positions to engage those who had fired upon them. Sgt. O fired 3 rounds at a man firing a pistol from behind a car parked in the courtyard. The man fell and was carried away. He fired a further 3 rounds at a man standing at first floor level on the cat-walk connecting Blocks 2 and 3, who was firing a fairly short weapon like an M1 carbine. The flashes at the muzzle were visible. Sgt. O caught a glimpse of Soldier S firing at a man with a similar weapon but his view was obscured by people "milling about." The sergeant returned to his vehicle, but later fired 2 more rounds at a man whom he said was firing an M1 carbine from an alleyway between Blocks 2 and 3. He later saw Soldier T splashed with acid and told him that if further acid bombs were thrown he should return fire. He heard Soldier T fire 2 rounds and saw another acid bomb which had fallen. Sgt. O described the firing from the Flats as the most intense that he had seen in Northern Ireland in such a short space of time.

(iv) *Pvt. Q*, after dismounting from his vehicle, was being stoned and so took cover at the end of Block 1 of the Rossville Flats. There he heard 4 or 5 low velocity shots, that is to say shots fired by someone other than the Army, though he could not say from what direction. Shortly afterwards he saw a man throwing nail bombs, 2 of which simply rolled away whilst another one exploded near to the houses backing on to Chamberlain Street. He shot at and hit the man as he was in the act of throwing another nail bomb. That bomb did not explode and the man's body was dragged away.

(v) *Pvt. R* heard one or 2 explosions like small bombs from the back of Rossville Flats. He also heard firing of high and low calibre weapons. He noticed a man about 30 yards along the eastern side of Block 1, who made as if to throw a smoking object, whereupon Pvt. R fired at him. He thought he hit him high up on the shoulder, but was not certain what happened to the man because he was at that moment himself struck on the leg by an acid bomb thrown from an upper window in the Flats. A few moments later R saw a hand firing a pistol from the alleyway between Blocks 2 and 3. R fired 3 times. . . .

(vi) *Pvt. S* said that he came under fire as soon as he dismounted from his vehicle. The fire was fairly rapid single shots, from the area of the Rossville Flats. He dodged across to the back of one of the houses in

Chamberlain Street, from which position he saw a hail of bottles coming down from the Flats onto one of the armored vehicles and the soldiers around it. He fired a total of 12 shots at a gunman or gunmen who appeared, or reappeared, in front of the alleyway between Blocks 1 and 2 of the Flats. The gunman was firing what he thought was an M1 carbine. He thought that he scored 2 hits.

(vii) *Pvt. T* heard a burst of fire, possibly from a semi-automatic rifle being fired very quickly, about 30 to 45 seconds after dismounting from his vehicle. It came from somewhere inside the area of the Rossville Flats. He was splashed on the legs by acid from an acid bomb and noticed a person throwing acid bombs, about 3 storys up in the Flats. On the orders of his sergeant he fired 2 rounds at the acid bomb thrower. He thought that he did not score a hit.

(viii) *Lance Cpl. V* heard 2 explosions, not baton rounds, or rifle fire, before his vehicle stopped. As soon as he jumped out he heard rifle fire and saw several shots spurting into the ground to his right. He thought that this fire was coming from the alleyway between Blocks 1 and 2 of the Rossville Flats. He saw a crowd of about 100 towards the end of Chamberlain Street who were throwing stones and bricks. Cpl. V moved further forward and shot at and hit a man about 50 or 60 yards away from him in the act of throwing a bottle with a fuse attached to it.

52. A number of soldiers other than those of 1 Para gave evidence about the opening of fire. Capt. 028, a Royal Artillery officer attached to 1 Para as a press officer, saw the leading vehicle struck by a round before it came to a halt and saw a man open fire with a sub-machine gun from the barricade as the soldiers jumped out of their vehicles. A few minutes later, during the gun battle, he saw a man armed with a pistol come out from the south end of Block 1 of the Rossville Flats, and another man with a rifle at a window in the Flats. Lt. 227 of the Royal Artillery, who was in command of an observation post on the City Walls, heard 2 bursts of automatic fire from the Glenfada Park area after the arrest operation had begun and before he had heard any other sort of ball ammunition. He subsequently heard 3 or 4 pistol shots from the Rossville Flats area. Gunner 030, who was in a slightly different position on the City walls, saw a youth fire 5 or 6 shots with a pistol from the south-east corner of the Rossville Flats courtyard in the direction of Rossville Street. This was before 030 heard any fire from the Paras. Later on he heard a burst of automatic fire and saw a man with a machine gun running in Glenfada Park.

53. There was also a considerable body of civilian evidence about the presence of gunmen in the Bogside that afternoon, including some to the effect that they were the first to open fire. Father Daly saw a man armed with a pistol fire 2 or 3 shots at the soldiers from the south end of Chamberlain Street. Mr. Dunne saw the same gunman. Father O'Gara saw a youth armed with a pistol fire 3 shots at the soldiers from Kells Walk. Both these episodes took place after the soldiers had opened fire. Mr. Donnelly, a photographer of the Dublin newspaper the *Irish Times*, heard a single revolver shot in William Street 20 minutes before the Paras appeared on the scene; and Mr. Capper, a BBC reporter, heard a single revolver shot fired from the crowd he was with at Kells Walk in the direction of soldiers in William Street. He heard this shot after the shooting of Mr. Johnson and Mr. Donaghy in William Street, but before the Paras moved into Rossville Street. Mr. Beggin, a BBC cameraman, who went through the William Street barrier with soldiers of C Company and watched the soldiers of Support Company

crossing the open ground in front of the Rossville Flats, heard a number of shots fired apparently from the Flats before the soldiers themselves opened fire. Mr. Phillips, Mr. Seymour, Mr. Wilkinson and Mr. Hammond, members of an Independent Television News team, who also went through the William Street barrier behind the Paras, all heard machine-gun fire as the soldiers went across the open space. They also heard single shots but were not unanimous as to whether or not the automatic fire came first. It has been established that the troops did not use automatic weapons. So though the ITN men were not able to throw much light on the question of who fired first, their evidence did add considerable weight to the probability that the soldiers were fired on very soon after getting out of their vehicles. After the initial firing at the Rossville Street barricade, Mr. Mailey, a resident of Londonderry and a free-lance photographer, heard 3 shots of a much lower caliber than that of the Army's weapons. Mr. Winchester of the *Guardian* heard a single rifle shot from the direction of the Little Diamond some time before the Paras came through the barriers. A few minutes later and still before the Paras appeared, he saw youths clearing people away from an entrance to Columbcille Court in a manner which suggested to him that they were clearing a field of fire for a sniper. After he had reached the south side of the Rossville Flats he heard some low-caliber fire in answer to the Army's fire and also some automatic fire from the general direction of the Flats. Mr. Winchester and Mr. Wade of the *Daily Telegraph* were fired at by a gunman armed with a low-caliber weapon, possibly a .22 rifle, as they made their way out of the Bogside at the end of the afternoon after the main shooting was over. Mr. Bedell, a Londoner who was on holiday in Northern Ireland, was present at the meeting at Free Derry Corner. From there he saw the armored vehicles arrive in Rossville Street and heard firing. Some minutes later he saw several cars drive down from the Creggan. About 2 dozen men armed with rifles and automatic weapons got out, dispersed amongst the flats on the north side of Westland Street and fired about 50 rounds at the soldiers. When the gunmen withdrew, Mr. Bedell saw a crowd of about 50 civilians surround and give cover to one of the gunmen who had been separated from the main body, so that he was able to rejoin the others in safety. Mr. Kunioka, a Japanese student at the London Film School, saw a man armed with a rifle in Westland Street.

54. To those who seek to apportion responsibility for the events of 30 January the question "Who fired first?" is vital. I am entirely satisfied that the first firing in the courtyard was directed at the soldiers. Such a conclusion is not reached by counting heads or by selecting one particular witness as truthful in preference to another. It is a conclusion gradually built up over many days of listening to evidence and watching the demeanor of witnesses under cross-examination. It does not mean that witnesses who spoke in the opposite sense were not doing their best to be truthful. On the contrary I was much impressed by the care with which many of them, particularly the newspaper reporters, television men and photographers, gave evidence. Notwithstanding the opinion of Sgt. O I do not think that the initial firing from the Flats was particularly heavy and much of it may have been ill-directed fire from pistols and like weapons. The soldiers' response was immediate and members of the crowd running away in fear at the soldiers' presence understandably might fail to appreciate that the initial bursts had come from the direction of the Flats. . . . [Photos] confirm that the soldiers' initial action was to make arrests and there was no reason why they should have suddenly desisted and begun to shoot unless they had come under fire themselves. If the soldiers are wrong they were

parties in a lying conspiracy which must have come to light in the rigorous cross-examination to which they were subjected.

(b) The Action in Rossville Street

55. When the vehicle convoy halted in Rossville Street the Anti-Tank Platoon and one of the Composite Platoon deployed to their right in the vicinity of the flats known as Kells Walk. From this point it is possible to look due south down Rossville Street to the rubble barricade in that street and beyond it to Free Derry Corner. . . . The distance from Kells Walk to Free Derry Corner would be of the order of 300 yards. A considerable number of rounds was fired from Kells Walk in the direction of the barricade, at which at least 4 of the fatal casualties occurred.

56. It will be remembered that when the vehicles entered Rossville Street a densely packed crowd of perhaps 500 people was already assembled round the speakers' platform at Free Derry Corner and that the arrival of the soldiers caused some of the crowd on the waste ground also to run towards Free Derry Corner.

57. The barricade in Rossville Street running across from Glenfada Park to Block 1 of the Rossville Flats had fallen into disrepair and was only about 3 feet high. There was a gap to allow a single line of traffic to go through but there were also reinforcements of barbed wire on wooden knife rests. . . . Perhaps the most ugly of all the allegations made against the Army is that the soldiers at Kells Walk fired indiscriminately on a large and panic-stricken crowd which was seeking to escape over the barricade. The principal witness to support this allegation was Mr. James Chapman, a civil servant who had previously been a regular soldier in the British Army with the rank of Warrant Officer Class 1. He had been a resident of Londonderry for 36 years, 30 of them in the Bogside itself. He lived at No. 6 Glenfada Park, so that his sitting room window directly overlooked the Rossville Street barricade. He described how the main crowd of marchers, which he estimated at 5 or 6,000, had passed peacefully down Rossville Street before the soldiers' vehicles appeared. When the armored personnel carriers appeared and the rest of the crowd began to run some 50 to 100 soldiers deployed from their vehicles and according to Mr. Chapman immediately opened fire into the crowd trying to flee over the barricade. Mr. Chapman is reported as having said in a television interview on 3 February "I watched them shooting indiscriminately into a fleeing crowd of several thousand people, not just as some people say a few hundred hooligans." In fairness to Mr. Chapman there may have been some confusion here and at the inquiry his estimate of the crowd crossing the barricade was of the order of 200 to 300. He maintained, however, that the Army fired indiscriminately upon the backs of that number of people who were scrambling over the barricade in an effort to escape and that no firearms or bombs were being used against the soldiers at that time.

58. Mr. Robert Campbell, the assistant chief constable of the Renfrew and Bute Constabulary, who was observing the scene from the City wall, gave a very different account of events at the barricade. He could not see the entry of the vehicles but he had a clear view of part of the barricade in Rossville Street and of the whole of the area to the south of it down to Free Derry Corner. . . . He described how people streamed through the barricade on their way to the meeting at Free Derry Corner, but he also observed a group of demonstrators who detached themselves from the main crowd and remained close to the barricade from which they threw stones and other missiles in the direction of the Army vehicles. Mr. Campbell described their stone throwing as very active. After a time he heard

automatic fire from the direction of the Rossville Flats. As this did not deter the stone-throwers he assumed that the rounds did not go near them. The automatic fire was followed by a single high velocity shot which caused them to take cover. Within 2 or 3 minutes, however, the militants were throwing stones again. Then came a cluster of 10 or 12 high velocity rounds which finally scattered them, leaving 3 or 4 bodies lying at the barricade. Father [T. M.] O'Keefe, a lecturer in philosophy at the University of Ulster in Coleraine, gave a version of this incident which supported Mr. Campbell rather than Mr. Chapman. He said that when the armored personnel carriers arrived the bulk of the marchers had already moved to Free Derry Corner. He held back to make contact with friends and when the soldiers arrived he was part of a group of 25 to 30 people standing near the Rossville Street barricade. Whilst he and others took cover behind the gable end of the Glenfada Park Flats, some 5 or 6 remained at the barricade and he had the impression that stones were being thrown. . . . He said that the soldiers opened fire on the people at the barricade and he saw one of them hit and 3 bodies on the ground. At the end of his evidence I put Mr. Chapman's account to him:

"Q. One witness has told me that when the soldiers fired and hit the 3 young men standing at the barricade of whom you speak at that time 100 or 150 people were trying to make their way over and through the barricade in order to get to Free Derry Corner and that the 3 who were shot as they were endeavoring to climb over the barricade. I take it that that is not the picture as you saw it?

"A. That is not the picture I have at all."

Mr. Ronald Wood, an English born citizen of Londonderry, who had served in the Royal Navy, also spoke of 30 to 40 people near the barricade, some of whom were throwing stones. Mr. Donnelly, an *Irish Times* photographer, spoke of a thin line of about 20 youths and men behind the barricade. . . . Further, the pathologist's evidence about the 4 young men who were casualties at the barricade, namely Kelly, Young, Nash and McDaid, was that they were not shot from behind.

59. I am entirely satisfied that when the soldiers first fired at the barricade they did not do so on the backs of a fleeing crowd but at a time when some 30 people, many of whom were young men who were or had been throwing missiles, were standing in the vicinity of the barricade.

60. It was not alleged that the shots fired in Glenfada Park, which are dealt with in paragraphs 83 to 85 below, constituted firing on the backs of a fleeing crowd. But it was alleged that the crowd at Free Derry Corner was so fired on. What really happened at Free Derry Corner is clear because the evidence is almost all one way. If the line of fire from Kells Walk to the Rossville Street barricade is projected southward it comes dangerously close to Free Derry Corner. . . . When the soldiers began to fire at the barricade the crowd around the speakers' platform, though agitated by the sound of the shooting, did not immediately break up. A 2d burst however caused the crowd to fall flat on their faces and at the next lull in the firing they quickly dispersed. There is no evidence that any soldier deliberately fired at this crowd. Lord Brockway, who was attempting to address the meeting at the time, acknowledged as much. No one in this crowd was injured. . . .

PART III: RESPONSIBILITY

61. Having dealt with the allegations of a general character made against the conduct of 1 Para on 30 January I turn to consider the conduct of the individual

soldiers who fired and the circumstances in which the individual civilians were killed.

62. The starting point of this part of the inquiry is that 108 rounds of 7.62-mm. ammunition were expended by members of Support Company. The Browning gun on the company commander's scout car was not fired nor were the 3 sub-machine guns. No shots were fired by the other companies of 1 Para. I have no means of deciding which soldiers fired or how many rounds each fired except the evidence of the soldiers themselves. According to that evidence the allocation is as follows:

	Rounds		*Rounds*
Corporal A	2	Private M	2
Private B	3	Lieutenant N	5 (4 plus 1 ejected unfired)
Private C	5	Sergeant O	8
L/Corporal D	2	Corporal P	9
Corporal E	3	Private Q	1
L/Corporal F	13	Private R	4
Private G	6	Private S	12
Private H	22	Private T	2
L/Corporal J	2	Private U	1
Sergeant K	1	L/Corporal V	1
Private L	4		108

The Army case is that each of these shots was an aimed shot fired at a civilian holding or using a bomb or firearm. On the other side it was argued that none of the deceased was using a bomb or firearm and that the soldiers fired without justification and either deliberately or recklessly.

63. To solve this conflict it is necessary to identify the particular shot which killed each deceased and the soldier who fired it. It is then necessary to consider the justification put forward by the soldier for firing and whether the deceased was in fact using a firearm or bomb. It has proved impossible to reach conclusions with this degree of particularity. In 2 instances a bullet was recovered from the body, so that the rifle, and thus the firer, was positively identified. But several shots fired by the same rifle cannot be distinguished from one another and there is no certainty that a bullet hit the person at which it was aimed and whose conduct had caused the soldier to fire.

64. Another difficulty is that there is no certainty that the known casualty list is exhaustive. According to the Army evidence at least 25 civilians were hit, possibly more, of whom 5 or 6 were hit whilst firing from buildings or doorways. The Army's estimate of the number hit corresponds closely to the total number of known dead and wounded. But all the known dead, and all the wounded who gave evidence or about whom evidence was given, were hit in the open. Furthermore some of those whom the Paras were confident they hit . . . cannot be identified with any of the known dead or wounded. In addition, soldiers of the Royal Anglian Regiment and the Royal Artillery believe that they hit 6 or 7 gunmen on whom they returned fire in other parts of Londonderry on 30 January; and nothing more is known about these casualties. There is a widely held belief that on some previous occasions when shots have been exchanged in Londonderry, casualties amongst the IRA and their supporters have been spirited away over the border into the Republic. . . .

A. Were the Deceased Carrying Firearms or Bombs?

65. Mr. Campbell, the Scottish police officer, and a substantial number of soldiers gave evidence that they heard nail bombs exploding. The civilians were at one in denying that there were any such explosions. I did not conclude that some of the witnesses were necessarily lying on this point. Soldiers under attack, or expecting to be attacked, might well be quick to identify as nail bombs bangs otherwise unexplained. Conversely the civilians, hearing bangs at a time of confusion and panic and to the accompaniment of shouts and other loud noises, might be just as quick to attribute the bangs to the Army. Although a number of soldiers spoke of actually seeing firearms or bombs in the hands of civilians none was recovered by the Army. None of the many photographs shows a civilian holding an object that can with certainty be identified as a firearm or bomb. No casualties were suffered by the soldiers from firearms or gelignite bombs. In relation to every one of the deceased there were eye witnesses who said that they saw no bomb or firearm in his hands. The clothing of 11 of the deceased when examined for explosive residues showed no trace of gelignite. The 2 others were Gerald McKinney, whose clothing had been washed at the hospital and could not be tested, and Donaghy, in the pockets of whose clothing there had, on any view, been nail bombs and whose case is considered later.

66. The only other relevant forensic test applied to the deceased was the so-called paraffin test. When a firearm is discharged minute particles of lead are carried by the propellant gases. The particles carried forward through the muzzle may be deposited over a distance of 30 feet in front of the weapon. Some gases escape from the breach however, and deposit lead particles on the hands or clothing of the firer. . . . If swabs are taken from the firing hand of a man who has fired such a weapon they may be expected to show an even distribution of minute particles on the back of that hand and between the forefinger and thumb. Such a deposit, if not otherwise explained, is strong if not conclusive evidence of firing.

67. Before such a conclusion is accepted other possible sources of the lead contamination must be examined. Amongst these are: (*a*) being close to someone else who is firing; (*b*) being within 30 feet of the muzzle of the weapon fired in one's own direction; (*c*) physical transfer of lead particles on contact with the body or clothing of someone who has recently fired a weapon; (*d*) the passing at close range of a bullet which has been damaged by contact with a hard substance and which may spread lead particles from its damaged surface; (*e*) direct contact with lead in, say, the trade of a plumber or whilst loading a firearm.

68. In deciding whether lead found on a subject's hand or clothing should be attributed to his having fired a weapon or to some other cause much depends upon the pattern of the deposit itself. The characteristic of lead deposit from a weapon is an even distribution of minute particles, whereas the deposit from the handling of a body or object contaminated with lead is more likely to be in the form of a smear. According to the expert evidence of Dr. Martin of the Northern Ireland Department of Industrial & Forensic Science and Prof. Keith Simpson a concentration of minute particles on the hand creates a "strong suspicion" that the subject has been firing.

The Deceased Considered Individually

John Francis Duddy

69. Age 17. He was probably the first fatal casualty and fell in the courtyard of Rossville Flats. . . . As already recounted (paragraph 50(i)) he was seen

to fall by Father Daly. Mrs. Bonnor and Mrs. Duffy both spoke of seeing a soldier fire at him. According to Mrs. Bonnor he was shot in the back. In fact the bullet entered his right shoulder and travelled through his body from right to left. As he ran he turned from time to time to watch the soldiers. This fits in with Father Daly having overtaken him while running and explains the entry wound being in his side. No shot described by a soldier precisely fits Duddy's case. The nearest is one described by Soldier V who spoke of firing at a man in a white shirt in the act of throwing a petrol bomb, but Duddy was wearing a red shirt and there is no evidence of his having a bomb. His reaction to the paraffin test was negative. I accept that Duddy was not carrying a bomb or firearm. The probable explanation of his death is that he was hit by a bullet intended for someone else.

Patrick Joseph Doherty

70. Age 31. His body was found in the area at the rear of No 2 Block of Rossville Flats between that Block and Joseph Place. His last moments are depicted in a remarkable series of photographs taken by Mr. Peress which show him with a handkerchief over the lower part of his face crawling with others near the alleyway which separates No 2 Block from No 3. . . . He was certainly hit from behind whilst crawling or crouching because the bullet entered his buttock and proceeded through his body almost parallel to the spine. There is some doubt as to whether he was shot when in the alleyway or at the point where his body was found. On the whole I prefer the latter conclusion. If this is so the probability is that he was shot by Soldier F, who spoke of hearing pistol shots and seeing a crouching man firing a pistol from the position where Doherty's body was found. Soldier F said that he fired as the man turned away, which would account for an entry wound in the buttock. Doherty's reaction to the paraffin test was negative. In the light of all the evidence I conclude that he was not carrying a weapon. If Soldier F shot Doherty in the belief that he had a pistol that belief was mistaken.

Hugh Pius Gilmore

71. Age 17. Gilmore died near the telephone box which stands south of Rossville Flats and near the alleyway separating Blocks 1 and 2. According to Miss Richmond he was one of a crowd of 30 to 50 people who ran away down Rossville Street when the soldiers appeared. She described his being hit just before he reached the barricade and told how she helped him to run across the barricade towards the point where he collapsed. A photograph of Gilmore by Mr. Robert White . . . , which according to Miss Richmond was taken after he was hit, shows no weapon in his hand. The track of the bullet is not consistent with Gilmore being shot from directly behind and I think it likely that the statement of Mr. Sean McDermott is more accurate on this point than the evidence of Miss Richmond. Mr. McDermott put Gilmore as standing on the barricade in Rossville Street when he was hit and in a position such that his front or side may have been presented to the soldiers.

72. Gilmore was shot by one of the soldiers who fired from Kells Walk at the men at the barricade. It is impossible to identify the soldier. Gilmore's reaction to the paraffin test was negative. There is no evidence that he used a weapon.

Bernard McGuigan

73. Age 41. This man was shot within a short distance of Gilmore, on the south side of No 2 Block of the Rossville Flats. According to Miss Richmond

a wounded man was calling for help and Mr. McGuigan, carrying a white handkerchief, deliberately left a position of cover to attend to him. She said that he
was shot almost at once. Other civilian witnesses confirmed this evidence and
photographs of McGuigan's body show the white handkerchief in question. . . .
Although there was some evidence that the shot came from Glenfada Park, which
means that the soldier who fired might have been Soldier F, another possibility is
that the shot came through the alleyway between Blocks 1 and 2. I cannot form
any worthwhile conclusion on this point.

74. Although the eye witnesses all denied that McGuigan had a weapon, the
paraffin test disclosed lead deposits on the right palm and the web, back and palm
of his left hand. The deposit on the right hand was in the form of a smear, those
on the left hand were similar to the deposits produced by a firearm. The earlier
photographs of McGuigan's body show his head uncovered but in a later one it
is covered with a scarf. . . . The scarf showed a heavy deposit of lead, the
distribution and density of which was consistent with the scarf having been used
to wrap a revolver which had been fired several times. His widow was called to
say that the scarf did not belong to him. I accept her evidence in concluding it is
not possible to say that McGuigan was using or carrying a weapon at the time
when he was shot. The paraffin test, however, constitutes ground for suspicion
that he had been in close proximity to someone who had fired.

John Pius Young

75. Age 17. This young man was one of 3 who were shot at the Rossville
Street barricade by one of the cluster of 10 to 12 shots referred to by Mr. Cam-
bell (paragraph 58 above refers). (Mr. Mailey's EP 23/4. Mr. Mailey said that 2
men fell immediately after he took this photograph.) Young was undoubtedly
associated with the youths who were throwing missiles at the soldiers from the
barricade and the track of the bullet suggests that he was facing the soldiers at the
time. Several soldiers, notably P, J, U, C, K, L and M all said that they fired from
the Kells Walk area at men who were using firearms or throwing missiles from the
barricade. It is not possible to identify the particular soldier who shot Young.

76. The paraffin test disclosed particles on the web, back and palm of the
left hand which were consistent with exposure to discharge gases from firearms.
The body of Young, together with those of McDaid and Nash, was recovered
from the barricade by soldiers of 1 Para and taken to hospital in an APC. It was
contended at the hearing that the lead particles on Young's left hand might have
been transferred from the hands of the soldiers who carried him or from the
interior of the APC itself. Although these possibilities cannot be wholly
excluded, the distribution of the particles seems to me to be more consistent with
Young having discharged a firearm. When his case is considered in conjunction
with those of Nash and McDaid and regard is had to the soldiers' evidence about
civilians firing from the barricade a very strong suspicion is raised that one or
more of Young, Nash and McDaid was using a firearm. No weapon was
found. . . .

Michael McDaid

77. Age 20. This man was shot when close to Young at the Rossville Street
barricade. The bullet struck him in the front in the left cheek. The paraffin test
disclosed abnormal lead particle density on his jacket and one large particle of
lead on the back of the right hand. Any of the soldiers considered in connection
with the death of Young might equally well have shot McDaid. Dr. Martin
thought that the lead density was consistent with McDaid having handled a

firearm, but I think it more consistent with his having been in close proximity to someone firing.

William Noel Nash

78. Age 19. He also was close to Young and McDaid at the Rossville Street barricade and the 3 men were shot almost simultaneously. The bullet entered his chest from the front and particles of lead were detected on the web, back and palm of his left hand with a distribution consistent with his having used a firearm. Soldier P (who can be seen in Mr. Mailey's photographs EP 23/7 and 8; he is looking up the alleyway in No 7) spoke of seeing a man firing a pistol from the barricade and said that he fired 4 shots at this man, one of which hit him in the chest. He thought that the pistol was removed by other civilians. In view of the site of the injury it is possible that Soldier P has given an accurate account of the death of Nash.

79. Mr. Alexander Nash, father of William Nash, was wounded at the barricade. From a position of cover he saw that his son had been hit and went to help him. As he did so he himself was hit in the left arm. The medical opinion was that the bullet came from a low velocity weapon and Soldier U described seeing Mr. Nash senior hit by a revolver shot fired from the entrance to the Rossville Flats. The soldier saw no more than the weapon and the hand holding it. I think that the most probable explanation of this injury is that it was inflicted by a civilian firing haphazardly in the general direction of the soldiers without exposing himself enough to take proper aim.

Michael Kelly

80. Age 17. Kelly was shot while standing at the Rossville Street barricade in circumstances similar to those already described in the cases of Young, Nash and McDaid. The bullet entered his abdomen from the front which disposes of a suggestion in the evidence that he was running away at the time. The bullet was recovered and proved that Kelly was shot by Soldier F, who described having fired one shot from the Kells Walk area at a man at the barricade who was attempting to throw what appeared to be a nail bomb. . . .

81. The lead particle density on Kelly's right cuff was above normal and was, I think, consistent with his having been close to someone using a firearm. This lends further support to the view that someone was firing at the soldiers from the barricade, but I do not think that this was Kelly nor am I satisfied that he was throwing a bomb at the time when he was shot.

Kevin McElhinney

82. Age 17. He was shot whilst crawling southwards along the pavement on the west side of No 1 Block of Rossville Flats at a point between the barricade and the entrance to the Flats. The bullet entered his buttock so that it is clear that he was shot from behind by a soldier in the area of Kells Walk. Lead particles were detected on the back of the left hand and the quantity of particles on the back of his jacket was significantly above normal, but this may have been due to the fact that the bullet had been damaged. Dr. Martin thought the lead test inconclusive on this account. Although McElhinney may have been hit by any of the rounds fired from Kells Walk in the direction of the barricade . . . it seems probable that the firer was Sgt. K. This senior NCO was a qualified marksman whose rifle was fitted with a telescopic sight and who fired only one round in the course of the afternoon. He described 2 men crawling from the barricade in the direction of the door of the flats and said that the rear man was

carrying a rifle. He fired one aimed shot but could not say whether it hit. Sgt. K obviously acted with responsibility and restraint. Though I hesitate to make a positive finding against a deceased man, I was much impressed by Sgt. K's evidence.

James Joseph Wray, Gerald McKinney, Gerald Donaghy and William McKinney

83. These 4 men were all shot somewhere near the south-west corner of the more northerly of the 2 courtyards of the flats at Glenfada Park. Their respective ages were 22, 35, 17 and 26. The 2 McKinneys were not related. 3 other men wounded in the same area were [Michael] Quinn, [Patrick] O'Donnell and [Joseph] Friel. I deal with the cases of these 4 deceased together because I find the evidence too confused and too contradictory to make separate consideration possible. One important respect in which the shooting in Glenfada Park differs from that at the Rossville Street barricade and in the forecourt of the Rossville Flats is that there is no photographic evidence.

84. 4 soldiers, all from the Anti-Tank Platoon, fired in this area, namely E, F, G and H. Initially the platoon deployed in the Kells Walk area and was involved in the firing at the Rossville Street barricade. It will be remembered that at this time some 30 or 40 people were in the region of the barricade, of whom some were engaging the soldiers whilst others were taking cover behind the nearby gable end of the flats in Glenfada Park. ... Cpl. E described how he saw civilians firing from the barricade and then noticed some people move towards the courtyard of Glenfada Park. He said that on his own initiative he accordingly led a small group of soldiers into the courtyard from the north-east corner to cut these people off. The recollection of the platoon commander (Lt. 119) was somewhat different; he said that he sent Soldiers E and F into the courtyard of Glenfada Park to cut off a particular gunman who had been firing from the barricade. The result in any event was that Soldiers E and F advanced into the courtyard and Soldiers G and H followed shortly afterwards. In the next few minutes there was a very confused scene in which according to civilian evidence some of the people who had been sheltering near the gable end of Glenfada Park sought to escape by running through the courtyard in the direction of Abbey Park and the soldiers fired upon them killing the 4 men named at the head of this paragraph. Soldiers E, F and G gave an account of having been attacked by the civilians in this group and having fired in reply. Soldier H gave an account of his activities with which I deal later. From the forensic evidence about a bullet recovered from the body it is known that Soldier G shot Donaghy. It is clear that the other 3 were shot by Soldiers E, F, G or H. Although several witnesses spoke of having seen the bodies there was a conflict of evidence as to whether they fell in the courtyard of Glenfada Park or between Glenfada Park and Abbey Park. The incident ended when the 20 to 30 civilians remaining in the courtyard were arrested on the orders of the platoon commander, who came into Glenfada Park just as the shooting finished.

85. In the face of such confused testimony it is difficult to reach firm conclusions but it seems to me more probable that the civilians in Glenfada Park were running away than that they were seeking a battle with the soldiers in such a confined space. It may well be that some of them had been attacking the soldiers from the barricade, a possibility somewhat strengthened by the forensic evidence. The paraffin tests on the hand swabs and clothing of Gerald McKinney and William McKinney were negative. Dr. Martin did not regard the results of the tests on Donaghy as positive but Prof. Simpson did. The 2 experts agreed that the results of the tests on Wray were consistent with his having used a firearm. However, the balance of probability suggests that at the time when these 4 men

were shot the group of civilians was not acting aggressively and that the shots were fired without justification. I am fortified in this view by the account given by Soldier H, who spoke of seeing a rifleman firing from a window of a flat on the south side of the Glenfada Park courtyard. Soldier H said that he fired an aimed shot at the man, who withdrew but returned a few moments later, whereupon Soldier H fired again. This process was repeated until Soldier H had fired 19 shots, with a break for a change of magazine. It is highly improbable that this cycle of events should repeat itself 19 times; and indeed it did not. I accepted evidence subsequently given, supported by photographs, which showed that no shot at all had been fired through the window in question. So 19 of the 22 shots fired by Soldier H were wholly unaccounted for.

86. A special feature of Gerald Donaghy's case has some relevance to his activities in the course of the afternoon although it does not directly bear on the circumstances in which he was shot.

87. After Donaghy fell he was taken into the house of Mr. Raymond Rogan at 10 Abbey Park. He had been shot in the abdomen. He was wearing a blue denim blouse and trousers with pockets of the kind that open to the front rather than to the side. The evidence was that some at least of his pockets were examined for evidence of his identity and that his body was examined by Dr. Kevin Swords, who normally worked in a hospital in Lincoln. Dr. Swords' opinion was that Donaghy was alive but should go to hospital immediately. Mr. Rogan volunteered to drive him there in his car. Mr. Leo Young went with him to help. The car was stopped at a military check-point in Barrack Street, where Mr. Rogan and Mr. Young were made to get out. The car was then driven by a soldier to the Regimental Aid Post of 1st Battalion Royal Anglian Regiment, where Donaghy was examined by the medical officer (Soldier 138) who pronounced him dead. The medical officer made a more detailed examination shortly afterwards but on neither occasion did he notice anything unusual in Donaghy's pockets. After another short interval, and whilst Donaghy's body still lay on the back seat of Mr. Rogan's car, it was noticed that he had a nail bomb in one of his trouser pockets (as photographed in RUC photographs EP 5A/26 and 27). An ammunition technical officer (bomb disposal officer, Soldier 127) was sent for and found 4 nail bombs in Donaghy's pockets.

88. There are 2 possible explanations of this evidence. First, that the bombs had been in Donaghy's pockets throughout and had passed unnoticed by the Royal Anglians' medical officer, Dr. Swords, and others who had examined the body; secondly that the bombs had been deliberately planted on the body by some unknown person after the medical officer's examination. These possibilities were exhaustively examined in evidence because, although the matter is a relatively unimportant detail of the events of the afternoon, it is no doubt of great concern to Donaghy's family. I think that on a balance of probabilities the bombs were in Donaghy's pockets throughout. His jacket and trousers were not removed but were merely opened as he lay on his back in the car. It seems likely that these relatively bulky objects would have been noticed when Donaghy's body was examined; but it is conceivable that they were not and the alternative explanation of a plant is mere speculation. No evidence was offered as to where the bombs might have come from, who might have placed them or why Donaghy should have been singled out for this treatment.

B. *Were the Soldiers Justified in Firing?*

89. Troops on duty in Northern Ireland have standing instructions for opening fire. These instructions are set out upon the yellow card which every soldier is required to carry. Soldiers operating collectively—a term which is not

itself defined—are not to open fire without an order from the commander on the spot. Soldiers acting individually are generally required to give warning before opening fire and are subject to other general rules which provide *inter alia:*

"2. Never use more force than the *minimum* necessary to enable you to carry out your duties.

"3. Always first try to handle the situation by other means than opening fire. If you have to fire: (*a*) Fire only aimed shots. (*b*) Do not fire more rounds than are absolutely necessary to achieve your aim."

The injunction to fire only aimed shots is understood by the soldiers as ruling out shooting from the hip. . . .

90. Other stringent restrictions apply to soldiers who have given warning of intention to fire. But the rule of principal significance to the events of 30 January is that which contemplates a situation in which it is not practicable to give a warning. It provides:

"You may fire without warning . . . 13. Either when hostile firing is taking place in your area, and a warning is impracticable, or when any delay could lead to death or serious injury to people whom it is your duty to protect or to yourself; *and then only:* (*a*) against a person using a firearm against members of the security forces or people whom it is your duty to protect; or (*b*) against a person carrying a firearm if you have reason to think he is about to use it for offensive purposes."

The term "firearm" is defined as including a grenade, nail bomb or gelignite-type bomb.

*   *   *

93. Many people will be surprised to learn that it is not open to the soldier to give warning by firing warning shots. As has already been seen, the soldier is required to "fire only aimed shots." Whilst the yellow card does not in terms forbid a soldier hard pressed by an advancing mob to fire over their heads, to do so is certainly a breach of the orders. The justification put forward for this somewhat surprising provision is that hooligans would rapidly note and take advantage of the regular firing of shots meant to pass harmlessly by; the carrying of firearms would cease to deter.

*   *   *

97. Those accustomed to listening to witnesses could not fail to be impressed by the demeanour of the soldiers of 1 Para. They gave their evidence with confidence and without hesitation or prevarication and withstood a rigorous cross-examination without contradicting themselves or each other. With one or 2 exceptions I accept that they were telling the truth as they remembered it. But did they take sufficient care before firing and was their conduct justified, even if the circumstances were as they described them?

98. There were infringements of the rules of the yellow card. Lt. N fired 3 rounds over the heads of a threatening crowd and dispersed it. Cpl. P did likewise. Soldier T, on the authority of Sgt. O, fired at a person whom he believed to be throwing acid bombs and Soldier V said he fired on a petrol bomber. Although these actions were not authorized by the yellow card they do not seem to point to a breakdown in discipline or to require censure. Indeed in 3 of the 4 cases it could be held that the person firing was, as the senior officer or NCO on the spot, the person entitled to give orders for such firing.

99. Grounds put forward for identifying gunmen at windows were sometimes flimsy. Thus Soldier F fired 3 rounds at a window in Rossville Flats after having been told by another soldier that there was a gunman there. He did not seem to have verified the information except by his observation of "a movement" at the window. Whether or not it was fired by Soldier H a round went through the window of a house in Glenfada Park into an empty room. The only people in the house were an old couple who happily were sitting in another room. In all 17 rounds were fired at the windows of flats and houses, not counting Soldier H's 19 rounds.

100. The identification of supposed nail bombers was equally nebulous—perhaps necessarily so. A nail bomb looks very much like half a brick and often the only means of distinguishing between a stone-thrower and a nail-bomber is that a light enough stone may be thrown with a flexed elbow whereas a nail bomb is usually thrown with a straight arm as in a bowling action.

101. Even assuming a legitimate target, the number of rounds fired was sometimes excessive. Soldier S's firing of 12 rounds into the alleyway between Blocks 1 and 2 of the Rossville Flats seems to me to have been unjustifiably dangerous for people round about.

102. Nevertheless in the majority of cases the soldier gave an explanation which, if true, justified his action. A typical phrase is "I saw a civilian aiming what I thought was a firearm and I fired an aimed shot at him." In the main I accept these accounts as a faithful reflection of the soldier's recollection of the incident; but there is no simple way of deciding whether his judgment was at fault or whether his decision was conscientiously made. Some of the soldiers showed a high degree of responsibility. Examples of this are the experienced Sgt. K, already referred to, and the 18-year-old Soldier R. At the other end of the scale are some of the soldiers who fired in Glenfada Park in the circumstances described in paragraphs 83 to 85 above. Between these extremes a judgment must be based on the general impression of the soldiers' attitudes as a whole. There is no question of the soldiers firing in panic to protect their own skins. They were far too steady for that. But where soldiers are required to engage gunmen who are in close proximity to innocent civilians they are set an impossible task. Either they must go all out for the gunmen, in which case the innocent suffer; or they must put the safety of the innocent first, in which case many gunmen will escape and the risk to themselves will be increased. The only unit whose attitude to this problem I have examined is 1 Para. . . . In 1 Para the soldiers are trained to go for the gunmen and make their decisions quickly. In these circumstances it is not remarkable that mistakes were made and some innocent civilians hit.

103. In reaching these conclusions I have not been unmindful of the numerous allegations of misconduct by individual soldiers which were made in the course of the evidence. I considered that allegations of brutality by the soldiers in the course of making arrests were outside my terms of reference. There is no doubt that people who resisted or tried to avoid arrest were apt to be roughly handled; but whether excessive force was used is something which I have not investigated.

104. There have also been numerous allegations of soldiers firing carelessly from the hip or shooting deliberately at individuals who were clearly unarmed. These were all isolated allegations in which the soldier was not identified and which I could not investigate further. If, and insofar as, such incidents occurred the soldier in question must have accounted for the rounds fired by giving some different and lying story of how they were expended. Though such a possibility

cannot be excluded, in general the accounts given by the soldiers of the circumstances in which they fired and the reasons why they did so were, in my opinion, truthful.

SUMMARY OF CONCLUSIONS

1. There would have been no deaths in Londonderry on 30 January if those who organized the illegal march had not thereby created a highly dangerous situation in which a clash between demonstrators and the security forces was almost inevitable.

2. The decision to contain the march within the Bogside and Creggan had been opposed by the chief superintendent of police in Londonderry but was fully justified by events and was successfully carried out.

3. If the Army had persisted in its "low key" attitude and had not launched a large scale operation to arrest hooligans the day might have passed off without serious incident.

4. The intention of the senior Army officers to use 1 Para as an arrest force and not for other offensive purposes was sincere.

5. An arrest operation carried out in battalion strength in circumstances in which the troops were likely to come under fire involved hazard to civilians in the area which commander 8 Brigade may have underestimated.

6. The order to launch the arrest operation was given by commander 8 Brigade. The tactical details were properly left to CO 1 Para who did not exceed his orders. In view of the experience of the unit in operations of this kind it was not necessary for CO 1 Para to give orders in greater detail than he did.

7. When the vehicles and soldiers of Support Company appeared in Rossville Street they came under fire. Arrests were made; but in a very short time the arrest operation took 2d place and the soldiers turned to engage their assailants. There is no reason to suppose that the soldiers would have opened fire if they had not been fired upon first.

8. Soldiers who identified armed gunmen fired upon them in accordance with the standing orders in the yellow card. Each soldier was his own judge of whether he had identified a gunman. Their training made them aggressive and quick in decision and some showed more restraint in opening fire than others. At one end of the scale some soldiers showed a high degree of responsibility; at the other, notably in Glenfada Park, firing bordered on the reckless. These distinctions reflect differences in the character and temperament of the soldiers concerned.

9. The standing orders contained in the yellow card are satisfactory. Any further restrictions on opening fire would inhibit the soldier from taking proper steps for his own safety and that of his comrades and unduly hamper the engagement of gunmen.

10. None of the deceased or wounded is proved to have been shot whilst handling a firearm or bomb. Some are wholly acquitted of complicity in such action; but there is a strong suspicion that some others had been firing weapons or handling bombs in the course of the afternoon and that yet others had been closely supporting them.

11. There was no general breakdown in discipline. For the most part the soldiers acted as they did because they thought their orders required it. No order and no training can ensure that a soldier will always act wisely, as well as bravely and with initiative. The individual soldier ought not to have to bear the burden of

deciding whether to open fire in confusion such as prevailed on 30 January. In the conditions prevailing in Northern Ireland, however, this is often inescapable.

WIDGERY

W. J. Smith, *Secretary*
10 *April* 1972

The British government announced Apr. 27 that it would offer "appropriate compensation" to innocent victims of the shootings in Londonderry.

Initial Reaction to Report

Catholics in Northern Ireland Apr. 19 largely dismissed Lord Widgery's report as a "whitewash." Bernadette Devlin called Widgery "a liar." Ivan Cooper, a Catholic politician in Londonderry, called him "an accessory to the actions of the paratroopers." Kevin McCorry, a leader of the Northern Ireland Civil Rights Association, said the report was "an attempt to excuse murder by saying that the Army was provoked." He predicted that the report would "have the effect of lessening still further" the credibility of the British government in its recent takeover of direct rule in Northern Ireland.

Bernard Weinraub of the *N.Y. Times* reported Apr. 19 that "Catholic moderates were angry, too." Weinraub quoted Tom Conaty, chairman of Belfast's Falls Road area Central Citizens Defense Committee, as saying: " 'I think it is the best recruiting pamphlet for the IRA I have seen in a long time. It destroys the credibility of anyone who says, "Give Britain a chance. She will do the right thing." ' " Weinraub continued: "In Londonderry, James Wray, whose 22-year-old son [James Joseph] was one of the 13 victims, said simply: 'I am glad I fathered the son who died, rather than fathered the son who murdered him.' And the Rev. Edward Daly, who testified before Lord Widgery, said: 'I'm flabbergasted. It's a disgraceful report.' "

Irish Republic Prime Min. John Lynch said Apr. 19 that he found "it difficult to see how Lord Widgery reached his conclusions" and called again for an "international examination" to study the British Army's rôle in Ulster. "The main lesson to be drawn from the events in the North and the now numerous reports on them is that Britain must prepare to move, in conjunction with Ireland, toward a general settlement which would end permanently and peacefully the remaining problem in Anglo-Irish relations," Lynch added.

British Defense Secy. Lord Carrington was one of the few public figures in Great Britain to express a favorable reaction. Carrington said Apr. 19 that he was "very satisfied" with the Widgery report's findings, in view of the allegations of "willful murder." The Defense Ministry ruled out any action against the soldiers involved in the clash.

The British journalist Simon Winchester, who had testified as an eye-witness in the Widgery inquiry, criticized Widgery in a commentary spread 5 columns wide over most of one page in the Apr. 29, 1972 Manchester *Guardian Weekly:* "According to Lord Widgery, the facts of 'Bloody Sunday' . . . vindicate the Army's operation in principle but imply serious criticism of the judgment with which some soldiers carried out their orders. His report has been 'accepted' by the [British] government but no formal action is contemplated. . . . Lord Carrington, secretary for defense, said that on the whole the Army had reason to be proud of itself and expressed the . . . hope that the events of Jan. 30 could now be forgotten. . . . The tribunal's conclusions were widely described as a 'whitewash' job which would arouse resentment and make Mr. William Whitelaw's job of conciliation in Northern Ireland more difficult. . . . The Army in Northern Ireland is privately delighted with the report and most Protestants are also happy. But Mr. Eddie McAteer, president of the Nationalist Party, who was at the Civil Rights March on Bloody Sunday, said of the report: 'This is a political judgment by a British officer and a British judge upon his darling British Army.' Catholic reaction in the streets was equally strong. One man in the Falls Road said: 'We knew they didn't mind murdering us but at least we thought they might admit it.' And in Londonderry itself the relatives of those who lost their lives were upset and dismayed that the tribunal had done nothing to clear their names. . . . To those of us who were in Derry on that ghastly, though brilliant winter's day 10 weeks ago—who lay in gutters and hid behind walls and saw the blood and the terrible grief of it—the report will come as a profound disappointment. The good and impartial judge comes to conclusions which disagree fundamentally with those most of us came to, or were forced to come to when we heard the casualty figures from Altnagevin Hospital. . . ."

Continuing Terrorism

The "Bloody Sunday Massacre" in Londonderry Jan. 30 had evoked IRA vows of vengeance on the British Army. The first act of reprisal took place Feb. 1, 1972 when a sniper shot to death a British sentry in Belfast.

A man was shot and killed during rioting in Belfast's Catholic districts Feb. 2 after funeral services for 12 of the 13 Londonderry dead, and a bomb exploded in a suburban Belfast pub, killing one person.

2 British soldiers were killed Feb. 10 when a mine destroyed their patrol car near the border with the Irish Republic at Cullyhanna. 2 other soldiers were killed by terrorists Feb. 13 and Feb. 16.

A Catholic bus driver was dragged from his bus by terrorists in Londonderry Feb. 16. His body was later found on the city outskirts, shot in the head. The victim was a member of the Ulster Defense Regiment, the equivalent of the national militia. (More than 200 Catholic and Protestant workers jointly staged a one-day strike in Londonderry Feb. 17 in protest against the bus driver's execution.)

The IRA's terrorist campaign struck in England Feb. 22 when a bomb explosion at the Aldershot Army base, 35 miles from London, killed 5 waitresses, a gardener and an Army chaplain, Father Weston. 17 other persons, 14 of them soldiers, were injured. The explosion ripped through the officers' mess of the parachute brigade that had been involved in the Londonderry shootings. The bomb had been planted in a car parked in front of the kitchen where the civilian staff was preparing lunch. The dining room was empty at the time of the blast. A spokesman for the IRA Officials claimed responsibility for the blast as retaliation for the "Londonderry massacre." In a subsequent statement, the IRA said that "any civilian casualties would be very much regretted, as our target was the officers responsible for the Derry outrages." An IRA statement issued Feb. 23 said the persons responsible for the blast had returned safely to Dublin. But an unidentified man was charged with murder Mar. 5 in the Aldershot bombing. The man had been arrested in London Mar. 3. 2 unidentified men had been charged Feb. 27 with conspiracy to cause the Aldershot explosion and with illegal possession of arms.

John Taylor, Stormont's minister of state for home affairs, was shot and seriously wounded in Belfast Feb. 25 by IRA terrorists. A right-wing hardliner in his attitude toward Catholic opponents of the Ulster régime, he was the first government minister to be shot by terrorists. Hospital bulletins reported that Taylor would not suffer permanent injury from the bullet wounds in his neck, jaw and chest. Taylor was attacked as he got into his car in the center of the city. The IRA Officials, in a statement issued Feb. 25 in Dublin, claimed responsibility for the assassination attempt. It said that Taylor was one of the principal architects of internment without trial and was "primarily responsible for the attitude of the British Army" in the Londonderry killings. The statement cited other tough anti-terrorist measures advocated by Taylor in explaining the attack.

A bomb explosion in a crowded Belfast restaurant Mar. 4 killed 2 women and injured 136 other persons, 27 of them seriously. The bomb exploded without warning while afternoon shoppers were taking a tea break. The police blamed the bombing on the IRA, but both IRA wings disclaimed responsibility for the blast and blamed Protestant extremists.

A bomb explosion in a parking lot behind a movie theater in downtown Belfast injured 52 persons Mar. 6, most of them women shoppers and office workers. The injuries were minor.

In an effort to halt the intensified terrorism in Belfast, Prime Min. Brian Faulkner Mar. 8 imposed new security regulations that called for searching anyone entering public buildings, closing off some entrances and searching all shopping bags, briefcases or overcoats carried by store customers.

The Ulster Volunteer Force, an extremist Protestant group banned 5 years previously, responded to the mounting terrorist campaign with a threat Mar. 8 "to kill 10 IRA men for every policeman or soldier murdered in Ulster." But an Agricultural Ministry official became the next fatal victim of terrorists; he was shot to death in Armagh County Mar. 8.

The IRA Provisionals Mar. 10 announced a 72-hour ceasefire, effective at midnight that night, as a "gesture of the sincerity of the leadership to secure a just and lasting peace" in Northern Ireland. The Provisionals listed the following conditions the British would have to meet in order to secure an end to the IRA terrorist campaign: immediate withdrawal of British troops from the streets of Northern Ireland, coupled with a statement of intent of complete eventual evacuation; abolition of the Stormont Parliament; and total amnesty for all political prisoners. The IRA Officials denounced the truce, and the truce was broken by 2 killings of civilians in Belfast Mar. 12-13. One of the deaths occurred Mar. 12 when a housewife was shot to death by bullets aimed at a British Army patrol.

British State Undersecy. for Defense Geoffrey Johnson Smith told the House of Commons Mar. 16 that the IRA was beginning to feel the effects of the anti-terrorist campaign being conducted by British troops. He said: "Attrition of the IRA's strength by the security forces continues, and this is one reason why the IRA has begun to arm young boys.... One boy estimated to be no more than 12 to 14 years of age was found at the end of February with a loaded carbine in his possession. The growing use of inexperienced young people by the IRA is also shown by premature explosions, such as the one which killed 4 terrorists in a car last month and the one in a house in Clonard Street last week which killed 3 or 4 more."

Claiming that the Catholic community was turning against the

IRA, Smith continued: "There are indications of increasing hostility on the part of ordinary Catholic people in some parts of Belfast towards the IRA—and there have been instances of members of the IRA Youth Organization being set upon by local people because of their acts of vandalism. I assure the House that the Army fully recognizes the tremendous strains under which these people are living. That is why the Army will continue, through community relations, to make every possible contact with all moderate members of the community.... Perhaps one of the best examples was that of Father Weston, tragically murdered at Aldershot, who spent his time when in Ulster talking to civilian clergy and to Catholics in the streets and truly earned his decoration for doing all possible to cool inflamed passions and restore a little peace to troubled areas."

Smith derided the IRA Provisionals' "truce": "What sort of truce was it? ... There were certainly few major explosions murdering civilians for 72 hours. But planning was going ahead for the next batch of killings to take place as soon as the so-called truce was over. At the same time shooting was approaching the level of an average weekend—there were 27 incidents against an average of 35."

6 persons, 2 of them policemen, were killed and 147 were injured Mar. 20 when a 100-pound gelignite bomb hidden in a car exploded in a central Belfast street crowded with midday shoppers. Police said that many of the victims had been lured by terrorists to the scene after misleading phone calls had warned that bombs had been placed in a nearby street. The IRA Provisionals claimed responsibility for the blast Mar. 23.

A British soldier was shot to death by a terrorist in Londonderry Mar. 23. He was the 55th British soldier killed in Ulster since 1969 and the 8th to die there in 1972.

A bomb Mar. 22 wrecked part of Belfast's biggest hotel, the Europa, injuring more than 70 persons. 2 of 3 bombs mailed to 3 IRA offices in Dublin had exploded Mar. 20 after the packages in which they were contained were opened. Seán MacStiofáin the Provisionals' chief of staff, was slightly injured.

Thousands of Protestants had staged a 4-hour work stoppage in factories throughout Northern Ireland Mar. 9 in protest against the continuing IRA terrorism. The workers cut off electrical power, forcing many industrial firms to close, and leaving homes and stores without power. The work stoppage was organized by the Loyalist Association of Workers, a militant Protestant organization.

50,000 to 60,000 Protestants staged a rally in a Belfast park Mar. 18 in defiance of a government ban on demonstrations. It was the biggest such rally in 60 years. Ex-Home Affairs Min. William Craig apparently caught the mood of growing Protestant militancy when he warned the crowd that the Protestants might have "to liquidate the enemy" if the politicians failed to resolve the Northern Irish crisis. He said Catholic terrorism had to be brought to an end. The rally was organized by the Ulster Vanguard, an 8-week-old organization of extreme right-wing Protestants, as a warning to the government against any British political initiative that would change the status of Ulster as a province of the United Kingdom.

Speaking of growing Protestant fears over the status of Northern Ireland, the U.S. news magazine *Time* commented Jan. 10: "Fear of a Westiminster 'sellout' now dominates the Protestant community, despite assurances by Faulkner and Heath. MacStiofáin contends that these fears are unjustified: 'We have no interest in treating the Protestants harshly: We don't want them to leave the North. We want them to accept that they are Irish, that they have a stake in the future of this country.' Such words are small reassurance to dedicated Unionists like Billy Hull, chairman of the Loyalist Association of Workers (LAW). Hull worries that Ulster may be abandoned by 'perfidious Albion' and that Protestants may share the fate of those prewar 'Czechoslovaks who woke up one morning and found themselves Germans.' Says Hull: 'If we're sold down the drain, there wouldn't be civil war. There would be armed rebellion against the government of Britain.' "

WESTMINSTER TAKES CONTROL

Direct British Rule Imposed

In an attempt to halt the continuing terrorist violence in Protestant Ulster, Great Britain suspended Northern Ireland's government and Parliament Mar. 30, 1972 and imposed direct rule over the province for at least a year. The action ended 51 years of semiautonomous rule by the Ulster government.

Northern Ireland's Prime Min. Brian Faulkner and his cabinet resigned the day of the British takeover. In an apparent retreat from his initial sharp opposition to the British move, Faulkner said on resigning that he hoped to make "a constructive contribution" to the new provincial administration. Faulkner demanded the restoration of the Ulster Parliament after a year or, failing that, the "complete integration" of Northern Ireland into the United Kingdom "with full and just representation in the Westminster Parliament." He also urged an end to strikes staged by Protestants in protest against the British move.

The new British policy had been announced to the House of Commons Mar. 24 by Prime Min. Edward Heath. Under the plan, Heath appointed William Whitelaw, leader of the House of Commons, to the newly created post of secretary of state for Northern Ireland. Whitelaw took all legislative and executive powers in the province and was directed to appoint a local advisory commission composed of representatives of the Protestant and Catholic communities.

3 ministers were named Mar. 26 to serve under Whitelaw in the new Northern Ireland office. Lord Windlesham, a Catholic currently serving as minister of state at the Home Office, was named minister of state for Northern Ireland. The 2 other appointees were Paul Channon, currently undersecretary of state at the Department of Environment, and David Howell, parliamentary secretary in the Civil Service Department.

The suspension of the Ulster provincial government came after the British Parliament Mar. 30, by 438-18 vote, adopted an enabling bill on direct rule. During the all-night debate preceding passage, the House of Commons added a new clause specifying that nothing in the legislation would alter the province's status as part of the United Kingdom.

In his statement to Parliament Mar. 24, Heath had announced plans to hold periodic plebiscites in Ulster on unification with the Irish Republic; to give "high priority" to economic aid for Northern Ireland, and to gradually end the internment without trial of suspected terrorists. He promised to release "internees whose release is no longer thought to be an unacceptable risk to security." The British government's aim, Heath said, was to "change the climate of political opinion in Northern Ireland" so that Catholics and Protestants could try to work out the "future structure" of their government.

Heath disclosed that he had presented 3 major proposals to Faulkner at a meeting in London Mar. 22. These were the holding of plebiscites, the ending of internment and Britain's takeover of responsibility for Northern Ireland's security. He reported that Faulkner had rejected British control over law and order Mar. 23 and that this had led to the Ulster government's resignation and Britain's imposition of direct rule. Heath said: "The first 2 of our proposals were in principle acceptable to the Northern Ireland government. But Mr. Faulkner told us that his government could not accept proposals for the transfer of responsibility for law and order from Stormont to Westminster. At a further meeting yesterday evening he confirmed, after having consulted his cabinet, that this was their unanimous view and that if any such proposal were implemented, it would entail the resignation of the Northern Ireland government. The United Kingdom government remain of the view that the transfer of this responsibility to Westminster is an indispensable condition for progress in finding a political solution in Northern Ireland. The Northern Ireland government's decision therefore leaves them with no alternative to assuming full and direct responsibility for the administration of Northern Ireland until a political solution to the problems of the province can be worked out in consultation with all those concerned."

In a nationally telecast speech Mar. 24, Heath urged the acceptance of his proposals. He said: "We must make a completely fresh start . . . if we are to break out of the vicious circle of violence and yet more violence." He said that the British Army would remain in Northern Ireland "as long as any faction seeks to terrorize or intimidate ordinary people." Heath ended his address with this special appeal to the people of Northern Ireland: "You are the ones who have had to endure the years of violence and fear. We admire the steadiness and courage with which you have done this. Now, only you can take the decision to live together in peace. . . . Now is your chance, a chance for fairness, a chance for prosperity, above all a chance for peace. A chance at last to bring the bombings and killings to an end. Memories of the past are long-lived. In all conscience you have suffered enough. What the government have done today is intended to give us the opportunity to put the past behind us and to concentrate on the future. Let us take that opportunity together. Goodnight."

Heath's proposals were hailed Mar. 24 by opposition Labor Party leader Harold Wilson, who promised his party's "full support" to ensure Parliamentary approval of the enabling bill. (A Labor Party motion censuring the Conservative government for procrastination in formulating a program for peace in Ulster had been defeated Mar. 20 by 294–257 vote. Prior to the vote, Home Secy. Reginald Maudling had indicated that the government's plans would provide "an active, permanent and guaranteed place" for Catholics in the Ulster government and for "massive" economic aid to the province.)

Speaking to the British House of Commons Mar. 28, Atty. Gen. Sir Peter Rawlinson, who by virtue of his office was also attorney general of Northern Ireland, explained in some detail Britain's policy:

> This bill [the direct rule enabling bill] . . . terminates any division of authority between Belfast and Westminster and ends a situation whereby the main instrument for maintaining order lay with Westminster, whereas the responsibility, constitutionally, for maintaining law and order rested mainly with Belfast. At times such as the present and in conditions such as now exist, few will doubt that central undivided responsibility offers the better prospect for law and order and for peace. . . . The purposes and intentions of [the British] government are to defeat the terrorists, reestablish peace, reduce tension by the running-down of internment, provide an opportunity when practical for the people of Northern Ireland to decide their future, provide conditions and opportunities whereby they can express their undoubted desire for peace and whereby talks can begin which could lead to an acceptable and just solution to this centuries-old problem.

While admitting that the takeover would not solve Northern Ireland's problems, Rawlinson declared: "It begins a new phase. What is needed is the will to succeed in the twin task of crushing terrorism and seeking a settlement." On the question of internment, he explained: "With regard to the Special Powers Review and the Special Powers Act . . . [the secretary of state] wants to make it clear that he intends not only to review the case of each and every person who is now interned under the Special Powers Act, but he also intends to review the whole operation of the act and of the regulations."

In an effort to reassure Protestants who feared a British "betrayal," Rawlinson declared: "It does not affect by one jot the borders of the United Kingdom or the territory over which her majesty exercises dominion. The status, citizenship and nationality of the people of Northern Ireland remain as they are, and will so remain unless and until they themselves decide otherwise. . . ."

Speaking at the annual conference of the Federation of Conservative Students at St. Peter's College, Saltby, Birmingham, Mar. 29, Prime Min. Heath sought to ease the fears of those Irish who believed direct rule was the first step in altering the constitutional status of

Northern Ireland. He said: "Let us be quite clear that the guarantee of the status of Northern Ireland as part of the United Kingdom has never depended on the existence of a government and parliament exercising responsibility for law and order at Stormont. The guarantee has always depended essentially on the determination and good faith of the sovereign Parliament at Westminster. That guarantee has been powerfully strengthened by our decision to hold a plebiscite in Northern Ireland as soon as possible."

A rôle in the events leading to Britain's assumption of direct rule over Northern Ireland appears to have been played by John Hume, president of the Social Democratic & Labor Party's Alternative Assembly (formed by and around Hume and 5 other Northern Irish MPs boycotting the Stormont Parliament before its suspension). Hume "used the . . . [Northern Irish] courts to test the legality of British Army activity in Northern Ireland" before the takeover, according to a report-and-interview account in "The Talk of the Town" section of the Apr. 8, 1972 issue of the weekly *New Yorker.* Hume was quoted as saying in New York Mar. 22:

Last August [1971], in the Bogside [district of Londonderry], I was arrested by the British Army. . . . I live there. And I had wanted to do something to prevent trouble, because the soldiers had been there since morning, trying to dismantle the barricades, and the people in the neighborhood were getting quite tense. So I sat down in the street in front of the soldiers, and some of the people sat down with me, and the soldiers ordered us to move. We refused, of course. Some more people sat down with me, and the soldiers fired CS gas and rubber bullets into the crowd. Also purple dye. We were drenched with dye. And then arrested. I was fined £20 [$48] for failing to move on the command of a member of her majesty's forces.

So I decided to test the constitutionality of the Army's action in arresting me. Actually, it was myself and 4 others who challenged the action. We took the challenge to the High Court of Northern Ireland, before 3 judges, including the Lord Chief Justice. [One of the 3 judges was, like Hume, a Catholic.] . . . I asked the court, 'Did the Army have the right to arrest me?' They had arrested me under the Special Powers Act of 1922—that is, in effect, under orders of the Northern Ireland Parliament—and I claimed that the Northern Ireland Parliament did not have the power to confer these rights on the British Army, that these rights were exclusive to the British Parliament and were prohibited to the Northern Ireland Parliament under the Government of Ireland Act, 1920, which is generally regarded as Northern Ireland's constitution. . . .

. . . We won the case by a unanimous decision. We showed that the Army was behaving illegally, that every arrest, every search the Army had made was unconstitutional. . . . The decision was announced one morning in February [Feb. 23, 1972]. But by 3:30 [p.m.] the same day a one-clause bill had been presented to the British Parliament legalizing, retrospectively, the British Army's rule in Northern Ireland. It was called the Northern Ireland Act, 1972, and [the] Westminster [Parliament passed it] . . . in a matter of hours. . . .

Here was the biggest constitutional case in 50 years, involving hundreds of people against whom illegal acts had been committed, and suddenly those people were left with no legal redress at all; any redress they may have had was wiped out by that one piece of retrospective legislation. What the British Parliament had done, of course, was to create an argument for extraparliamentary activity—which means an argument for the IRA.

The High Court of Northern Ireland's ruling would also have covered the British Army's authority to search, enter homes and make arrests without warrant. The opposition British Labor Party accepted the one-clause Northern Ireland Act, 1972, because, according to party leader Harold Wilson, the Northern Irish of either side in the controversy might otherwise be incited "to an orgy of violence in the hope that troops would be inhibited in dealing with it." Wilson, a former British prime minister in whose administration British troops had first been ordered into Northern Ireland in Apr. 1969, was reported to have been embarrassed at discovering that the troops had, until Feb. 24, 1972, no legal justification for any activities beyond guard duty at utility installations and public property.

Reaction to British Takeover

U.S. Sen. Edward M. Kennedy (D., Mass.) joined Mar. 24 with Sen. Abraham A. Ribicoff (D., Conn.) and Rep. Hugh L. Carey (D., N.Y.) to praise Britain's imposition of direct rule over Northern Ireland. The 3 had previously sponsored Congressional resolutions calling for the suspension of Ulster Parliament, the abolition of internment without trial, and the withdrawal of British troops.

"It was a dramatic turn in the endless blood-drenched conflict between Britain and Ireland, Protestant and Catholic," *Time* magazine commented Apr. 3 in reference to the British takeover. "It was also the boldest step of British Prime Min. Edward Heath's career." While applauding the move, however, the U.S. weekly warned that "in appeasing the Catholics, Heath had unavoidably offended the Protestants, now deprived of the political dominance they had historically enjoyed through Stormont."

Irish Republic Prime Min. John Lynch Mar. 24 welcomed the British takeover as a "step forward in seeking a lasting solution" and called on Catholics and Protestants to shun violence. He also ordered the Irish ambassador to Britain, Dr. Donal O'Sullivan, to return to his post in London. (O'Sullivan had been recalled after the killings in January.) Later Mar. 24 Lynch called the British move "a step toward the ultimate reunification of the Irish people."

In Northern Ireland, reaction to the British moves ranged from expressions of satisfaction by Catholic moderates at the end of the

Protestant-dominated Faulkner régime to bitter denunciations and threats from Protestant extremists. William Craig, leader of the militant Protestant Ulster Vanguard, warned Mar. 24: "Ulster is closer to civil war today than it was yesterday." He said Protestants would organize "defensive mechanisms, vigilante organizations. We will succeed because no British government can stay here without the consent of the majority."

Prime Min. Faulkner, who announced his resignation Mar. 24 on the steps of Stormont Castle, the seat of the Ulster government, said that he had opposed Britain's control of law and order in Northern Ireland because it would "be widely construed as an acceptance of totally baseless criticism of our stewardship." He expressed the fear that "many people will draw a sinister and depressing message from these events: that violence can pay; that violence does pay." The ruling Protestant Ulster Unionist parliamentary party voted Mar. 24 to "withhold cooperation" from the proposed provincial advisory commission.

A moderate political group in Northern Ireland, the nonsectarian Alliance Party, backed the British measures Mar. 25 and called on all citizens to work for the restoration of the rule of law and to reestablish the system of regional government.

Within the Irish Catholic community, the 6 Parliament members of the Social Democratic & Labor Party, the Catholic party that had boycotted the Stormont Parliament since mid-1971, hailed the proposals Mar. 25 as "the first serious steps on the road to peace" and promised their "fullest cooperation" with the authorities. They called for an end to terrorist violence "to enable us to bring internment to a speedy end."

The Northern Ireland Civil Rights Association, the organizer of anti-internment protest marches earlier in 1972, denounced Heath Mar. 25 for his failure to end internment without trial immediately. The leaders announced a one-month moratorium on illegal demonstrations but said they would be resumed unless the British government announced immediate moves toward a "full civil rights program."

Both the Marxist Official and the militant Provisional wings of the outlawed IRA in Dublin denounced direct rule Mar. 24. Cathal Goulding, chief of staff of the Officials, said that the measures were tantamount to martial law, and Seán MacStiofáin, the Provisional leader, warned that IRA violence would continue until Britain permanently abolished the Stormont government, recalled its troops from Ulster streets and declared its intention to withdraw them totally and granted amnesty to all internees. (A split between IRA Provisionals in Northern Ireland and in the Irish Republic was reported Mar. 27 when an IRA leader in Londonderry allegedly ordered a cease-fire in response to the British plan. The report was denied by the Londonderry and Dublin headquarters later the same day.)

Northern Ireland's militant Protestants expressed their disapproval of the British measures with a 2-day general strike Mar. 27-28 organized by the Ulster Vanguard. Airline, train, bus and postal services were halted and eletricity and phone service were sharply curtailed. Estimates on the number of strikers ranged from 180,000 to 300,000.

In Belfast Mar. 27, nearly 25,000 Protestants applauded William Craig as he urged noncooperation with the new Ulster adminstration. A larger rally of 50,000 to 100,000 Protestants organized by Craig and his Ulster Vanguard gathered Mar. 28 in front of Stormont Castle, where the provincial Parliament was holding its final session. Prime Min. Faulkner made a surprise appearance at the rally to urge Protestants not to cooperate with "any undemocratic commission." The most striking aspect of the rally was a public display of reconcil-iation between Faulkner and Craig, formerly political opponents. Faulkner and Craig warmly shook hands on the Stormont Castle balcony.

Craig Mar. 29 promised further militant Protestant protests, including a civil disobedience campaign and "lightning strikes" against electricity and industrial plants. But another right-wing extremist leader, the Rev. Ian Paisley, had urged his fellow Protestants Mar. 28 to follow a moderate course of action and to avoid violence in opposing British rule.

Direct British Rule in Effect

The British government took direct control over Northern Ire-land's government and public affairs Mar. 30, 1972, made House of Commons Leader William Whitelaw secretary of state for Northern Ireland and assumed responsibility for those of the Stormont govern-ment's policies still in effect.

After 2 weeks of direct rule, Whitelaw Apr. 14 expressed optimism at the course of affairs. In a speech to the Omskirk Conservative Association in Prescot, Liverpool, Whitelaw said he had been "immensely heartened . . . in my task of bringing peace and work to Northern Ireland by the tremendous wave of support that has reached me from people throughout the country." Acknowledging that it would "take time to win back confidence and understanding,"

Whitelaw compared the mood in the 6 counties to "a very tender plant struggling to keep alive." Gunmen would not be permitted to determine events, he affirmed. He expressed the hope that the Catholic residents of Bogside would dismantle their barricades and would "decide for themselves that the democratic principle is far superior to the rule of the gun."

Evaluating Whitelaw's first week on the job, the American magazine *Newsweek* Apr. 17 expressed cautious optimism. It commented that, while bombings continued, "there was increasing signs of moderation in both the Protestant and Catholic camps." *Newsweek* concluded that "there was a growing feeling last week that it was deeds, not words, that mattered."

Whitelaw Apr. 27 revoked the ban on traditional parades and declared an amnesty for the 283 persons convicted of organizing or participating in illegal marches since Dec. 1971. Among those to benefit from the amnesty were Bernadette Devlin and Frank McManus, both Northern Irish members of the British Parliament. Whitelaw said that he had made his decisions after consultations with the security authorities and the organizers of the main Roman Catholic and Protestant parades. The revocation of the parade ban covered only traditional processions. Other parades including all civil rights marches, would require organizers to give 5 days' notice to security authorities, who would be authorized to reroute or even ban the processions.

Whitelaw May 11 introduced in the British House of Commons special legislation designed to create a Northern Ireland Finance Corp., which would give financial support to private business "so as to help to reduce the very serious levels of unemployment in Northern Ireland, which [Whitelaw said] are themselves conducive to social unrest." The vast majority of private business in the 6 counties was in the hands of Protestant proprietors, but many of their employes were Catholics. Whitelaw added: "This is an extremely urgent need, and a bill to establish a finance corporation to give financial support to undertakings in the province had passed all but the very last stages at Stormont. But for the prorogation [of the Stormont Parliament Mar. 28] it would almost certainly be in operation now. . . ."

(It had been reported earlier that 10 Northern Irish enterprises, employing more than 600 persons in all, had been forced to cease operations since the onset of the crisis in 1969.)

Prospects for Reunification

Britain's assumption of direct rule in Northern Ireland aroused considerable speculation again over the prospects for an eventual reunification of Protestant Ulster's 6 counties with the Irish Republic's 26 to form an island country. (Such a political entity had been unknown to the world since the decline of the medieval confederation of the kingdoms of Connaught, Leinster, Munster and Ulster 801 years earlier, when Henry II Plantagenet of England established his papal-sanctioned overlordship in Ireland.)

33 days before the British government announced its intention of taking over from Stormont, Irish Republic Prime Min. John Lynch had proposed at a conference of the ruling Fianna Fáil party in Dublin Feb. 19 a 3-point peace plan. Lynch urged: the ultimate establishment of a "specifically Irish institution" to rule Northern Ireland; talks between the Irish and British governments, with the assistance of elected representatives of Ulster's Catholic and Protestant communities, to agree on the form of the new administration; and the creation of an interim commission to administer Northern Ireland during the talks. He reiterated that any lasting solution would have to take into consideration the desire of the majority of Irish people for unity.

A tougher government policy toward IRA terrorists was indicated Feb. 20 when Justice Min. Desmond O'Malley told the Fianna Fáil party conference that the attorney general would order the retrial of certain persons who had been freed recently by "inexplicable" court decisions. His statement was thought to refer to a case in which illegal arms possession charges against 7 IRA suspects had been dismissed the previous week by a court at Dundalk because of insufficient evidence. The suspects included Anthony (Dutch) Doherty and Martin Meehan, 2 escapees from Crumlin Road prison in Belfast. O'Malley also warned that illegal organizations would not be allowed to interfere with the government's policy of seeking reunification of Ireland by peaceful means.

Summarizing the dilemma of the Irish Republic government and of its prime minister, the *Economist* of London had commented Feb. 5: "Mr. Lynch needs the IRA to give him any leverage in the North, but he does not like it in the South, not at all; nor do his policemen; nor do the people who might invest in the Republic if they felt it was not on the brink of a civil war. So Mr. Lynch, embarrassed by the presence of Mr. Dutch Doherty and others on his side of the border, let his policemen do what they wanted a week ago. Only very simple people imagined that a Southern jury would ever convict IRA men, so the effect of what has happened since in Londonderry is not important in that way. But if Mr. Lynch's government did not like gunmen running around and Irish juries would not convict, even the very simple could see that internment had to loom up in the South, too. Mr. Lynch plainly cannot contemplate that now, nor for some time ahead; so the gunmen may be expected to run loose. Mr. Lynch's friends will increasingly dislike being powerless to stop them."

Signaling an apparent crackdown on the IRA guerrillas, Irish police arrested 8 IRA leaders in Dublin Feb. 23 under an act authorizing detention of suspects for 48 hours without charges. The action was ordered by Lynch. Among those detained for questioning were Cathal Goulding, chief of the IRA Officials, and his son. A Dublin court dropped charges Mar. 10 against Goulding and 3 other men after the prosecution failed to produce witnesses to testify against them. The defendants had been charged with membership in the outlawed IRA and illegal activities in connection with the group. A Dublin court Mar. 27 dropped charges against Thomas MacGiolla, head of the Official Sinn Fein party (the political arm of the IRA), because of insufficient evidence. MacGiolla had been accused of membership in an outlawed organization, attempts to raise an illegal military force and possession of incriminating documents.

British Prime Min. Edward Heath, in an interview published in the *N.Y. Times* Feb. 27, had reiterated his government's intention to seek a political solution to the Northern Ireland crisis that would keep Protestant Ulster within the United Kingdom. He argued that significant differences between the Irish people of the North and South made Irish unification no more justified than the absorption of Portugal by Spain. He reiterated, however, that Britain would accept Irish unification if a majority of Northern Irish wanted it but insisted that this was not yet the case because the Irish Republic had "theocratic government" and a lower standard of living than Northern Ireland.

Further opinion on the matter had been expressed by Sen. Edward M. Kennedy (D., Mass.) when the U.S. House Foreign Affairs Subcommittee on Europe held hearings Feb. 28–Mar. 1 on the Northern Ireland crisis. Kennedy opened the testimony Feb. 28 with his previously stated demands for the dissolution of the Stormont Parliament and the unification of Northern Ireland with the Irish Republic. Irish Republic Prime Min. John Lynch, in an interview in the *Washington Post* Mar. 2, criticized Kennedy's call for the immediate removal of British troops from Northern Ireland. He advocated instead that British troops withdraw immediately from Ulster's Catholic areas as a first step toward reducing tensions and eventual total withdrawal from Northern Ireland. Lynch said Kennedy did not "understand the situation as fully as we do."

In response to growing Congressional and public demands that Pres. Richard M. Nixon intervene in the Ulster crisis, Martin J. Hillenbrand, U.S. assistant secretary of state for European affairs, warned the House subcommittee Feb. 29 that resolutions currently before Congress on the crisis "would not advance the interests of Ireland but could, in fact, set them back."

Britain in Charge of Internees

One of the responsibilities assumed by Britain when it took direct rule of Northern Ireland was the problem of internment.

Even before he became state secretary for Northern Ireland, William Whitelaw had flown to Belfast Mar. 25 to confer with Army and police officials. He told reporters he would personally study the file of each internee and detainee to determine who should be released. He linked a complete abolition of internment to an end of terrorism. (Whitelaw reportedly had been among those of the Conservative Party's leadership to approve the internment policy's imposition when the Stormont government invoked the policy early in Aug. 1971.)

Whitelaw announced in Belfast Apr. 7 that 47 internees and 26 detainees were being freed and that HMS *Maidstone* in Belfast Harbor would no longer serve as a prison ship for these suspects. Whitelaw declared that he had become more optimistic about Northern Ireland's future since arriving in Belfast: "I have been encouraged by the willingness to think again by those who may have reacted strongly to the measures which were so recently taken by Her Majesty's Government. Equally I have been impressed by the courage of those who have been prepared to speak up against the law of the gun."

Whitelaw announced that he had undertaken an official review of Northern Ireland's 8-month-old internment policy: "As I promised, I have begun to review personally the cases of the 728 people still interned under the Special Powers Act. This of course takes time. Initially, I have looked at those cases which the security authorities have advised might be considered for early release, and last night I signed orders authorising the release of 47 internees. It did not seem to me to be right to delay the release of any internees until I had been able to complete my review of every case. I shall now proceed as quickly as possible to review the remaining cases and intend to authorize the release of any whom I consider suitable as soon as I have completed each one." He asserted that Northern Ireland could return to normal whenever the people of the province were ready to do so.

Whitelaw's assistant, State Min. Lord Windlesham, announced Apr. 15 that all detainees had been removed from the Crumlin Road prison and that the use of HMS *Maidstone* as a place of detention had been discontinued as of Apr. 7. It was also announced that the internment center at Long Kesh had been enlarged and that efforts to improve its accommodation and facilities were continuing. These improvements included a reduction of some 20% in the numbers of internees in each compound and the construction of a new playing field. A board of visitors had been appointed and members had already made several visits.

Whitelaw told the House of Commons May 4 that he had interned nobody since taking office as Northern Ireland's administrator. It was reported May 4 that 182 men—130 internees and 52 detainees—had been released from the internment camps since Apr. 1, that the Magilligan Camp had been closed Apr. 30 and its 44 internees and 35 detainees transferred to Long Kesh and that, as of May 4, Long Kesh remained the only internment or detention center in operation, with 747 men in custody—598 internees and 149 detainees.

Terrorism Continues

The daily violence that had terrorized Northern Ireland was sharply reduced in the aftermath of British Prime Min. Heath's announcement of direct British rule.

A bomb explosion in the town of Maghera Mar. 24, 1972 injured 8 persons, none seriously. In Belfast the same day, bombs damaged a bank, a service station and houses, but caused no casualties.

Protestant youths threw stones at a Catholic housing project in Belfast Mar. 27, but troops dispersed them. In Lurgan the same day, British troops fired rubber bullets at a Protestant crowd stoning a bus. These were the first clashes between British troops and Protestants in a year.

2 deaths occurred when a van was blown up Mar. 28 outside a police station in the town of Limavady, 15 miles east-northeast of Londonderry.

Another upsurge of terrorism occurred in mid-April after the death Apr. 15 of Joseph McCann, 25, a battalion commander of the IRA Officials. He was shot by British soldiers in Belfast when he allegedly attempted to flee an Army patrol. In subsequent violence Apr. 16, 3 British soldiers were killed and 2 wounded in Belfast and Londonderry. The IRA Officials claimed responsibility for the killings and said that they were in retaliation for McCann's death.

The body of James Elliott, 33, was found shot through the head and tied up in a sack on a deserted road Apr. 19 outside Newton-Hamilton near the Irish border. 6 claymore mines, 200 pounds of other explosives and a large bomb lay around or near the sack. Elliott, the father of 3, had been kidnapped at gunpoint near Newry the night of Apr. 17 as he crossed into the North driving his company's truck. Elliott, a Presbyterian, had been a member of the Ulster Defense Regiment, a target of the IRA.

Protestant and Catholic youths clashed Apr. 23 in Londonderry's Waterside district, the only area in Londonderry where the 2 communities lived together in peace. The clash erupted when Protestant youths attacked Catholic homes after attending a rally organized by the Ulster Vanguard. Protestant youths rioted in Belfast Apr. 27-28 after 2 Protestant youngsters were gunned down. The rioters, blaming the shootings on the IRA, attacked policemen, burned cars and set up barricades in east Belfast in the first major outbreak of violence by Protestants since the British takeover of direct rule in March. 3 policemen were injured. 2 Protestant teenagers were wounded by gunfire in continued rioting in Belfast April 29.

Amid mounting controversy over the "no go" sections of Northern Ireland's Catholic districts where the IRA openly patrolled the streets and barred entry to British soldiers, ministers of the suspended provincial government urged Britain Apr. 24 to launch a military offensive against the IRA strongholds in the Creggan and Bogside districts of Londonderry. Northern Ireland State Secy. Whitelaw rejected the demand because of probable casualties among innocent civilians.

The Ulster Vanguard movement, an extreme right-wing Protestant group, warned Apr. 30 that it would take "appropriate action" against Catholic terrorists unless Britain crushed the IRA. The threat, made in a letter delivered by hand to Prime Min. Edward Heath in London, charged that the IRA was "operating without hindrance in many parts" of Protestant Ulster.

A series of bomb explosions destroyed a $31 million textile complex under construction in Carrickfergus, near Belfast, May 1. One worker was killed and about 15 were injured, 8 seriously.

Whitelaw May 11 introduced in the British House of Commons special legislation that would widen Britain's Explosives Act to include control over ammonium nitrate and sodium chlorate. Whitelaw said: "The first Order [in Council for the House's approval] extends the Northern Ireland explosives legislation so as to enable control to be exercised over substances which, although not in themselves explosives, are capable of being used for explosive purposes in combination with other substances. As many honorable members may be aware, ammonium nitrate and sodium chlorate, both of which are readily available for agricultural use, have been used with deadly effect, of which we may have seen another example at the Belfast Cooperative Building yesterday. This order and the regulations which it empowers me to make and which I intend to make as soon as possible, will enable these substances to be put under control: measures which I hope will help to save lives which might otherwise have been lost."

The total of persons killed in 3 years of violence in Northern Ireland reached 332 May 18, 1972 with the deaths of Harold Morris, 15, of Belfast and British Lance Cpl. John H. Hillman. Morris was hit by 2 bursts of machine-gun fire from a neighboring Catholic enclave in the Lower Falls Road area of Belfast May 18 while he was playing with friends in a Protestant neighborhood. Hillman had been mortally wounded May 17 in a shooting incident in Belfast. (This was one of 4 such incidents in Northern Ireland that day. The British Army said May 18 that 7 gunmen were shot in separate skirmishes in Londonderry.) Hillman was the 67th British soldier to be killed in Northern Ireland since 1969.